DATE DUE

DECODED

JAY-Z

SPIEGEL & GRAU

NEW YORK · 2011

2011 Spiegel & Grau Trade Paperback Edition

Published in the United States by Spiegel & Grau, an imprint of The Random House
Publishing Group, a division of Random House, Inc., New York.

SPIEGEL & GRAU and Design is a registered trademark of Random House, Inc.

Originally published in hardcover in the United States by Spiegel & Grau, an imprint
of The Random House Publishing Group, a division of Random House, Inc., in 2010.

Song lyric credits are located beginning on page 327.

Library of Congress Cataloging-in-Publication Data
Jay-Z.
Decoded / Jay-Z.
p.   cm.
ISBN 978-0-8129-8115-5
eBook ISBN 978-1-58836-959-8
1. Jay-Z. 2. Rap musicians—United States—Biography. I. Title.
ML420.J29A3 2010   782.421649092—dc22   [B] 2010015063

Printed in the United States of America

www.spiegelandgrau.com

9876543

DESIGNED BY RODRIGO CORRAL DESIGN

To Gloria Carter and Adnis Reeves

Without your love and love for music none of this would be possible

CONTENTS

I saw the circle before I saw the kid in the middle. I was nine years old, the summer of 1978, and Marcy was my world. The shadowy bench-lined inner pathways that connected the twenty-seven six-story buildings of Marcy Houses were like tunnels we kids burrowed through. Housing projects can seem like labyrinths to outsiders, as complicated and intimidating as a Moroccan bazaar. But we knew our way around.

THE STREET
SIGNS FOR
FLUSHING,
MARCY,
NOSTRAND,
AND MYRTLE
AVENUES
SEEMED LIKE
METAL FLAGS
TO ME:
BED-STUY
WAS MY
COUNTRY,
BROOKLYN
MY PLANET.

Marcy sat on top of the G train, which connects Brooklyn to Queens, but not to the city. For Marcy kids, Manhattan is where your parents went to work, if they were lucky, and where we'd yellow-bus it with our elementary class on special trips. I'm from New York, but I didn't know that at nine. The street signs for Flushing, Marcy, Nostrand, and Myrtle avenues seemed like metal flags to me: Bed-Stuy was my country, Brooklyn my planet.

When I got a little older Marcy would show me its menace, but for a kid in the seventies, it was mostly an adventure, full of concrete corners to turn, dark hallways to explore, and everywhere other kids. When you jumped the fences to play football on the grassy patches that passed for a park, you might find the field studded with glass shards that caught the light like diamonds and would pierce your sneakers just as fast. Turning one of those concrete corners you might bump into your older brother clutching dollar bills over a dice game, *Cee-Lo* being called out like hard-core bingo. It was the seventies and heroin was still heavy in the hood, so we would dare one another to push a leaning nodder off a bench the way kids on farms tip sleeping cows. The unpredictability was one of the things we counted on. Like the day when I wandered up to something I'd never seen before: a cipher—but I wouldn't have called it that; no one would've back then. It was just a circle of scrappy, ashy, skinny Brooklyn kids laughing and clapping their hands, their eyes trained on the center. I might have been with my cousin B-High, but I might have been alone, on my way home from playing baseball with my Little League squad. I shouldered through the crowd toward the middle—or maybe B-High cleared the way—but it felt like gravity pulling me into that swirl of kids, no bullshit, like a planet pulled into orbit by a star.

His name was Slate and he was a kid I used to see around the neigh-borhood, an older kid who barely made an impression. In the circle, though, he was transformed, like the church ladies touched by the spirit, and everyone was mesmerized. He was rhyming, throwing out couplet after couplet like he was in a trance, for a crazy long time—thirty min-utes straight off the top of his head, never losing the beat, riding the handclaps. He rhymed about nothing—the sidewalk, the benches—or he'd go in on the kids who were standing around listening to him, call out someone's leaning sneakers or dirty Lee jeans. And then he'd go in on how clean he was, how nice he was with the ball, how all our girls loved him. Then he'd just start rhyming about the rhymes themselves, how good they were, how much better they were than yours, how he was the best that ever did it, in all five boroughs and beyond. He never stopped moving, not dancing, just rotating in the center of the circle, looking for his next target. The sun started to set, the crowd moved in closer, the next clap kept coming, and he kept meeting it with another rhyme. It was like watching some kind of combat, but he was alone in the center. All he had were his eyes, taking in everything, and the words inside him. I was dazzled. *That's some cool shit* was the first thing I thought. Then: *I could* do *that*.

That night, I started writing rhymes in my spiral notebook. From the beginning it was easy, a constant flow. For days I filled page after page. Then I'd bang a beat out on the table, my bedroom window, whatever had a flat surface, and practice from the time I woke in the morning until I went to sleep. My mom would think I was up watching TV, but I'd be in the kitchen pounding on the table, rhyming. One day she brought a three-ring binder home from work for me to write in. The paper in the binder was unlined, and I filled every blank space on every page. My rhymes looked real chaotic, crowded against one another, some vertical, some slanting into the corners, but when I looked at them the order was clear.

I connected with an older kid who had a reputation as the best rapper in Marcy—Jaz was his name—and we started practicing our rhymes into a heavy-ass tape recorder with a makeshift mic attached. The first time I heard our voices playing back on tape, I realized that a recording captures you, but plays back a distortion—a different voice from the one you hear in your own head, even though I could recognize myself instantly. I saw it as an opening, a way to re-create myself and reimagine my world. After I recorded a rhyme, it gave me an unbelievable rush to play it back, to hear that voice.

One time a friend peeked inside my notebook and the next day I saw him in school, reciting my rhymes like they were his. I started writing real tiny so no one could steal my lyrics, and then I started straight hiding my book, stuffing it in my mattress like it was cash. Everywhere I went I'd write. If I was crossing a street with my friends and a rhyme came to me, I'd break out my binder, spread it on a mailbox or lamppost and write the rhyme before I crossed the street. I didn't care if my friends left me at the light, I had to get it out. Even back then, I thought I was the best.

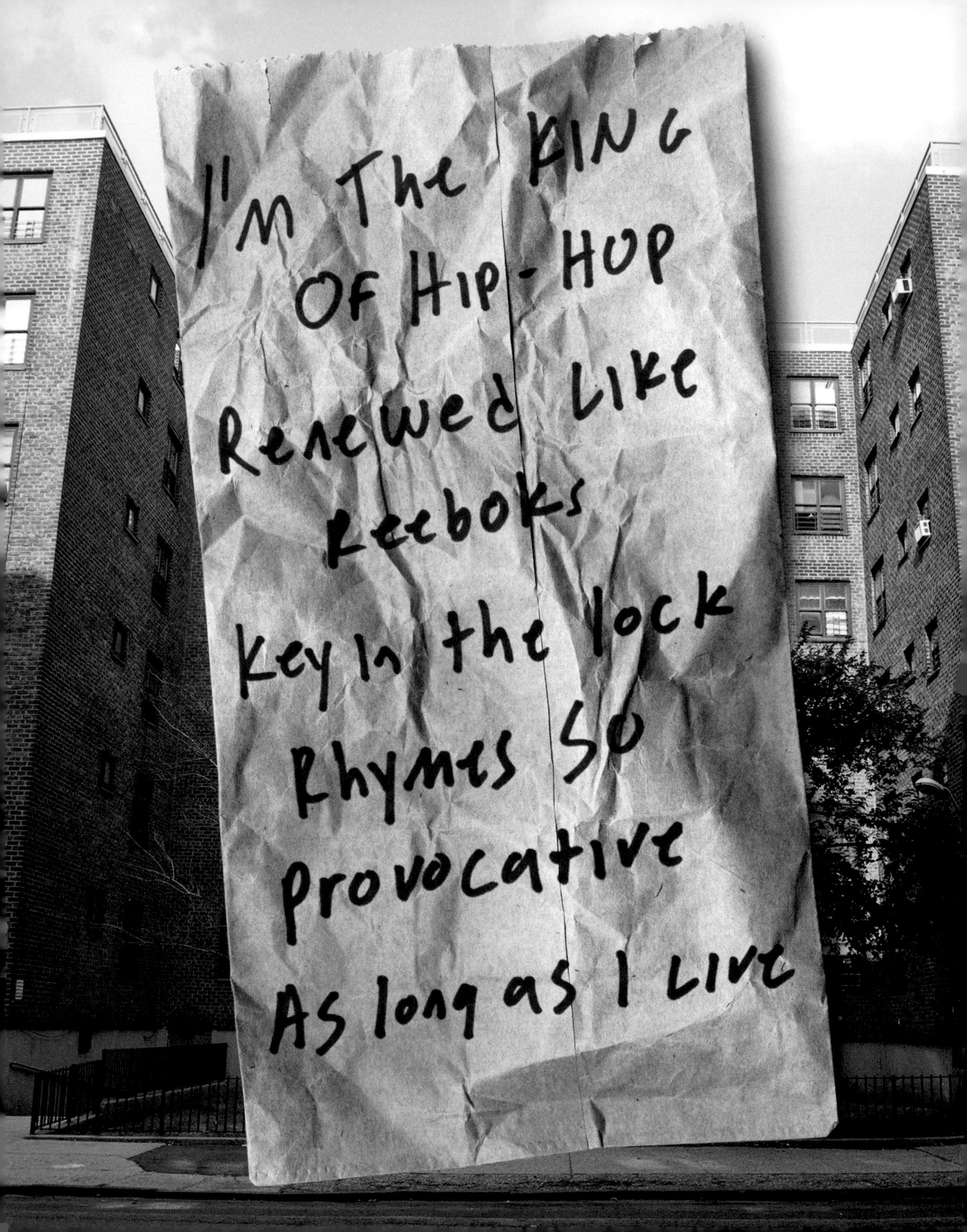
I'm The KING
Of Hip-Hop
Renewed Like
Reeboks
Key in the lock
Rhymes So
provocative
As long as I Live

I'm the king of hip-hop / Renewed like Reeboks / Key in the lock / Rhymes so provocative / As long as I live

There were some real talents in Marcy. DJs started setting up sound systems in the project courtyards and me and Jaz and other MCs from around the way would battle one another for hours. It wasn't like that first cipher I saw: the crowds were more serious now and the beat was kept by eight-foot-tall speakers with subwoofers that would rattle the windows of the apartments around us. I was good at battling and I practiced it like a sport. I'd spend free time reading the dictionary, building my vocabulary for battles. I could be ruthless, calm as fuck on the outside, but flooded with adrenaline, because the other rapper was coming for me, too. It wasn't a Marquess of Queensberry situation. I saw niggas get swung on when the rhymes cut too deep. But mostly, as dangerous as it felt, it stayed lyrical. I look back now and it still amazes me how intense those moments were, back when there was nothing at stake but your rep, your desire to be the best poet on the block.

I wasn't even in high school yet and I'd discovered my voice. But I still needed a story to tell.

FIRST THE FAT BOYS GONNA BREAK UP

Hip-hop was looking for a narrative, too. By the time the eighties came along, rap was exploding, and I remember the mainstream breakthroughs like they were my own rites of passage. In 1981, the summer before seventh grade, the Funky Four Plus One More performed "That's the Joint" on *Saturday Night Live* and the Rock Steady Crew got on *ABC Nightly News* for battling the Dynamic Rockers at Lincoln Center in a legendary showdown of b-boy dance crews. My parents watched *Soul Train* every Saturday when we cleaned up, but when my big sister Annie and I saw Don Cornelius introduce the Sugar Hill Gang, we just stopped in the middle of the living room with our jaws open. What are *they* doing on TV?

I remember the 12-inch of Run-DMC's "It's Like That" backed with "Sucker M.C.'s" being definitive. That same year, 1983, the year I started high school, Bambaataa released "Looking for the Perfect Beat" and shot a wild-ass video wearing feathered headdresses that they'd play on the local access channel. Annie and I would make up dance routines to those songs, but we didn't take it as far as the costumes. Herbie Hancock's "Rockit" came out that year, too, and those three records were a cultural trifecta. Disco, and even my parents' classic R&B records, all faded into the background. Everywhere we went there were twelve-pound boom boxes being pulled on skateboards or cars parked on the curb blasting those records. DJ Red Alert debuted his show on Kiss FM and Afrika Islam had a show, "Zulu Beats," on WHBI. The World's Famous Supreme Team did a show you had to catch early in the morning. Kids would make cassettes and bring them to school to play one another the freshest new song from the night before. I'm not gonna say that I thought I could get rich from rap, but I could clearly see that it was gonna get bigger before it went away. Way bigger.

The feeling those records gave me was so profound that it's sometimes surprising to listen to them now. Like those three songs that shook my world back in the early eighties: "Rockit" had complicated-sounding scratching by Grand Mixer DXT, which was big for me because I wanted to be a DJ before I wanted to be a rapper—I would practice scratching at my friend Allen's house on two mismatched turntables mounted on a long piece of plywood. But "Rockit" had no real voice aside from a looping synthetic one. "Looking for the Perfect Beat" was true to its title, obsessed with beats, not lyrical content. Then there was "Sucker M.C.'s."

From the first listen, Run-DMC felt harder than the Sugar Hill Gang or even Kool Moe Dee and other serious battle rappers of the time. Run-DMC's songs were like the hardest rock you'd ever heard stripped to its core chords. Their voices were big, like their beats, but naturally slick, like hustlers'. The rhymes were crisp and aggressive. Run's lyrics described the good life: champagne, caviar, bubble baths. He rapped about having *a big long Caddy, not like a Seville,* a line that seems like a throwaway, but to me felt meaningful—he was being descriptive and precise: Run didn't just say a car, he said a Caddy. He didn't just say a Caddy, he said a Seville. In those few words he painted a picture and then gave it emotional life. I completely related. I was the kid from public housing whose whole hood would rubberneck when an expensive car drove down the block.

Run had the spirit of a battle rapper—funny, observant, charismatic, and confrontational—but his rhymes were more refined. When he passed the mic to his partner, DMC followed with a story told in short strokes that felt completely raw and honest.

It was like he was looking around his hood in Queens—and around

his bedroom, his mom's kitchen—and just calling out what he saw. But the beat and DMC's delivery elevated that humble life into something iconic. *I'm light skinned, I live in Queens / and I love eatin chicken and collard greens.*

With that song hip-hop felt like it was starting to find its style and swagger and point of view: It was going to be raw and aggressive, but also witty and slick. It was going to boast and compete and exaggerate. But it was also going to care enough to get the details right about our aspirations and our crumb-snatching struggles, our specific, small realities (*chicken and collard greens*) and our living-color dreamscapes (*big long Caddy*). It was going to be real. Before Run-DMC, rappers dressed like they were headed to supper clubs for after-dinner drinks, or in full costume. Run-DMC looked like the streets, in denim, leather, and sneakers.

But for all of Run-DMC's style and showmanship, there was something missing in their songs. A story was unfolding on the streets of New York, and around the country, that still hadn't made it into rap, except as an absence. We heard Melle Mel's hit "The Message," with its lyrics about *broken glass everywhere,* and we heard about Run's *big long Caddy,* but what was missing was what was happening in between those two images—how young cats were stepping through the broken glass and into the Caddy.

The missing piece was the story of the hustler.

IF I'M NOT A HUSTLER WHAT YOU CALL THAT?

The story of the rapper and the story of the hustler are like rap itself, two kinds of rhythm working together, having a conversation with each other, doing more together than they could do apart. It's been said that the thing that makes rap special, that makes it different both from pop music and from written poetry, is that it's built around two kinds of rhythm. The first kind of rhythm is the meter. In poetry, the meter is abstract, but in rap, the meter is something you literally hear: it's the beat. The beat in a song never stops, it never varies. No matter what other sounds are on the track, even if it's a Timbaland production with all kinds of offbeat fills and electronics, a rap song is usually built bar by bar, four-beat measure by four-beat measure. It's like time itself, ticking off relentlessly in a rhythm that never varies and never stops.

When you think about it like that, you realize the beat is everywhere, you just have to tap into it. You can bang it out on a project wall or an 808 drum machine or just use your hands. You can beatbox it with your mouth.

PROFILE

RUN·D.M.C.

HARD TIMES 3:53
(J. Simmons·L. Smith·W. Waring·D. McDaniels)
Protoons, Inc./Mofunk Music/Rush-Groove

ROCK BOX 5:28
(L. Smith·D. McDaniels·J. Simmons)
Mixed by DJ Starchild

SIDE ONE
STEREO
33⅓ RPM

PRO·1202A

JAM-MASTER JAY   3:21
(J. Mizel·J. Simmons·D. McDaniels·R. Simmons·L. Smith)
HOLLIS CREW   3:12
(J. Mizel·J. Simmons·D. McDaniels)
SUCKER M.C.'S   3:15
(L. Smith·J. Simmons·D. McDaniels)
Produced by Russell Simmons and Larry Smith for
Rush-Groove Productions
Assistant Producer: Roddey Hui
All songs published by Protoons, Inc./
Rush-Groove ASCAP except where noted.
* 1984 Profile Records Inc.

But the beat is only one half of a rap song's rhythm. The other is the flow. When a rapper jumps on a beat, he adds his own rhythm. Sometimes you stay in the pocket of the beat and just let the rhymes land on the square so that the beat and flow become one. But sometimes the flow chops up the beat, breaks the beat into smaller units, forces in multiple syllables and repeated sounds and internal rhymes, or hangs a drunken leg over the last *bap* and keeps going, sneaks out of that bitch. The flow isn't like time, it's like life. It's like a heartbeat or the way you breathe, it can jump, speed up, slow down, stop, or pound right through like a machine. If the beat is time, flow is what we do with that time, how we live through it. The beat is everywhere, but every life has to find its own flow.

Just like beats and flows work together, rapping and hustling, for me at least, live through each other. Those early raps were beautiful in their way and a whole generation of us felt represented for the first time when we heard them. But there's a reason the culture evolved beyond that playful, partying lyrical style. Even when we recognized the voices, and recognized the style, and even personally knew the cats who were on the records, the content didn't always reflect the lives we were leading. There was a distance between what was becoming rap's signature style—the relentlessness, the swagger, the complex wordplay—and the substance of the songs. The culture had to go somewhere else to grow.

It had to come home.

CRACK'S IN MY PALM

No one hired a skywriter and announced crack's arrival. But when it landed in your hood, it was a total takeover. Sudden and complete. Like losing your man to gunshots. Or your father walking out the door for good. It was an irreversible new reality. What had been was gone, and in its place was a new way of life that was suddenly everywhere and seemed like it had been there forever.

Cocaine wasn't new and neither was selling it. There had always been older dudes who grew their pinkie fingernails out to sniff coke. There were always down-low dealers who partied with their customers as they supplied them. Melle Mel had a song called "White Lines (Don't Do It)" and of course Kurtis Blow called himself "Blow," but for the most part doing coke was something that happened at private parties, something you might've of heard about but had never really seen. Crackheads were different. They'd smoke in hallways, on playgrounds, on subway station staircases. They got no respect. They were former neighbors, "aunts" and "uncles," but once they started smoking, they were simply crack-heads, the lowest on the food chain in the jungle, worse than prostitutes and almost as bad as snitches.

Most of these fiends were my parents' age or a little younger. They had no secrets. Skeletal and ashy, they were as jittery as rookie beat cops and their eyes were always spinning with schemes to get money for the next hit. Kids my age were serving them. And these new little kamikazes, who simply called themselves hustlers (like generations before us did), were everywhere, stacking their ones. Fuck waiting for the city to pass out summer jobs. I wasn't even a teenager yet and suddenly everyone I knew had pocket money. And better.

When Biggie rhymed about how *things done changed* he could've meant from one summer to the next. It wasn't a generational shift but a genera-tional split. *Look at our parents, they even fukn scared of us.* With that line, Big captured the whole transformation in a few words. Authority was turned upside down. Guys my age, fed up with watching their moms struggle on a single income, were paying utility bills with money from hustling. So how could those same mothers sit them down about a truant report? Outside, in Marcy's courtyards and across the country, teenagers wore automatic weapons like they were sneakers. Broad-daylight shoot-outs had our grand-mothers afraid to leave the house, and had neighbors who'd known us since we were toddlers forming Neighborhood Watches against us. There was a separation of style, too. Hip-hop was already moving fashion out of the disco clubs and popularizing rugged streetwear, but we'd take it even further: baggy jeans and puffy coats to stash work and weapons, con-struction boots to survive cold winter nights working on the streets.

New York wasn't big for gang banging, but every era has its gangs, and during my high school years it was the Decepticons, the Lo-Lifes, even girl gangs like the Deceptinettes. Those broads would just walk up to grown men and punch them in their faces so hard they'd drop. The proliferation of guns on the streets added a different dynamic than the nunchucks, clackers, and kitchen knives kids my older brother's age used to use as weapons in their street fights. The trains were wild. In the early eighties, before I was thirteen, you had graffiti writers tagging trains, knocking conductors out with cans of Krylon if they tried to protect their trains. You had stickup kids looking for jewelry. Forty-fives made it much more likely for you to lose your sheepskin coat—or your life—on the A express. So my friends and I rolled hard for one another.

WITH THAT LINE, BIG CAPTURED A SOCIAL TRANSFOR-MATION IN A FEW WORDS. AUTHORITY WAS TURNED UPSIDE DOWN.

My man Hill (names changed to protect the guilty) and I were close, and even before we got in the game we were living through the changes it brought. I'd ride the train all the way to East New York with him, he'd get off, go see his girl, and I'd ride back to Marcy alone. One time we were on the train heading to Hill's chick's house and these niggas across the aisle just started ice grilling us. We were outnumbered and only had one gun between us, but we grilled them right back. Nothing jumped off and eventually we got off the train. East New York was one of the most serious neighborhoods in the city, so we agreed that he'd hold on to the gun when he decided to spend the night out there. I hit the train alone to head back to Marcy. On the way back, I ran into the same dudes. Unbelievable. I was sitting on the train next to another young guy who just happened to be there when they came through the car. They sat across the aisle from me. They wanted something with me real bad, but they couldn't figure out if the guy sitting next to me was with me. He wasn't. Still, I was looking at them like I'd murder them for staring at me. When the guy next to me got off they grilled at me for a minute. It was on. It wasn't a rare thing to have to fight your way home. Something as meaningless as a glance often ended up in a scuffle—and worse. You could get killed just for riding in the wrong train at the wrong time. I started to think that since I was risking my life anyway, I might as well get paid for it. It was that simple.

One day Hill told me he was selling crack he was getting from a guy named Dee Dee. I told him I wanted to be down and he took me to meet the dude. I remember Dee Dee talking to us in a professional tone, taking his time so we'd really understand him. He explained that hustling was a business but it also had certain obvious, inherent risks, so we had to be disciplined. He knew that, like him, neither of us even smoked weed, so he wasn't worried that we'd get high off of the work, but he wanted to stress how real the game was, that as a hustle it required vision and dedication. We thought we had both. Plus, my friend had a cousin in Trenton, New Jersey, doing the same thing. All we needed were Metroliner tickets to join him. When Dee Dee was murdered, it was like something out of a mob movie. They cut his balls off and stuffed them in his mouth and shot him in the back of the head, execution style. You would think that would be enough to keep two fifteen-year-olds off the turnpike with a pocketful of white tops. But you'd be wrong.

YOU COULD GET KILLED JUST FOR RIDING IN THE WRONG TRAIN AT THE WRONG TIME.

LIFE STORIES TOLD THROUGH RAP

I was still rhyming, but now it took a backseat to hustling. It was all moving so fast, it was hard to make sense of it or see the big picture. Kids like me, the new hustlers, were going through something strange and twisted and had a crazy story to tell. And we needed to hear our story told back to us, so maybe we could start to understand it ourselves.

Hip-hop was starting to catch up. Fresh Gordon was one of Brooklyn's biggest DJs. He was also seeing some action as a producer after he worked on Salt 'N' Pepa's big hit "Push It." Like a lot of the DJs in the city, Gordy was doing mix tapes, and he had a relationship with my friend Jaz, so he invited us to come rhyme on a track he was recording with Big Daddy Kane. I laid my little verse down, but when I went home I couldn't get Kane's freestyle out of my head. I remember one punchline in Kane's verse: *put a quarter in your ass / cuz you played yourself.* "Played yourself" wasn't even a phrase back then. He made it up right there on that tape. Impressive. I probably wrote a million rhymes that night. That tape made it all around New York. It even traveled as far as Miami. (This was back when black radio had slogans that assured listeners they were "rap free," so hip-hop moved on an underground railroad for real.) People were talking about the second kid on the tape, the MC before Kane—I was getting great feedback. I couldn't believe people even noticed my verse, Kane's was so sick.

Kane was Brooklyn's superhero, and an all-time great, but among New York MCs there was no one like Rakim. In Rakim, we recognized a poet and deep thinker, someone who was getting closer to reflecting the truth of our lives in his tone and spirit. His flow was complex and his voice was ill; his vocal cords carried their own reverb, like he'd swallowed an amp. Back in 1986, when other MCs were still doing party rhymes, he was dead serious: *write a rhyme in graffiti and every show you see me in / deep concentration cause I'm no comedian.* He was approaching rap like literature, like art. And the songs still banged at parties.

Then the next wave crashed. Outside of New York, pioneers, like Ice-T in L.A. and Schoolly D in Philly, had rhymed about gang life for years. But then New York MCs started to push their own street stories. Boogie Down Productions came out with a hard but conscious street album, *Criminal Minded,* where KRS-One rhymed about catching a crack dealer with an automatic: *he reached for his pistol but it was just a waste / cuz my nine millimeter was up against his face.* Public Enemy came hard with songs about baseheads and black steel. These songs were exciting and violent, but they were also explicitly "conscious," and anti-hustling. When NWA's *Straight Outta Compton* claimed everything west of New Jersey, it was clear they were ushering in a new movement. Even though I liked the music, the rhymes seemed over the top. It wasn't until I saw movies like *Boyz n the Hood* and *Menace II Society* that I could see how real crack culture had become all over the country. It makes sense, since it came from L.A., that the whole gangsta rap movement would be supported cinematically. But by the time Dre produced *The Chronic,* the music was the movie. That was the first West Coast album you could hear knocking all over Brooklyn. The stories in those songs—about gangbanging and partying and fucking and smoking weed—were real, or based on reality, and I loved it on a visceral level, but it wasn't my story to tell.

IT'S LIKE THE BLUES, WE GON RIDE OUT ON THIS ONE

As an MC I still loved rhyming for the sake of rhyming, purely for the aesthetics of the rhyme itself—the challenge of moving around couplets and triplets, stacking double entendres, speed rapping. If it hadn't been for hustling, I would've been working on being the best MC, technically, to ever touch a mic. But when I hit the streets for real, it altered my ambition. I finally had a story to tell. And I felt obligated, above all, to be honest about that experience.

That ambition defined my work from my first album on. Hip-hop had described poverty in the ghetto and painted pictures of violence and thug life, but I was interested in something a little different: the interior space of a young kid's head, his psychology. Thirteen-year-old kids don't wake up one day and say, "Okay, I just wanna sell drugs on my mother's stoop, hustle on my block till I'm so hot niggas want to come look for me and start shooting out my mom's living room windows." Trust me, no one wakes up in the morning and wants to do that. To tell the story of the kid with the gun without telling the story of why he has it is to tell a kind of lie. To tell the story of the pain without telling the story of the rewards— the money, the girls, the excitement—is a different kind of evasion. To talk about killing niggas dead without talking about waking up in the middle of the night from a dream about the friend you watched die, or not getting to sleep in the first place because you're so paranoid from the work you're doing, is a lie so deep it's criminal. I wanted to tell stories and boast, to entertain and to dazzle with creative rhymes, but every thing I said had to be rooted in the truth of that experience. I owed it to all the hustlers I met or grew up with who didn't have a voice to tell their own stories—and to myself.

My life after childhood has two main stories: the story of the hustler and the story of the rapper, and the two overlap as much as they diverge. I was on the streets for more than half of my life from the time I was thirteen years old. People sometimes say that now I'm so far away from that life—now that I've got businesses and Grammys and magazine covers—that I have no right to rap about it. But how distant is the story of your own life ever going to be? The feelings I had during that part of my life were burned into me like a brand. It was life during wartime.

I lost people I loved, was betrayed by people I trusted, felt the breeze of bullets flying by my head. I saw crack addiction destroy families—it almost destroyed mine—but I sold it, too. I stood on cold corners far from home in the middle of the night serving crack fiends and then balled ridiculously in Vegas; I went dead broke and got hood rich on those streets. I hated it. I was addicted to it. It nearly killed me. But no matter what, it is the place where I learned not just who I was, but who we were, who all of us are. It was the site of my moral education, as strange as that may sound. It's my core story and, just like you, just like anyone, that core story is the one that I have to tell. I was part of a generation of kids who saw something special about what it means to be human—something bloody and dramatic and scandalous that happened right here in America—and hip-hop was our way of reporting that story, telling it to ourselves and to the world. Of course, that story is still evolving—and my life is, too—so the way I tell it evolves and expands from album to album and song to song. But the story of the hustler was the story hip-hop was born to tell—not its only story, but the story that found its voice in the form and, in return, helped grow the form into an art.

Chuck D famously called hip-hop the CNN of the ghetto, and he was right, but hip-hop would be as boring as the news if all MCs did was report. Rap is also entertainment—and art. Going back to poetry for a minute: I love metaphors, and for me hustling is the ultimate metaphor for the basic human struggles: the struggle to survive and resist, the struggle to win and to make sense of it all.

This is why the hustler's story—through hip-hop—has connected with a global audience. The deeper we get into those sidewalk cracks and into the mind of the young hustler trying to find his fortune there, the closer we get to the ultimate human story, the story of struggle, which is what defines us all.

THE
REVOLUTIONARY T-SHIRT

●

PUBLIC SERVICE ANNOUNCEMENT
(*THE BLACK ALBUM*, 2003)

AMERICAN DREAMIN'
(*AMERICAN GANGSTER*, 2007)

EARLY THIS MORNING
(Unreleased)

Just Blaze was one of the house producers at Roc-A-Fella Records, the company I co-founded with Kareem Burke and Damon Dash. He's a remarkable producer, one of the best of his generation. As much as anyone, he helped craft the Roc-A-Fella sound when the label was at its peak: manipulated soul samples and original drum tracks, punctuated by horn stabs or big organ chords. It was dramatic music: It had emotion and nostalgia and a street edge, but he combined those elements into something original. His best tracks were stories in themselves. With his genius for creating drama and story in music, it made sense that Just was also deep into video games. He'd written soundtracks for them. He played them. He collected them. He was even a character in one game. If he could've gotten bodily sucked into a video game, like that guy in *Tron* did, he would've been happy forever. I was recording *The Black Album* and wanted Just to give me one last song for the album, which was supposed to be my last, but he was distracted by his video-game work. He'd already given me one song, "December 4th," for the album—but I was still looking for one more. He was coming up empty and we were running up against our deadlines for getting the album done and mastered.

At the same time, the promotion was already starting, which isn't my favorite part of the process. I'm still a guarded person when I'm not in the booth or onstage or with my oldest friends, and I'm particularly wary of the media. Part of the pre-release promotion for the album was a listening session in the studio with a reporter from *The Village Voice,* a young writer named Elizabeth Mendez Berry. I was playing the album unfinished; I felt like it needed maybe two more songs to be complete. After we listened to the album the reporter came up to me and said the strangest thing: "You don't feel funny?" I was like, *Huh?,* because I knew she meant funny as in weird, and I was thinking, *Actually, I feel real comfortable; this is one of the best albums of my career. . . .* But then she said it again: "You don't feel funny? You're wearing that Che T-shirt and you have—" she gestured dramatically at the chain around my neck. "I couldn't even concentrate on the music," she said. "All I could think of is that big chain bouncing off of Che's forehead." The chain was a Jesus piece—the Jesus piece that Biggie used to wear, in fact. It's part of my ritual when I record an album: I wear the Jesus piece and let my hair grow till I'm done.

This wasn't the first time I'd worn a Che T-shirt—I'd worn a different one during my taping of an MTV *Unplugged* show, which I'd taped with the Roots. I didn't really think much of it. Her question—*don't you feel funny?*—caught me off guard and I didn't have an answer for her. The conversation moved on, but before she left she gave me a copy of an essay she wrote about me for a book about classic albums. The essay was about three of my albums: *Reasonable Doubt, Vol. 3 . . . Life and Times of S. Carter,* and *The Blueprint.* That night I went home and read it. Here are some highlights:

> *On "Dope Man" he calls himself, "the soul of Mumia" in this modern-day time. I don't think so.*

And:

> *Jay-Z is convincing. When he raps, "I'm representing for the seat where Rosa Parks sat / where Malcolm X was shot / where Martin Luther was popped" on "The Ruler's Back," you almost believe him.*

And, referring to my MTV *Unplugged* show:

> *When he rocks his Guevara shirt and a do-rag, squint and you see a revolutionary. But open your eyes to the platinum chain around his neck: Jay-Z is a hustler.*

Wow. I could've just dismissed her as a hater; I remember her going on about "bling-bling," which was just too easy, and, honestly, even after reading her essays I was mostly thinking, "It's a T-shirt. You're buggin." But I was fascinated by the piece and thought some more about what she was saying. It stuck with me and that night I turned it around in my head.

WE REBELLIOUS, WE BACK HOME

One of Big's genius lines wasn't even a rhyme, it was in the ad lib to "Juicy," his first big hit:

> *Yeah, this album is dedicated to all the teachers that told me I'd never amount to nothin, to all the people that lived above the buildings that I was hustlin in front of that called the police on me when I was just tryin to make some money to feed my daughters, and all the niggas in the struggle.*

I loved that he described what a lot of hustlers were going through in the streets—dissed and feared by teachers and parents and neighbors and cops, broke, working a corner to try to get some bread for basic shit—as more than some glamorous alternative to having a real job.

He elevated it to "the struggle." That's a loaded term. It's usually used to talk about civil rights or black power—*the seat where Rosa Parks sat / where Malcolm X was shot / where Martin Luther was popped*—not the kind of nickel-and-dime, just-to-get-by struggle that Biggie was talking about. Our struggle wasn't organized or even coherent. There were no leaders of this "movement." There wasn't even a list of demands. Our struggle was truly a something-out-of-nothing, do-or-die situation. The fucked-up thing was that it led some of us to sell drugs on our own blocks and get caught up in the material spoils of that life. It was definitely different, less easily defined, less pure, and harder to celebrate than a simple call for revolution. But in their way, Biggie's words made an even more desperate case for some kind of change. Che was coming from the perspective, "We deserve these rights; we are ready to lead." We were coming from the perspective, "We need some kind of opportunity; we are ready to die." The connections between the two kinds of struggles weren't necessarily clear to me yet, but they were on my mind.

THE RENEGADE, YOU BEEN AFRAID

The day after the listening session, Just finally played a track for me. It opened with some dark minor organ notes and then flooded them with brassy chords that felt like the end of the world. It was beautiful. When a track is right, I feel like it's mine from the second I hear it. I own it. This was the record I'd been waiting for. I spit two quick verses on it—no hook, no chorus, just two verses, because we were running out of time to get the album done and mastered and released on schedule. I called it "Public Service Announcement."

The subject of the first verse wasn't blazingly unique. It's a variation on a story I've been telling since I was ten years old rapping into a tape recorder: I'm dope. Doper than you. But even when a rapper is just rapping about how dope he is, there's something a little bit deeper going on. It's like a sonnet, believe it or not. Sonnets have a set structure, but also a limited subject matter: They are mostly about love. Taking on such a familiar subject and writing about it in a set structure forced sonnet writers to find every nook and cranny in the subject and challenged them to invent new language for saying old things. It's the same with bragga-dacio in rap. When we take the most familiar subject in the history of rap—why I'm dope—and frame it within the sixteen-bar structure of a rap verse, synced to the specific rhythm and feel of the track, more than anything it's a test of creativity and wit. It's like a metaphor for itself; if you can say how dope you are in a completely original, clever, powerful way, the rhyme itself becomes proof of the boast's truth. And there are always deeper layers of meaning buried in the simplest verses. I call rhymes like the first verse on "Public Service Announcement" Easter-egg hunts, because if you just listen to it once without paying attention, you'll brush past some lines that can offer more meaning and resonance every time you listen to them.

The second verse for "Public Service Announcement" was almost entirely unrelated to the first verse. I wrote the second verse, which opens with the lyric, *I'm like Che Guevara with bling on, I'm complex,* as a response to the journalist. When someone asked me at the time of the Unplugged show why it was that I wore the Che T-shirt, I think I said something glib like, "I consider myself a revolutionary because I'm a self-made millionaire in a racist society." But it was really that it just felt right to me. I knew that people would have questions. Some people in the hip-hop world were surprised by it. There are rappers like Public Enemy and Dead Prez who've always been explicitly revolutionary, but I wasn't one of them. I also wasn't a Marxist like Che—the platinum Jesus piece made that pretty clear.

Later I would read more about Guevara and discover similarities in our lives. I related to him as a kid who had asthma and played sports. I related to the power of his image, too. The image on the T-shirt had a name: *Guerrillero Heroico,* heroic guerrilla. The photo was taken after the Cuban Revolution and by the time I wore the T-shirt, it was probably one of the most famous photographs in the world. Like a lot of people who stumble across the image with no context, I was still struck by its power and charisma.

The journalist was right, though. Images aren't everything, and a T-shirt doesn't change who you are. Like I said in the song "Blueprint 2," *cause the nigger wear a kufi, it don't mean that he bright.* For any image or symbol or creative act to mean something, it has to touch something deeper, connect to something true. I know that the spirit of struggle and insurgency was woven into the lives of the people I grew up with in Bed-Stuy, even if in sometimes fucked up and corrupted ways. Che's failures were bloody and his contradictions frustrating. But to have contradictions—especially when you're fighting for your life—is human, and to wear the Che shirt and the platinum and diamonds together is honest. In the end I wore it because I meant it.

PUBLIC SERVICE ANNOUNCEMENT

This is a public service announcement / Sponsored by Just Blaze and the good folks at Roc-A-Fella Records / [Just Blaze] **Fellow Americans, it is with the utmost pride and sincerity that I present this recording, as a living testament and recollection of history in the making during our generation.**[1] / [*Jay-Z*] Allow me to re-introduce myself / My name is Hov, OH, H-to-the-O-V / I used to move snowflakes by the O-Z / I guess even back then you can call me / **CEO of the R-O-C,**[2] Hov! / Fresh out the fryin pan into the fire / I be the music biz number one supplier / **Flyer**[3] than a piece of paper bearin my name / Got the hottest chick in the game wearin my chain, that's right / **Hov, OH—not D.O.C.**[4] / But similar to them letters, "No One Can Do It Better"/ **I check cheddar like a food inspector**[5] / My homey Strict told me, **"Dude finish your breakfast"**[6] / So that's what I'ma do, take you back to the dude / with the Lexus, fast-forward the jewels and the necklace / **Let me tell you dudes what I do to protect this**[7] / I shoot at you actors like movie directors [*laughing*] / This ain't a movie dog *(oh shit)* / [*Just Blaze*] *Now before I finish, let me just say I did not come here to show out, did not come here to impress you. Because to tell you the truth when I leave here I'm GONE!*

1. This is Just Blaze's voice, although he recorded it in a way that made it sound older, like a political speech from the Black Power era captured on a distant tape recorder.

2. A simple double entendre of "Roc-A-Fella," our company, which we call the Roc, and "rock," common slang for crack because of the way the coke crystallizes when you cook it. I drop the "frying pan" into the next line to keep the comparison going. In the line after that I complete the connection between selling rock and selling the Roc, supplying the streets and supplying the music biz. Both take ruthlessness. In fact, the music industry is the fire to the crack game's frying pan.

3. The *flier/flyer* homonym also carries the momentum of the *fire/supplier* rhyme for one more line.

4. The D.O.C.'s "No One Can Do It Better" was an early classic of the West Coast's golden age.

5. This line combines two separate pieces of slang—"check" means to collect, "cheddar" means money—to create a third piece of new slang—"a food inspector"—that only makes sense if you decode the first two phrases. "Check cheddar" is an alliteration that adds force to the image.

6. My friend Strict uses the phrase "finish your breakfast" as a way of saying that you need to finish your job up strong.

7. In these four lines I use five different variations on "do" and "dude" (plus "jewels," whose hard "j" sounds almost like a "d") to create a percussive rhythm within the beat.

And I don't care WHAT you think about me—but just remember, when it hits the fan, brother, whether it's next year, ten years, twenty years from now, you'll never be able to say that these brothers lied to you JACK! / [*Jay-Z*] thing ain't lie / I done came through the block in everything that's fly / **I'm like Che Guevara**[8] with bling on I'm complex / I never claimed to have wings on nigga I get my / **by any means on**[9] whenever there's a drought / Get your umbrellas out because / **that's when I brainstorm**[10] / You can blame Shawn, but I ain't invent the game / I just rolled the dice, tryin to get some change / And I do it twice, ain't no sense in me / lyin as if I am a different man / And I could blame my environment / but there ain't no reason / **why I be buyin expensive chains**[11] / Hope you don't think users / are the only abusers niggaz / **Gettin high within the game**[12] / If you do, then how would you explain? / I'm ten years removed, still the vibe is in my veins / **I got a hustler spirit, nigga period**[13] / Check out my hat yo, peep the way I wear it / Check out my swag' yo, / I walk like a ballplayer / No matter where you go / you are what you are player / And you can try to change but that's just the top layer / **Man, you was who you was 'fore you got here**[14] / Only God can judge me, so I'm gone / **Either love me, or leave me alone**[15]

8. "Jay-Z sported a white T emblazoned with Che's image, perhaps a case of game recognizing game . . ." —Elizabeth Mendez Berry, "The Last Hustle," *The Village Voice,* November 25, 2003.

9. Just to amplify the connection I'm trying to make between revolutionaries and hustlers, I invoke Malcolm's famous "By Any Means Necessary" slogan.

10. A drought in the game is when the supply or demand starts to dry up—and that's when resourceful hustlers have to start getting creative. If that means getting violent, the "brainstorming" might just lead to someone getting wet, as in bloody, which is why you need to get your umbrella out, for protection. It's a dramatic, violent image to convey the way desperation and hunger can explode.

11. Here's where life gets "complex." I'm innocent because I didn't invent the game; the game came to the hood via a bunch of people from the outside: the big drug suppliers, the gun merchants, the corrupt officials who, at best, let it happen, or, at worst, were actively involved. And we—the hustlers at the street level—definitely didn't invent the poverty and hopelessness that drove a generation of desperate kids to start selling drugs. But then there's a point where I'm not so innocent anymore. It's when I "do it twice." The second time is not out of desperation to survive or to resist the status quo, but out of greed for the spoils of the game.

12. And it's not just the material spoils that keep you going: You start getting addicted to the thrill of it, the adrenaline rush of going to see your connect in a small building in Harlem in a lobby that you've never been in, where you go in with a bag of money and come out with a bag of work. Or the feeling when you come around the corner back home and all eyes turn to you because everyone knows who you are—you represent something successful and free and dangerous, all at once. You have the best car, the best jewelry, the whole package. You taste a strange kind of fame. It's as addictive as the shit you're selling, and just as deadly.

13. "The ghetto people knew I never left the ghetto in spirit." —Malcolm X

14. You can put a new shirt on your back, slide a fresh chain around your neck, and accumulate all the money and power in the world, but at the end of the day those are just layers. Money and power don't change you, they just further expose your true self.

15. Elizabeth Mendez Berry wrote in her essay: "Squint and you see a revolutionary. But open your eyes to the platinum chain around his neck: Jay-Z is a hustler." No doubt. It's a simple truth, but complex, too. Identity isn't a prison you can never escape, but the way to redeem your past is not to run from it, but to try to understand it, and use it as a foundation to grow.

AMERICAN DREAMIN'

This is the shit you dream about / with the homies steamin out / **Back-back-backing them Beemers out**[1] / Seems as our plans to get a grant / Then go off to college didn't pan or even out / We need it now, we need a town / **We need a place to pitch, we need a mound**[2] / For now, I'm just a lazy boy / Big dreaming in my La-Z-Boy / **In the clouds of smoke, been playin this Marvin**[3] / Mama forgive me, should be thinkin bout Harvard / But that's too far away, niggas are starving / **Ain't nothin wrong with aim, just gotta change the target**[4] / **I got dreams of baggin snidd-ow**[5] the size of pillows / I see pies everytime my eyes clidd-ose / **I see rides, sixes, I gotta get those**[6] / Life's a bitch, I hope to not make her a widow / Now see, the life's right there / And it seems right there / It's not quite near, / And it's not like we're / professionals movin the decimals / **Know where to cop? Nah! Got a connect? No!**[7] / Who in the F knows how to be successful / **Need a Personal Jesus, I'm in Depeche Mode**[8] / They say it's celestial, it's all in the stars / It's like Tony La Russa / **How you play your cards**[9] / Y'all ain't fucking with me! / The ironies are / **And at all costs better avoid these bars**[10] / Now let's start, on your mark / Get set, let's go—get out the car! / Going in circles, it's a vicious cycle / This is a crash course, this ain't high school / Wake up, Muttley, you're dreamin again / Your own reality show, the season begins / **Step one in this process, scramble up in your projects**[11] / And head to the heights where big coke is processed / You gotta convince 'em that you not from the Precinct / Please speak slow, 'cause he no speakey no English / If he takes a liking after a couple of trips / If your money is straight, he's gonna give you consignment / You're now in a game where only time can tell / Survive the droughts, I wish you well . . . / **Survive the droughts? I wish you well?**[12] / How sick am I? I wish you HEALTH / I wish you wheels, I wish you wealth / **I wish you insight so you could see for yourself**[13] / You could see the signs, when the jackers is schemin / And the cops is comin, you could read they mind / **You could see from behind,**[14] you could redefine / The game as we know it, one dream at a time / I'm American dreamin

1. This is really where it begins, in a room with your feet up with your dudes. Too young to shave, dreaming about the big body Benzes you're gonna push. Obviously for me, it's in Marcy, but this could be anywhere—a basement in the midwest, a backyard in Cali, an Oldsmobile somewhere down South. The danger is that it's just talk; then again, the danger is that it's not. I believe you can speak things into existence.

2. "Pitch" was slang for a hustle. Hustlers hoped to take a "mound" of work and turn it into a mountain of money. A mound is also the place you pitch from—which is why "we need a town."

3. This song samples Marvin Gaye's "Soon I'll Be Loving You Again," a track that transports you to a blue-lit room in the seventies; you can practically smell the smoke from a joint coming out of the speakers.

4. Our aim is the same as everyone, shooting for the American dream of success and wealth, but the target is a little different: Instead of trying to land in college or in a good job, I'm trying to get rich in the streets.

5. The image of bags of coke the size of pillows connects with the image of a kid dreaming.

6. In this verse I jump from it being about starving, a real and literal need, to desiring a 600-series Benz. It happens that quickly in the Life, too, in the real-life equivalent of two bars.

7. Initially the decision to hustle is freestyled. These kids in the cipher, the ones with their feet up and the dreams of foreign cars, have absolutely no idea how to go into business, even one that surrounds them like the drug game. Do they know where to go to cop the work? No. Do they have a drug connect? No. They're like anyone starting out in business; they need someone to give them the plan.

8. A reference to Depeche Mode's "Personal Jesus."

9. Tony La Russa is the manager of the St. Louis Cardinals, often called the Cards.

10. The "irony" refers back to the song's wordplay and is itself a play on words: The "iron" in "ironies" also refers to the "bars" in the next line, the iron bars of a penitentiary.

11. As with anything, you begin locally, in your own projects. The trip from Brooklyn to upper Manhattan once seemed as great a distance as going down South, or to a foreign country, with a foreign language. Repeat trips mean more money, familiarity with Papi, better relationships and credit. But credit is a vice, debt, a door-knocker.

12. The repeated lines are just me creating an echo chamber. The well is a literal place to store and draw water. So I'm wishing my fellow hustlers the foresight to stash, to be resourceful, to see droughts and setbacks and attacks before they come, to have a plan from which to draw.

13. The "insight" is a play on words—I'm not just wishing you insight, but sight in, the ability to see beyond what's visible, to see even within your own soul.

14. This series—about seeing the signs, seeing the scheming jackers, seeing inside the minds of the cops so you know when they're coming—is meant to show how impossible it is for anyone to have the level of vision you'd need to make the dream of the hustler really come true. There are too many threats, too many hazards; even the smartest, most discerning hustler can't anticipate it all. This song is like the blues; it's about the inevitable tragedy of the hustler's life, the inevitable piercing of the hustler's dream. It's about a wish that can't come true. Can it?

EARLY THIS MORNING

It was the best of times it was the worst of times / **I wake up hit my shoe box**[1] I snatch out a few rocks / Put the rest inside now I'm ready to ride / Put the bomb in my socks so cops can't locate the vials / I ain't freshly dressed but got a Colgate smile / That's right / (I woke up early this morning) / **Throw on the same clothes I had on last night**[2] / I got loads of capers to come up with this paper / **I got money schemes that come to me in my dreams**[3] / Hit the block like a veteran / Fiends need they medicine / **I'm the relief pitcher**[4] / Their clean-up hitters / It works I hit the Ave stash the bag in the dirt / Put the rest in my small pocket I start clockin / (I woke up early this morning) / Same routine I'm runnin game to fiends / Exchangin cash for crack rocks / Back and forth to my stash box / **Hundred dollars a week**[5] / Shorties got the Ave watched / **Fiends swarm I'm gettin rid of this bomb**[6] / As I / (I woke up early this morning with a new sight over life) / Good morning / (Never read the Qu'ran or Islamic scriptures) / (Only Psalms I read was on the arms of my niggaz) / (I woke up early this morning with a new sight over life) / (The sunshine was shinin' you were on my mind) / (I woke up early this morning)

1. The shoe box tells us from the first line that this is a low-level hustler.

2. This song is about the true nature of the work. You get up early. You wear the same clothes.

3. You obsess over making money. The work doesn't have a social value. It's not like you can motivate yourself by thinking about all the good you're doing for the world. You start off doing it for all kinds of dumb reasons—because it's cool, because you get to hang out with your friends all day—but the only thing you get out of it is money. And the money becomes your obsession.

4. They came to us suffering for more of that shit. We relieved them and then cleaned up whatever money they had. This line is meant somewhat ironically in the song, but the truth is that drug addicts have a disease. It only takes a short time in the streets to realize that out-of-control addiction is a medical problem, not a form of recreational or criminal behavior. And the more society treats drug addiction as a crime, the more money drug dealers will make "relieving" the suffering of the addicts.

5. "Hundred dollars a week" is not a lot of money for a cat waking up early in the morning, working all day dealing drugs to "fiends." The narrator here is still dreaming of big money, not making it. This is the reality of the low rungs of the drug game. But the ambition is still clear, not just in the scheming but in the work he's doing to get what he wants, waking up early, throwing on yesterday's clothes, and hitting the block hard.

6. This is *the best of times and worst of times,* but it's also the best and worst of who we are and what we can be. The narrator is caught up in a crazy system, one that treats addicts like criminals and forces the young and ambitious into a life that might end with him shot up or locked up. To me, there's something moving about the kid who goes to sleep dreaming about plans to make money, wakes up early with a Colgate smile, buries his work in the dirt, and fills his small pocket with crack rocks (*pockets full of hope,* I call them in "Renegade"). When he's swarmed by fiends, lost souls driven by addiction, it's hard to know if we should be happy for him because he's unloading his work, getting closer to his dream, or if we should feel fucked up because we know the shit is so hopeless. I like leaving the listener without an easy answer.

HONOR AMONG PREDATORS

COMING OF AGE
Featuring Memphis Bleek
(*Reasonable Doubt*, 1996)

COMING OF AGE (DA SEQUEL)
Featuring Memphis Bleek
(*Volume 2...Hard Knock Life*, 1998)

D'EVILS
(*Reasonable Doubt*, 1996)

BUT THE
RHYMING WAS
ALWAYS
FORCEFUL
AND NIMBLE,
SO THE GUYS
IN THE
AUDIENCE
WOULD GET
THEIR MINDS
BLOWN BY
KANE'S MIC
SKILLS AND
IGNORE THE
LADIES'-MAN
ROUTINES.

When Big Daddy Kane's first album, *Long Live the Kane,* came out, in 1988, I was still in the streets. I basically accepted that I'd be a hustler who happened to rap in his spare time. I thought the rap game was crooked and a little fake back then, but I admired people like Kane for making it work. Kane was playing a role, hip-hop's first playboy: He had the silk robes and pretty girls in all his videos, all that. But his flow was sick: *cuz I get ill / and kill / at will / teaching the skill / that's real / you're no thrill / so just stand still and chill as I build* . . . He was condensing, stacking rhymes one on top of another. Trying to keep up with him was an exercise in breath control, in wordplay, in speed and imagination. He was relentless on the mic.

I went on the road with Kane for a while—he knew me from that mix tape I was on with him and Jaz. I think he was considering starting his own label and might've had me in mind for a slot. I'm not sure, and nothing like that ever materialized. But I got an invaluable education watching him perform. Kane was like a hip-hop James Brown when it came to his live show. He had a bag of tricks for creating momentum, where to put in his hits, where to pull back. He would have his DJ, Mister Cee, cut off his big hit "Ain't No Half Steppin' " after one verse, and before the crowd could relax, he'd throw on something even hotter and dial up the energy even more. Kane would hit the stage with the gold rope and the double-breasted silk suit with no shirt and the girls would go crazy. Scoop and Scrap—his dancers—would do choreographed moves that Kane would step in and out of. But the rhyming was always forceful and nimble, so the guys in the audience would get their minds blown by Kane's mic skills and ignore the ladies'-man routines. He just had an incredible amount of showmanship—even today I use some of the ideas I picked up back then about pacing and performance in my own live show. He was generous, too: He'd stop the show and bring me out when nobody knew who the hell I was. Cee would put on a break beat—"Spread Love," by Take 6—and I'd just go in on it in the breakneck double- and triple-time rhyming that me and Jaz thought we'd pioneered. The crowd would go nuts.

Kane put me on a song on his *Daddy's Home* album in the early nineties. The video for the song was pretty low-budget, which worked out okay, because all the director could afford to do was something that looked real: They ran the cameras in the middle of the projects and filmed a bunch of hungry New York MCs spitting in a cipher, surrounded by a crowd. It was me, Scoob Lover, my man Sauce Money from Marcy, Ol' Dirty Bastard, fresh off Wu-Tang's debut, *Enter the Wu-Tang (36 Chambers),* and a kid named Shyheim, a sixteen-year-old babyfaced kid who was down with the Wu.

Shyheim was almost a decade younger than me but was already making some moves in the business. On "Show & Prove" he was rapping with grown men—including some veterans and future legends. In the video he waded through a grimy crowd, arms dicing up the air, oversized fitted to the side, stalking the concrete circle like he owned it. He looked even younger than he was, but he had a voice that sounded like it had been through something in Shaolin. I knew kids like that in Marcy. Maybe I'd been one.

WASN'T BORN HUSTLERS, I WAS BIRTHIN' 'EM

In the game there's always a younger guy who has an old soul and an understanding of things beyond his years. I mean in the street game, but it also applies to the music industry. An older guy will see a kid and think, *Man, that kid moves differently from the rest. He's ready for this life.* They know that if they find the right kid, they can put him under their tutelage and he'll get it fast, step right into the rhythm of the life. But it starts by the other guy watching him, trying to pick up clues.

If that sounds predatory, it's because recruiting new workers is one of the most predatory aspects of the game. When you're doing it, it's hard to see it that way because everyone comes into the game as a recruit—including the ones who eventually become recruiters. And most of the "older guys" doing the recruiting are barely out of their teens themselves, so they still know what it feels like to *want* to be put on.

When I wrote a song for my first album inspired by the tension between older guys and new recruits in the streets, I called Kane and told him, "Man, I wrote this song and I really want Shyheim on it." We tracked down Shyheim's people and in the end they said he couldn't do it for whatever reason—and at this point, I hadn't even made an album yet, so they weren't feeling pressed to let him do the song. But even though Shyheim is the one I was thinking about for the record, it didn't really matter that he said no. It was still a record I felt like I needed to make, I just needed someone who could represent what I thought I saw in Shyheim.

PEOPLE SET
BROTHERS
AGAINST
EACH OTHER
BY FEEDING
POISON TO
THE LESS
EXPERIENCED
ONE.

The next day I saw this kid I knew walking across Marcy. He looked like a little star already—the swagger in his bop, the clean gear. I knew his older brother, Andre, a little better, but Andre was a kid to me, too. I had this verse that needed a younger voice on it, but a young voice that was rough and full of ambition, and I just got a feeling from this kid. His name was Malik, but he'd soon rename himself Memphis Bleek.

I didn't just give him the verse, which I'd already composed. After all, I had no idea if he could pull it off. First there was a test. I collared him and said, "Look, I'm making an album and you can be on it, but you have to learn this song in twenty-four hours. You don't learn it, then you're not on it." He took the paper I handed him and looked it over. I'd written the verse down for him in some chicken scratch, and when he held it up, I could tell he was thinking, *Shit, I can't hardly read this*. But he took it and went home.

He came to my apartment the next day and spit the whole thing like he'd been doing it his whole life. That same day we went over to the producer Clark Kent's house, where Clark had a basement studio. When we got there, I ordered food for everyone. I asked Bleek what he wanted and he sort of casually ordered six bacon cheeseburgers. I looked at this kid, and back then Bleek was a thin dude, and I was like, *Word?* I'm thinking he's trying to take advantage of me. But I went ahead and ordered them, and when they came, I sat the bag in front of Bleek and told him to get busy because I was going to make sure he ate all six of them. As he unwrapped the first burger I was thinking that the stomach-ache he was about to have would be lesson number one for this little nigga: Don't take advantage of people's kindness. But Bleek wasn't paying me any mind. He hunched over those wrappers and ate every single one of those burgers and was like, *Bet, let's get to the booth*. He was hungry. And nervous.

These little tests I gave Bleek had a direct parallel in the lyrics to the song I'd given him. It was called "Coming of Age," and the key line is when my character in the song offers Bleek a thousand dollars to ride around the hood. He replies *A G? / I ride witchu for free / I want the long-term riches*. He passes the test by showing that he's down to learn and is already thinking about the bigger picture rather than coming for a handout.

AND EVEN IF I DIE HE'S IN MY WILL SOMEWHERE

For my third album, I decided to come back to the story of the two characters from "Coming of Age." By the time we get to "Coming of Age (Da Sequel)," the dynamic is a little different. This kid you recruited to be a member of your team now wants to be the star player. He's got a little crew of his own, and people are telling him he should be the boss, that he should take you out. The first verses of the song, when so much of the action happens, are all written as internal thoughts. The words we're rapping are unspoken. It's a conversation that's happening in the two characters' heads. But that's real life. The person that betrays you won't yell out his plans to turn on you—but he might think them so loud you can practically hear it.

I'd seen this kind of thing happen in the streets a million times—people set brothers against each other by feeding poison to the less experienced one. But it happens all over, not just in the streets. In fact, the inspiration for coming back to the "Coming of Age" story was what was happening with Bleek in real life. Just like the character in the song, after the original song Bleek got a little fame in the hood. He built up a following of chicks in Marcy and started feeling himself—which is understandable. But then it came time to record the next album. I made plans to meet Bleek at the studio to work on some new material and he didn't show. I called his house and his moms told me he wasn't feeling well. Now this was the same kid who ate six bacon cheeseburgers without blinking. I wasn't buying it.

So I broke down to the projects and knocked on his door. His moms cracked it open.

"Hey, Val, what's up? Where's Bleek?"

She just pointed to the back of the apartment and told me, "Go get him." I knocked on his bedroom door, and he was in there with some chick. And that was it for me. I told him, "Look, you want to be here? Be here." And I left. He called later about the tour and I told him, "What tour?" He asked about the new album and I was like, "What new album?" I cut him off. He'd forgotten why I put him on in the first place. I loved his hunger. But he got full real quick.

Bleek was still just a kid and took the lesson like a man. And when it came time for album number three, he was back, and after that he launched his own career. Today he's running his own label—and still touring with me. I can't even count the times over the years niggas have tried to bait Bleek into a battle with me about his position. They don't see the respect I have for him or the strength of character it takes for him to play a supporting role while he's also trying to build his own thing. Bleek has turned out to be one of the most secure guys I've met or done business with, which is ironic, given that he started off being the youngest.

When people say hustling is easy money they couldn't be more wrong. Paranoia and fear worm their way into every interaction you have. When somebody says hi to you, you can't just say hi back and keep it moving. You have to watch the person's body language, silently speculate about their intent. Was it too enthusiastic and artificial? Was it reticent, a way of pulling away? Most important, is he working with the cops? It can wear you down.

The second "Coming of Age" song is meant to reflect the constant internal cycling that's never spoken and the intense way we analyze each other, with even slight body language serving as a life-or-death clue. It's also meant to capture the power of brotherhood: They say that soldiers in armies don't fight for the cause, they fight for each other, and that's the same motivation for a lot of kids in the streets. Of course, just like in war, older guys use that kind of loyalty as a way to exploit the kids working for them. But I wanted to show how easily young guys are drawn into that life and into danger—from the almost pathetic eagerness to become a hood star in the first song to the weed-and-peer-pressure ambition of the second. It's easy to get in, and to get deeper and deeper, but like the lyric says, till death do us part. In the end it's a song about mutual loyalty, a rare thing on the streets, and just as rare off of them.

COMING OF AGE / FEATURING MEMPHIS BLEEK

*[Jay-Z] Yeah . . . / Come experience . . . life as we know it / As some of you should know it, yeah, yeah / Place, Marcy, Brooklyn / Actions . . . well, y'all know the action*s / Uhh, I got this shorty on my block always clockin **my rocks**[1] / He likes the style and profile I think he wanna mock / He likes the way I walk, he sees my money talkin / **the honies hawkin I'm the hottest nigga**[2] in New York and / **I see his hunger pains, I know his blood boils**[3] / He wanna run with me, I know this kid'll be loyal / I watched him make a few ends, to cop his little sneakers and gear / **then it's just enough for re-up again**[4] / I see myself in his eyes, I moved from Levi's / to Guess to Versace, now it's diamonds like Liberace / That's just the natural cycle, nobody wanna **be like Michael** / **where I'm from, just them niggaz who bounced**[5] from a gun / We out here trying to make hard white into cohhhhld green / I can help shorty blow out like Afro-Sheen / Plus I can relive my days of youth which is gone / That little nigga's peeps, it's time to put him on / *[Jay-Z and Memphis Bleek]* It's time to come up (and hold my own weight, defend my crown) / Gots to lock it down and when they rush (stand my ground) / It's time to come up (stick up my chest, and make some loot) / Gots to lock it down and when they rush (stand on my own two) / *[Memphis Bleek]* **I'm out here slingin**[6] bringin the drama, tryin to come up / in the game and add a couple of dollar signs to my name / **I'm out here servin**[7] disturbin the peace, life could be better / like my man reclined in plush leather seats /

1. Rocks here refer to jewelry, diamonds specifically; shorties can refer to girls or to any kid, which is how I'm using it here.

2. "In reality, we from the same building. He was the guy coming through with the fine women, fly cars . . . I was always the young guy looking up." —Memphis Bleek, *Making of Reasonable Doubt* documentary.

3. The "hunger pains" refer to being hungry with ambition or literally hungry, because he's broke. Feeding someone makes him loyal, at least in the short term.

4. He's making just enough money to get more supply—"re-up"—and get a little gear, but he's still in the minor leagues, looking for a promotion.

5. This refers to the old "be like Mike" commercials. The guys who didn't have the stomach for this life bounced from it.

6. *Slingin* is slang for selling drugs. I like the way it makes you think of reckless Old West outlaws, gunslingers, which makes it work well with "bringin the drama."

7. *Servin* is also slang for selling drugs. While "slingin" feels cocky and aggressive, "servin" feels more workmanlike and submissive, which works with the lyrics here—"life could be better."

He's sellin weight, I'm sellin eight . . . balls / sixteen tryin to graduate to pushin quarters y'all / I ain't gon' sweat him I'ma let him come to me / If he give me the nod then these niggaz gon' see / I'm tired of bein out here round the clock / and breakin day, **and chasin crackheads up the block for my pay**[8] / I'm stayin fresh, so chickens check / I'm tryin to step up to the next level, pushin Vettes to the Jets / Diamonds reflect from the sun, directly in your equilibirum / is stunned I'm waitin for my day to come / I got the urge to splurge, **I don't wanna lifetime sentence / just give me the word**[9] [*JZ*] Hey fella I been watchin you clockin / [*MB*] **Who me holdin down this block it ain't nothin**[10] / You the man nigga now stop frontin / [*JZ*] Hahahh I like your style / [*MB*] Nah, I like YO' style / [*JZ*] Let's drive around awhile / [*MB*] Cool nigga / [*JZ*] Here's a thou' / [*MB*] A G? I ride witchu for free / **I want the long-term riches and bitches**[11] / [*JZ*] Hold up; now listen to me / You let them other niggaz get the name, skip the fame / **Ten thou' or a hundred G keep yo' shit the same**[12] / [*MB*] On the low? / [*JZ*] Yeah, the only way to blow / You let your shit bubble quietly / [*MB*] AND THEN YOU BLOW! / [*JZ*] Hey keep your cool / The only way to peep a fool is let him show his hand / Then you play your cards / [*MB*] Then he through dealin, I understand / [*JZ*] Don't blow your dough on hotties / [*MB*] The only thing I got in this world is my word and my nuts / **and won't break em for nobody!**[13] [*JZ*] Hah, I like your résumé, pick a day, you can start [*MB*] **From now until death do us part . . .**[14]

8. This is the glamorous life of the young hustler. It wasn't always a simple transaction—you might find yourself doing crazy things to get paid, holding people's welfare cards hostage, literally chasing people down the streets, staying up all night and watching the sun come up on the corner. But you do it for the possibility that one day someone will pick you as the one to step up to the next level.

9. A little play on words that's meant to keep the listener's mind on how deep this conversation really is: If Bleek gets "the word" and gets deeper in the game, he's not just going to get the Vettes and diamonds, he's also going to have more serious consequences to pay if he fucks up—his life, in fact.

10. This conversation starts casually then turns into an interview and then a test.

11. These are the key lines in the song. It's about loyalty, but it's also a little heartbreaking how much this little nigga wants to get down. In our live shows around this time, I used to literally hand Bleek a stack of bills when we hit this line, and he would toss it out to the crowd. Dramatic shit.

12. This is a classic piece of OG advice. It's amazing how few people actually stick to it.

13. "All I have in this world is my balls and my word, and I don't break them for no one." —Tony Montana, *Scarface*

14. The word "résumé" makes it sound like the end of any other job interview, but then Bleek ends with a blood vow, "until death do us part," which reminds us that the stakes are higher than a nine to five.

COMING OF AGE (DA SEQUEL) / FEATURING MEMPHIS BLEEK

[*Jay-Z*] Uh-huh uh yeah, gi-gi-geyeah / Time to come up, hold my own weight, defend my crown / Gots to lock it down and when they rush—part two / [*MB*] Cocaine whiter now / [*JZ*] Operation is sweet / [*MB*] Whole game tighter now / [*JZ*] Movin a brick a week / [*MB*] Plus a nigga price is down / [*JZ*] We them niggaz to see / [*MB*] Time to start the arisin now / [*JZ*] I don't know what's wrong with Bleek / [*Jay-Z*] **It seems I'm like Keenan, pickin up on the vibe**[1] / that he ain't too happy, I could just see it in his eyes / I don't know if it's the chicks or how we dividin the loot / Time to pay his ass a visit 'fore he decide to get cute / Jumped out like a star with the flyest car / **Matchin the gator shirt, softer than my next door neighbors**[2] / These young niggaz think I fell out the loop / cause the last time they seen me hoppin out the Coupe / I hopped out in a suit / [*Memphis Bleek*] Look at this nigga Jay frontin tryin to take my shine / **I didn't say this verbally, just had some shit on my mind**[3] / Plus I'm puffin like an ounce, more than I used to puff / **Takin advice from these niggaz but they ain't used to stuff**[4] / They had me thinkin, "Shit, I'm the one that moved the stuff / while he drive around town in brand new Coupes and stuff" / Swear to God, they had me practically hatin his guts / As he approached I spoke, "Jigga whattup?" / [*Memphis Bleek*] **I done came up (uhh) put my life on the line (uhh)**[5] / Soaked the game up (yeah) now it's my time to shine / Time to change up (what?) no more second in line / Nine-eight, these streets is mine (uh-huh, uh-huh, uh-huh-uh-huh-uh-huh) / [*Jay-Z*] Look at that fake smile he just gave me, it's breakin my heart / **Should I school him or pull the tools out and just break**[6] him apart / I felt his hatred it was harsh, 'fore this fakin shit start / **I should take him in back of the building and blaze**[7] him / [*Memphis Bleek*] Uh-oh, this nigga Jay he ain't slow, he musta picked up on the vibe / and had I not been so high I woulda been able to hide / Tried to cover up myself, as I gave him a five / Hugged him, as if I loved him / [*Jay-Z*] To the naked eye / It woulda seemed we was the closest, but to those that know us / **could see that somethin**[8] was about to go down / [*Memphis Bleek*] Stay focused / I'm tryin to concentrate, but it's like he's reading my mind / **As if he can see through this fog and all this weed in my mind**[9] / Could he see I had plans on, bein the man / **Ever since we first spoke and he put that G in my hand**[10]/ And I gave it back to show him, I was down for the cause / As he approached ("Whattup Bleek?") and I paused . . . / [*Chorus: Memphis Bleek and Jay-Z*] / [*Jay-Z*] Right, yo we wild out in Vegas, styled on haters / Mouthed off at the cops, I done crammed in every drop **Copped whips the same color, we tighter than brothers**[11] / with different fathers but same mothers, **this life don't love us / So till death do us,**[12] I'm never breakin my bond / Nigga we Lex movers, V-12 pushers / [*Memphis Bleek*] / As I stand / One leg of my pants up, in a stance like, "And what?" / I know these niggaz are feedin my mind cancer / But in time's the answer / Seems mind-blowin, this weed and Hennessey / Got my mind goin, trust me nigga, I'm knowin / Chicks used to ignore me, in my ear sayin I need fifty / not sixty-forty / [*Jay-Z*] / Oh God, don't let him control y'all / **Your gun is my gun, your clip is my clip baby**[13] / [*Memphis Bleek*] Your fun is my fun (uh-huh) your bitch is my bitch / Any nigga tryin to harm Jay I'm feelin for you / I ain't only touchin you, I'm killin your crew / [*Jay-Z*] / **Give it a year, you'll be sittin on a million or two / records sold nigga,**[14] perfect your roll

1. Keenan Ivory Wayans hosted a late-night talk show that ran at the same time as *Vibe*'s late-night talk show, a rare moment when two late-night shows hosted by black people ran at the same time. They competed against each other, which is why Keenan was trying to "pick up on the vibe."

2. These details are meant to show that I'm no longer living in the same neighborhood. Instead I'm driving in from the suburbs, wearing a polo shirt, looking like the good life has made me softer than my new neighbors, who are themselves wealthy professionals, not gangsters.

3. All of these lyrics are internal, unspoken thoughts as the two men walk toward each other. The only lines spoken aloud are the last lines in the first two verses.

4. It's always the one who knows the least who is the first to start trying to tell someone what to do. The farther outside the circle someone is, it seems, the more they want to stir up resentment, mostly because they don't know better, or they're bored and have nothing better to do.

5. While in the first "Coming of Age" Bleek's character was almost casual about "until death do us part," now he realizes how serious it is to have real responsibility and actually put your life on the line.

6. *Tools* is obviously slang for a gun. I like that word here because it lets you know how at the end of the day I'm a professional, and even something as personal as this can be handled as coldly and impersonally as taking a hammer to a piece of defective machinery. At the same time the rhyme here—*breaking my heart/break him apart*—lets you know it's still more complicated than that for me.

7. The shift in slang—from talking about guns as tools that break things to talking about shooting as *blazing*—matches the shift in tone, from cold and professional to hot and emotional. In the streets we had as many words for guns and shooting as Eskimos had for snow. A single act had a million variations in emotion and intent.

8. All of this back and forth is happening with no actual words exchanged, but perceptive observers can see it all. The only spoken words occur at the end of each verse.

9. I wasn't trying to make some kind of anti-weed public service announcement, but the truth is even a minor slip can expose you. No matter how comfortable you feel, it's best to keep your mind clear.

10. This is a reference to the first "Coming of Age" and is the beginning of a change in tone in the song. He goes from bold to scared to humbled.

11. This is the key line in this verse. The bond they share isn't just that they "wilded out" in Vegas together, it's that they're both, ultimately, outcasts—unloved—who can depend only on each other. It's more than the money, it's a sense of brotherhood that bonds them.

12. Another reference to the original "Coming of Age," but this time it's my character repeating Bleek's vow from the first song: *until death.*

13. This third verse, which is spoken aloud, is about loyalty that goes deep—not just two guys who came together to make money and move on, but a relationship that's closer to kinship. You don't make these kinds of declarations of loyalty to just anyone you happen to hustle with.

14. In the end, I bring it back to music—and to the actual relationship between me and Bleek.

D'EVILS

This shit is wicked on these mean streets / None of my friends speak / **We're all trying to win,**[1] but then again / Maybe it's for the best though, 'cause when they're seeing too much / You know they're trying to get you touched / **Whoever said illegal was the easy way out couldn't understand the mechanics**[2] / And the workings of the underworld, granted / Nine to five is how you survive, I ain't trying to survive / **I'm trying to live it to the limit and love it a lot**[3] / Life ills, poison my body / **I used to say "fuck mic skills,"**[4] and never prayed to God, I prayed to / **Gotti**[5] / That's right it's wicked, that's life I live it / **Ain't asking for forgiveness for my sins, ends**[6] / I break bread with the late heads, picking their brains for angles on / all the evils that the game'll do / It gets dangerous, money and power is changing us / **And now we're lethal, infected with D'Evils . . .**[7] / We used to fight for building blocks / **Now we fight for blocks with buildings that make a killing**[8] / The closest of friends when we first started / But grew apart as the money grew, and soon grew blackhearted / Thinking back when we first learned to use rubbers / **He never learned so in turn I'm kidnapping his baby's mother**[9] / **My hand around her collar, feeding her cheese**[10] / She said the taste of dollars was shitty so I fed her fifties / About his whereabouts I wasn't convinced / **I kept feeding her money till her shit started to make sense**[11] / Who could ever foresee, we used to stay up all night at slumber parties / **now I'm trying to rock this bitch to sleep**[12] / All the years we were real close / Now I see his fears through her tears, know she's wishing we were still / close / Don't cry, it is to be / **In time, I'll take away your miseries and make it mine, D'Evils . . .**[13] / My flesh, no nigga could test / My soul is possessed by D'Evils in the form of diamonds and Lexuses / The exorcist got me doing sticks like / **Homie, you don't know me, but the whole world owe me / Strip!**[14] / Was thought to be a pleasant guy all my fucking life / So now I'm down for whatever, ain't nothing nice / Throughout my junior high years it was all friendly / But now this higher learning got the Remy in me / Liquors invaded my kidneys / Got me ready to lick off, mama forgive me / I can't be held accountable, D'Evils beating me down, boo / Got me running with guys, making G's, telling lies that sound true / Come test me, I never cower / For the love of money, son, I'm giving lead showers / Stop screaming, you know the demon said it's best to die / **And even if Jehovah witness, bet he'll never testify, D'Evils . . .**[15]

1. "Coming of Age" and "D'Evils" are two songs on the same basic theme. They're both about being in the game and they both deal with competition and friendship. But the "Coming of Age" songs are about a boss dealing with the rise of someone younger, while "D'Evils" is about the relationship between peers, two people who grew up together.

2. The "mechanics" here aren't about the technical details of the business, but the psychological and emotional machinery that's always working under the surface.

3. The first defense of a lot of people who take the criminal route is that they had no choice, which is almost true: Most of us had choices, but the choices were bleak. The street life was tough and morally compromised and sometimes ugly, but a dead-end nine-to-five job at permanent entry level wasn't all that attractive, either. The righteous seed in a hustler's mentality was this: He wanted something more for himself.

4. This reflects the way I actually thought: I ignored my god-given ability, never believing that someone from where I came from could make it out.

5. The whole idea of "D'Evils" is that the narrator is no longer just expressing his ambition to live a full life—he's been poisoned somehow, possessed with a desire for money, alienated from all that's good, and focused on the underworld, here represented by Mafia references.

6. The narrator isn't thinking about redemption or turning back—he's totally focused on making money, "ends."

7. "D'Evils"—this obsession with getting paid—is something the narrator picks up after he "breaks bread with the late heads," who school him in ruthlessness.

8. I'm describing childhood friends, who went from fighting for those blocks with ABCs on them to fighting to control buildings where they can move crack and "make a killing."

9. Here's where the song takes a sudden turn from a general analysis and reminiscences to a clear narrative. I tried to convey a lot of information in one line: that we were friends so close that we learned basic sex ed at the same time; that he "never learned," which sets him up as someone sloppier, less calculating and cunning than me; that he had a child as a result, and "a baby's mother"; and that I kidnapped her, which shows how profoundly "blackhearted" I had become, violently exploiting any opening—even the innocent mother of his child. The line goes from the innocence of two dumb kids learning to use condoms together, bypasses any happiness or joy about the birth of a child, and ends in a truly dark place. It's the poison of "D'Evils" sketched out in a few words.

10. The "cheese" is money, which I'm feeding her to try to get her to rat out the location of her man.

11. Extending the money-as-food metaphor, I keep feeding her larger bills till she shits out some information, the dollars breaking down to cents/sense as she digests them.

12. This reflects another movement from innocence to violence, from slumber parties to putting her to sleep forever.

13. In the end, I get her to do what I want, but it's a grim victory. Not only will blood be shed based on the information she's given me—hers and his—but the last vision of her, tears like a veil over her eyes, begging for both of their lives, is going to haunt me. Her miseries become mine.

14. Another quick scene: Possessed by material lust, the narrator sticks up random people. The quick line of dialogue is meant to show someone completely blinded by desire, reckless and aggressive, but also haunted, the kind of character who talks to his vics as he's robbing them, making jokes and justifying himself by saying the whole world has done him wrong, so now everyone owes him. This could be the same character from the opening verses; driven over the edge by the killing of his best childhood friend, now he's just a raging psychopath.

15. The song ends with a dizzying carousel of conversations: First the narrator addresses his mother, then his girl ("boo"), and finally a last victim. The narrator is completely lost to the "D'Evils." He taunts his victims, defends himself, brags about how low he gets down, invites niggas to try to come get him, like George Bush saying "bring 'em on" to the terrorists. The final two lines, contrasting the demons in his head with a God he thinks is powerless, show how deeply he's fallen into a moral vacuum. The song isn't about literal demonic possession, of course, even if some sloppy listeners claim that it is; the truth is you don't need some external demon to take control of you to turn you into a raging, money-obsessed sociopath, you only need to let loose the demons you already have inside of you.

99 PROBLEMS
(*THE BLACK ALBUM*, 2003)

NEGATIVE
•
SPACE

IGNORANT SHIT
FEATURING BEANIE SIGEL
(*AMERICAN GANGSTER*, 2007)

Hip-hop has always been controversial, and for good reason. When you watch a children's show and they've got a muppet rapping about the alphabet, it's cool, but it's not really hip-hop. The music is meant to be provocative—which doesn't mean it's necessarily obnoxious, but it is (mostly) confrontational, and more than that, it's dense with multiple meanings. Great rap should have all kinds of unresolved layers that you don't necessarily figure out the first time you listen to it. Instead it plants dissonance in your head. You can enjoy a song that knocks in the club or has witty punch lines the first time you hear it. But great rap retains mystery. It leaves shit rattling around in your head that won't make sense till the fifth or sixth time through. It challenges you.

Which is the other reason hip-hop is controversial: People don't bother trying to get it. The problem isn't in the rap or the rapper or the culture. The problem is that so many people don't even know how to listen to the music.

ART WITH NO EASEL

Since rap is poetry, and a good MC is a good poet, you can't just half-listen to a song once and think you've got it. Here's what I mean: A poet's mission is to make words do more work than they normally do, to make them work on more than one level. For instance, a poet makes words work sonically—as sounds, as music. Hip-hop tracks have traditionally been heavy on the beats, light on melody, but some MCs—Bone Thugs 'N Harmony, for example—find ways to work melodies into the rapping. Other MCs—think about Run from Run-DMC—turn words into percussion: *cool chief rocka, I don't drink vodka, but keep a bag of cheeba inside my locka.* The words themselves don't mean much, but he snaps those clipped syllables out like drumbeats, *bap bap bapbap.* It's as exciting as watching a middleweight throw a perfect combination. If you listened to that joint and came away thinking it was a simple rhyme about holding weed in a gym locker, you'd be reading it wrong: The point of those bars is to bang out a rhythmic idea, not to impress you with the literal meaning of the words.

But great MCing is not just about filling in the meter of the song with rhythm and melody. The other ways that poets make words work is by giving them layers of meaning, so you can use them to get at complicated truths in a way that straightforward storytelling fails to do. The words you use can be read a dozen different ways: They can be funny *and* serious. They can be symbolic *and* literal. They can be nakedly obvious *and* subliminally effective at the same time. The art of rap is deceptive. It seems so straightforward and personal and real that people read it completely literally, as raw testimony or autobiography. And sometimes the words we use, *nigga, bitch, motherfucker,* and the violence of the images overwhelms some listeners. It's all white noise to them till they hear a *bitch* or a *nigga* and then they run off yelling "See!" and feel vindicated in their narrow conception of what the music is about. But that would be like listening to Maya Angelou and ignoring everything until you heard her drop a line about drinking or sleeping with someone's husband and then dismissing her as an alcoholic adulterer.

But I can't say I've ever given much of a fuck about people who hear a curse word and start foaming at the mouth. The Fox News dummies. They wouldn't know art if it fell on them.

BILL O'REILLY YOU'RE ONLY RILING ME UP

"99 Problems" is almost a deliberate provocation to simpleminded listeners. If that sounds crazy, you have to understand: Being misunderstood is almost a badge of honor in rap. Growing up as a black kid from the projects, you can spend your whole life being misunderstood, followed around department stores, looked at funny, accused of crimes you didn't commit, accused of motivations you don't have, dehumanized—until you realize, one day, it's not about you. It's about perceptions people had long before you even walked onto the scene. The joke's on them because they're really just fighting phantoms of their own creation. Once you realize that, things get interesting. It's like when we were kids. You'd start bopping hard and throw on the ice grill when you step into Macy's and laugh to yourself when the security guards got nervous and started shadowing you. You might have a knot of cash in your pocket, but you boost something anyway, just for the sport of it. Fuck 'em. Sometimes the mask is to hide and sometimes it's to play at being something you're not so you can watch the reactions of people who believe the mask is real. Because that's when they reveal themselves. So many people can't see that every great rapper is not just a documentarian, but a trickster—that every great rapper has a little bit of Chuck and a little bit of Flav in them—but that's not our problem, it's their failure: the failure, or unwillingness, to treat rap like art, instead of acting like it's just a bunch of niggas reading out of their diaries. Art elevates and refines and transforms experience. And sometimes it just fucks with you for the fun of it.

This is another place where the art of rap and the art of the hustler meet. Poets and hustlers play with language, because for them simple clarity can mean failure. They bend language, improvise, and invent new ways of speaking the truth. When I was a kid in New York and the five Mafia families were always on the front page of the newspaper, the most intriguing character wasn't John Gotti, it was Vinnie Gigante. I'd see him in the *New York Post* under a headline like THE ODDFATHER, always in his robe, caught on camera mumbling to himself as he wandered around the Village. His crazy act kept him out of the pen for decades. He took it all the way, but every hustler knows the value of a feint. It keeps you one step ahead of whoever's listening in, which is also a great thing about the art of hip-hop. And it makes it all the more gratifying to the listener when they finally catch up. Turning something as common as language into a puzzle makes the familiar feel strange; it makes the language we take for granted feel fresh and exciting again, like an old friend who just revealed a long-held secret. Just that easily your world is flipped, or at least shaken up a little. That's why the MCs who really play with language—I'm talking about cryptic MCs like Ghostface who invent slang on the spot—can be the most exciting for people who listen closely enough, because they snatch the ground out from under you, and make the most familiar shit open up until it feels like you're seeing it for the first time.

RIDDLE ME THAT

So, "99 Problems" is a good song to use to talk about the difference between the art of rap and the artlessness of some of its critics. It's a song that takes real events and reimagines them. It's a narrative with a purposefully ambiguous ending. And the hook itself—*99 problems but a bitch ain't one*—is a joke, bait for lazy critics. At no point in the song am I talking about a girl. The chorus really makes that clear if you bother listening: the obvious point of the chorus is that I wasn't talking about women. It almost makes my head hurt to think that people could hear that and twist its meaning the full 180 degrees. But even as I was recording it, I knew someone, somewhere would say, "Aha, there he goes talking about them hoes and bitches again!" And, strangely, this struck me as being deeply funny. I couldn't wait to release it as a single. My only mistake was that I accidentally explained the joke in an early interview and that defused it for some listeners.

The phrase has become one of my most often repeated lyrics, because it works on all those levels, in its literal meaning, its ironic meaning, and in its sonic power (the actual sound of the words *but a bitch ain't one* is like someone spitting out a punch). And the joke of it is still potent: during the presidential primaries in 2008, some Hillary Clinton supporters even claimed that Barack Obama was playing the song at his rallies, which would've been hilarious if it was true. It's hard to beat the entertainment value of people who deliberately misunderstand the world, people dying to be insulted, running around looking for a bullet to get in front of.

But if you get caught up in the hook of the song, you miss something. Because between the incendiary choruses—on top of the guitar and cowbell Rick Rubin came up with—is a not-quite-true story. The story—like the language used to tell it—has multiple angles. It's a story about the anxiety of hustling, the way little moments can suddenly turn into life-or-death situations. It's about being stopped by cops with a trunk full of coke, but also about the larger presumption of guilt from the cradle that leads you to having the crack in your trunk in the first place. But forget the sermon: This isn't a song written from a soapbox, it's written from the front seat of a Maxima speeding down the highway with a trunk full of trouble.

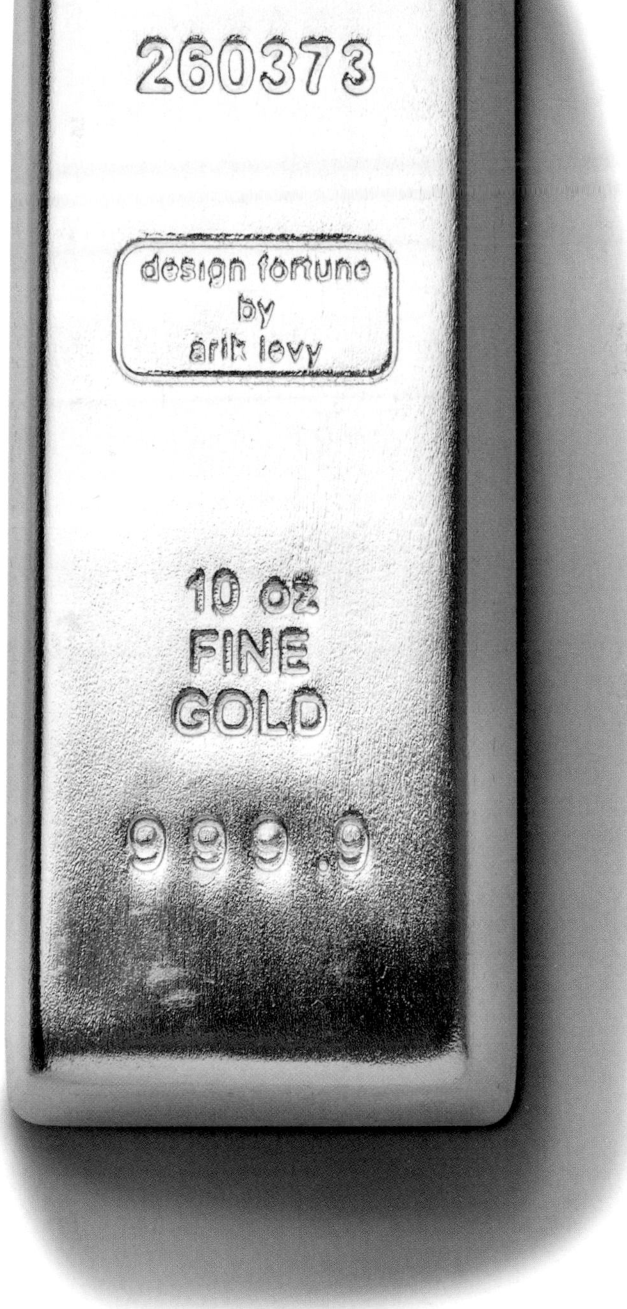
260373
design fortune
by
arik levy
10 oz
FINE
GOLD
999.9

The year is '94[1] **and in my trunk**[2] is raw / in my rearview mirror is the motherfucking law / I got two choices y'all, pull over the car or / bounce on the double put the pedal to the floor / **Now I ain't trying to see no highway chase with jake**[3] / Plus I got a few dollars I can fight the case / So I . . . pull over to the side of the road / And I heard "Son do you know why I'm stopping you for?" / **"Cause I'm young and I'm black and my hat's real low?**[4] / Do I look like a mind reader sir, I don't know / Am I under arrest or should I guess some mo?" / **"Well you was doing fifty-five in a fifty-four**[5] / License and registration and step out of the car / **Are you carrying a weapon on you, I know a lot of you are"**[6] / "I ain't stepping out of shit all my papers legit" / "Do you mind if I look round the car a little bit?" / "Well my glove compartment is locked, so is the trunk and the back / And I know my rights so you go'n need a warrant for that" / **"Aren't you sharp as a tack, some type of lawyer or something**[7] / Or somebody important or something?" / "Nah I ain't pass the bar but I know a little bit / Enough that you won't illegally search my shit" / "We'll see how smart you are when the K-9's come" / **"I got 99 problems but a bitch**[8] ain't one" / Hit me

1. This is based on a true story, but ultimately it's fictional. Our hero here is riding dirty, road-tripping down the turnpike from somewhere farther north, which is how things worked back in the eighties and early nineties. New York guys had better connects and opened up drug markets down the I-95 corridor. It was one of the factors that made coke money so thick in New York during that period, and the competition turned the game bloody from Brooklyn to Baltimore to D.C. to the Carolinas.

2. The car might've been a Maxima, which were big on the streets in '94. In the real-life version of this story, the trunk wasn't raw, it was a compartment in the sunroof that doubled as a "stash."

3. Jake is one of a million words for the boys in blue, but it's particularly dismissive and used mostly in New York, so it works as a way of establishing the character of the narrator. He's a slick New York kid.

4. "Driving while black" was usually a sufficient reason for the police to stop us. The first offense wasn't the crack in the ride but the color of the driver.

5. When we did work out of state, we would have everything planned down to the finest detail—but then get caught by a cop for no good reason, like "driving fifty-five in a fifty-four." Of course, the sarcasm in the speed limit being fifty-four is another way of saying that we're being pulled over for no good reason.

6. "A lot of you are" is another statement with racial undertones that he and I are both aware of.

7. This dialogue is about the tension between a cop who knows that *legally* he's dead wrong for stopping someone with no probable cause other than race, and a narrator who knows that legally *he's* dead wrong for moving the crack. But legality aside, they both think they're justified—and the fact is they're both used to getting away with it. So they're playing this cat-and-mouse game, taking sarcastic shots at each other, arguing over the law. The confrontation is casual and consequential all at once and shows how slippery language is, depending on which side of the conversation you're on.

8. In every verse of the song I use the word "bitch" in a different way. In this verse, the bitch is a female dog, the K-9 cop coming to sniff the ride. When I was living my version of this story, we got away—the K-9 was late, and the cop let me go. We were back on the road again, hearts pounding, crack still tucked untouched in the stash, when I saw the K-9 unit screaming up the highway, going in the opposite direction. It would've changed my life if that dog had been a few seconds faster. We had a strange kind of luck, some kind of rogue angel watching over us. But in the song I left the outcome ambiguous—does he get away or not? That's the writer in me. I like ambiguous endings, like Shane staggering off into the sunset at the end of the movie. Does he die or does he live? And the larger question: Should he die or live? I leave it to the listener to decide.

IGNORANT SHIT / FEATURING BEANIE SIGEL

Yessir! / Just the sound of his voice is a hit! / Y'all niggas got me really confused out there / I make "Big Pimpin" or "Give It 2 Me," one of those . . . / **Y'all hail me as the greatest writer**[1] of the 21st century / I make some thought-provoking shit / Y'all question whether he falling off / I'ma really confuse y'all on this one / Follow . . . / When them tops come down, chicks' tops come down / **Like when them shots come out make cops come around**[2] / When the blocks come out I can wake up a small town / **Finish off the block**[3] then I make my mall rounds / When them stares get exchanged then the 5th come out / The tough guy disappears then the bitch come out / "That's him"—I'm usually what they whisper about / Either what chick he with, or his chip amount / Cause I been doing this since **CHiPs was out**[4] / **Watchin Erik Estrada baggin up at the Ramada**[5] / Table full of powder, AC broke / **'Bout to take another shower on my 25th hour**[6] / **Spike Lees**[7] everywhere, game or the flight / You might see me anywhere, day in the life / Only thing changed the tail number on the flight / I can touch down and take off the same night / I'm so bossy / Bitch get off me / Trick get off me / You can't get shit off me / I'm so flossy / **No sixes on Sprees**[8] / laid back, Maybachs / Don't even talk to me! / [*first verse*] This is that ignorant shit you like / **Nigga, fuck, shit, ass, bitch, trick, plus ice**[9] / C'mon, I got that ignorant shit you love / **Nigga, fuck, shit, *maricon, puta,* and drugs**[10] / C'mon, I got that ignorant shit you need / Nigga, fuck, shit, ass, bitch, trick, plus weed / I'm only trying to give you what you want / Nigga, fuck, shit, ass, bitch, you like it don't front / **They're all actors**[11] / Looking at themselves in the mirror backwards / **Can't even face themselves,**[12] don't fear no rappers / They're all weirdos, DeNiros in practice / So don't believe everything your earlobe captures / It's mostly backwards / Unless it happens to be as accurate as me / And everything said in song you happen to see / Then actually believe half of what you see / **None of what you hear even if it's spat by me**[13] / And with that said, I will kill niggas dead / Cut niggas short, give you wheels for legs / I'm a K-I-double-L-E-R / See y'all in hell / **Shoot niggas straight through the E.R.**[14] / Whoa— this ain't BR, no / It's SC, CEO, the next Lyor? / No, the next leader of the whole free world / And the first thing I'ma do is free Sigel, go! [*third verse*]I missed the part where it stopped being about Imus / **What do my lyrics got to do with this SHIT?**[15] *Scarface* the movie did more than Scarface the rapper to me / **Still that ain't the blame for all the shit that's happened to me**[16] / Are you saying what I'm spittin / Is worse than these celebutantes showin they kitten, you kidding? / Let's stop the bullshittin / Till we all without sin, let's quit the pulpitting / *Scarface* the movie did more than Scarface the rapper to me / Still that ain't the blame for all the shit that's happened to me / Let's stop the bullshittin / Till we all without sin, let's quit the pulpitting, c'mon! / This is that ignorant shit you like / Nigga, fuck, shit, ass, bitch, trick, plus ice / C'mon, I got that ignorant shit you love / Nigga, fuck, shit, *maricon, puta,* and drugs / C'mon, I got that ignorant shit you need / Nigga, fuck, shit, ass, bitch, trick plus weed / I'm only trying to give you what you want / Nigga, fuck, shit, ass, bitch, you like it don't front

1. This is a slight exaggeration.

2. In the opening four lines of the song, I made sure to include the big four "ignorant" subjects: chicks taking off their clothes, guns popping, drugs getting sold, and spending money. The rest of the song follows from there.

3. The first block is a block of coke; the second is the actual city block.

4. The television show *CHiPs* ran from 1977 to 1983. Truthfully, I wasn't doing this since I was eight, but close.

5. There are a lot of motel references in my songs. Motels are where a lot of our work got done, where we bagged our powder.

6. In Spike Lee's movie, the 25th hour was the moment right before the main character went to prison. Every hour is the 25th hour when you're on the streets; it can end at any moment.

7. "Spike Lees" are slang for the best seats in the house—in this case, whether it's at the arena or in the jet.

8. Sprewells are custom rims that have an internal disk that spins when the car stops, named after Latrell Sprewell, who started

selling them in his custom shop. Fun for kids, but for grown-ups, a sign that you might be trying too hard.

9. A satisfying list of ignorant words—childish and adult at the same time, like a rapper with Tourette's.

10. A bilingual list of ignorant words, just to make sure everyone's included.

11. When I say that rappers are actors, I mean it in two ways: First, a lot of them are pretending to be something they're not outside the booth; second, it also means that even rappers who are being real often use a core reality as the basis for a great fantasy, the way a great Method actor like DeNiro does.

12. They're standing in the "mirror backwards" because they can't face themselves. No matter how convincing you are to the rest of the world, you still know the truth, and in a private moment it shames you enough to turn away from your own reflection. I bring back the idea a few lines later, when I say that what they're saying in their rhymes is as backward as their posture in the mirror.

13. This Marvin Gaye reference also makes the point that even an honest rapper has the liberty to make things up, because it's entertainment.

14. The concept of this song was a license to go completely over the top. But there's a serious point in the end.

15. Imus called the Rutgers women's basketball team a "bunch of nappy-headed hoes," and the debate over his dismissal somehow got turned into a debate about the language used in rap.

16. We give violent movies a pass but come down hard on a rapper like Scarface, who is ultimately a storyteller just like Brian de Palma. And neither of them is responsible for the poverty and violence that really do shape people's lives—not to mention their individual choices.

PART II

ILL

OSE

I met Bono years ago, in the cigar room of a bar in London with Quincy Jones and Bobby Shriver. I'd spent most of the night quizzing Quincy about *Thriller*, the greatest album ever made. Quincy graciously answered all of my detailed questions, questions he's probably asked four times a week, and then gave me a history lesson about his days as a jazz musician, telling stories about touring Europe in the fifties and sixties with Dizzy, Miles, and Ray Charles.

Bono was beaming and laughing the whole time. I liked him right away. I knew who he was, of course, as a musician and philanthropist and human rights activist. I knew U2's hits like everyone else on the planet, but I was completely unprepared for what a genuine, humble, and open person he is. Bono's got such a pure soul and positive energy—his eyes almost literally light up and dance when he's excited. He's one of those people who always seem hungry—for new information and experiences, and then impatiently generous to share the things he's consumed.

After Quincy talked for more than an hour, Bono pulled out a song U2 had recorded earlier in the day. I was traveling with one of those boom-boxes that are built into backpacks, the ones skateboarders use, and at three in the morning in that cigar room Bono played his new song for us on that box, eager to hear what we thought—including me, even though he'd never met me before. Later, when he heard me tell Quincy I was going to meet some friends in the morning and head to the south of France for the first time, he offered to fly me to Nice in his plane. I didn't tell him just how many friends I was traveling with—which was a lot, too many for his plane—but I really didn't want to impose anyway.

We became friends after that night. Years later, we both became investors in a restaurant in New York, the Spotted Pig in Greenwich Village. One night I ran into him there and he told me he'd read an interview I'd done somewhere. The writer had asked me about the U2 record that was about to be released and I said something about the kind of pressure a group like that must be under just to meet their own stan-dard. Bono told me that my quote had really gotten to him. In fact, he said it got him a little anxious. He decided to go back to the studio even though the album was already done and keep reworking it till he thought it was as good as it could possibly be.

I really wasn't trying to make him nervous with that quote—and I was surprised to find out that at this point in his career he still got anxious about his work. What I thought I was doing was expressing sympathy. Here he is, Bono, star, master musician, world diplomat, philanthropist, all of that. It was only right that I met him and Quincy Jones on the same night—they're both already in the pantheon.

I tried to explain all of that to him and we ended up trading stories about the pressure we felt, even at this point in our lives. I explained how I've always believed there's a real difference between rock and hip-hop in terms of how the artists relate to each other. In hip-hop, top artists have the same pressure a rock star like Bono has—the pressure to meet

expectations and stay on top. But in hip-hop there's an added degree of difficulty: While you're trying to stay on top by making great music, there are dozens of rappers who don't just compete with you by putting out their own music, but who are trying to pull you down at the same time. It's like trying to win a race with every runner behind you trying to tackle you. It's really not personal—at least it shouldn't be—it's just the nature of rap. Hip-hop is a perfect mix between poetry and boxing. Of course, most artists are competitive, but hip-hop is the only art that I know that's built on direct confrontation.

TAKE YOUR LAST TWO DEEP BREATHS AND PASS THE MIC

There are rap groups, of course, but one thing you'll hardly ever find in hip-hop is rappers harmonizing on the mic. The rule is one person on the mic at a time. And you have to earn the right to get on the mic. No one just passes you a mic because you happen to be standing there. In the earliest days of hip-hop, MCs had to prove themselves to DJs before they could rock a party. The competition grew from there—after a while it wasn't just about who could rock the party or the park or the rec center, it was about who could rep the hood, the borough, the city. Then when people started getting record deals, the battles exploded again, but now they were over national dominance and sales.

Sales battles are a hip-hop phenomenon that you just don't see played out in the same explicit, public way in other genres of music. Rappers can be like gambling addicts who see a potential bet everywhere they look. Everywhere we look, we see competition. A couple years back, when I was still running Def Jam, 50 Cent challenged Kanye West to a battle over who would get the biggest first-week sales numbers. This was when 50's *Curtis* album and Kanye's *Graduation* were scheduled to come out the same day. The whole thing was fun and useful marketing—and 'Ye won by close to three hundred thousand units—but it was also kind of strange to watch people, regular fans, get so caught up in this battle over numbers. Only in hip-hop.

I'm not complaining. I love the competition—even the sales battles. Before the Kanye situation, I had my own relatively low-key battle with 50 Cent. When I was about to release *The Black Album* we had to push up the release date to get the jump on bootleggers, which put us into the same initial sales week as *Beg For Mercy,* the first album from 50's crew, G-Unit. 50, in his showman style, got on the radio and announced that he was putting money on *Beg For Mercy* outselling *The Black Album*. This was the same year that 50's first album, *Get Rich or Die Trying*, had an incredible run, including huge first-week numbers. Kevin Liles at Def Jam called me asking if I wanted to push the date back a couple of weeks to give 50's album—and some other high-profile releases that week—a chance to breathe. I love Kevin; he's one of the nicest people you'll ever meet. But I told him to put my shit out as planned.

The Black Album debuted at number one, *Beg For Mercy* was third, and the soundtrack to *Resurrection,* the Tupac documentary, was the number two album on the charts. There was something beautiful about Pac being my closest competition on the charts that week. Aside from the heartbreak of losing two great MCs—and one great friend—I've always felt robbed of my chance to compete with Tupac and Biggie, in the best sense, and not just over first-week sales numbers. Competition pushes you to become your best self, and in the end it tells you where you stand. Jordan said the same thing about Larry Bird and Magic. He'd spent this whole career at North Carolina waiting to have the chance to play with them, and by the time Jordan and the Bulls were really coming into their own, Bird and Magic both retired.

But there's a risk in this kind of indirect, nonmusical "battling": the spectacle of competition can overshadow the substance of the work. That's when the boxing analogy breaks down and the more accurate comparison becomes professional wrestling, an arena where the showmanship is more important than actual skill or authentic competition. I'm not a professional wrestler. Rappers who use beef as a marketing plan might get some quick press, but they're missing the point. Battles were always meant to test skill in the truest tradition of the culture. Just like boxing takes the most primal type of competition and transforms it into a sport, battling in hip-hop took the very real competitive energies on the street— the kind of thing that could end in some real life-and-death shit—and transformed them into art. That competitive spirit that we learned growing up in the streets was never just for play and theater. It was real. That desire to compete—and to win—was the engine of everything we did. And we learned how to compete the hard way.

KNOCKED A NIGGA OFF HIS FEET, BUT I CRAWLED BACK

When I was sixteen years old, my friend Hill and I set up shop in Trenton, hustling, literally, on a dead-end street. There were a couple of

Hero relives 130-ft. rescue leap
SEE STORY PAGE 4

U.S. sends 5,000 troops to Kuwa
SEE STORY PAGE 2

DAILY ◉ NEWS

NEW YORK'S HOMETOWN NEWSPAPER

Saturday, September 14

Tupac Shakur dies of gunshot wounds

RAP REQUIEM

D.C. pols in uproar
PAGE 2

Stomp suspect nabbed
PAGE 3

Montauk house burns
PAGE 7

DAILY ◉ NEWS

NEW YORK'S HOMETOWN NEWSPAPER

http://www.mostnewyork.com

Wednesday, March 19, 1997

THE B.I.G. SLEEP

Thousands line Brooklyn streets to say goodbye to rapper Biggie Smalls

areas close by where other hustlers were working: in front of the grocery store, in front of a club on the main strip, out in the park. So we competed on price because we were getting our supply at lower numbers.

We started making some money, and we were styling, too—brand-new Ewings, new gear that wasn't even sold in Jersey yet. The local girls were loving us. Hill enrolled in the high school just to fuck with the girls. My dumb ass went up to meet him one day at the end of school and I got arrested by the school cop for trespassing; I had crack in my pockets, but since it was my first arrest and I had no prior offenses, they released me on my own recognizance and sealed it once I turned eighteen. But the damage was done—they confiscated the work I was holding. That combined with a series of other setbacks, and suddenly we were in a hole.

I went back to Brooklyn, stressed. I needed to make some money fast to cover the loss. A kid from Marcy owed me money, so I went out with him on the streets and worked for sixty straight hours. I would give him work to sell, wait while he turned it around, then take that money uptown to cop more work. I kept him working three nights in a row. His girl brought him sandwiches in the middle of the night. I stayed awake by eating cookies and writing rhymes on the back of the brown paper bags. Once I'd recovered my money, we headed back to Trenton.

When we got back, we worked even harder, determined to never be in a position where a loss would set us that far back. Meanwhile, kids in Trenton were really starting to hurt from the drop in prices we'd forced on them. Word got back to us that we weren't welcome in the park. This one kid, a boxer with a missing tooth, got into a hand-to-hand fight with Hill when he walked through the park anyway. We weren't gonna let some dudes in the park shut us down. It was like playground beef all over again, except niggas are damn near grown men, and holding. So how did we react to the scrap? We went to the park and confronted these cats at four in the afternoon, both sides armed and ready to shoot it out. We faced off and guns were drawn, but luckily nobody got shot. We did get respect. It was stupid and stressful, but we felt we didn't really have a choice. It was win or go home.

HAD A DREAM I SAID

You hear rappers talk a lot about winning, about being number one and taking out whoever's on top. There are very few beta rappers—it's alphas all the way. Even in rap groups or crews where you think there's an obvious leader, believe me, the other dude thinks he should be on top. Even the weed carrier thinks he could be the top guy. This is another way the streets bled into and shaped hip-hop.

What's the basic motivation for a hustler? I hit the streets for the same reason a lot of other kids do: I wanted money and excitement and loved the idea of cutting myself loose from the rules and low ceilings of the straight world. The truth is that most kids on the corner aren't making big money—especially if you break their income down to an hourly wage.* But they're getting rewarded in ways that go beyond dollars and cents. The kid on the streets is getting a shot at a dream. The dream is that he will be the one to make this hustling thing pay off in a big way. He sees the guy who gets rich and drives the nice car and thinks, yep, that'll be me. He ignores the other stories going around, about dudes who get shot or beaten to death with bricks and chains, the young guy in a wheelchair for life, the nigga out of state who never came home, the nigga upstate who'll never come home. But they're working that corner for more than whatever small cut they get of the crack they sell—they're working because they think they're due for a miracle. The kid in McDonald's gets a check and that's it. There's no dream in fast food. Manager? That's a promotion, not a dream. It took me a long time to realize how much courage it took to work at McDonald's, to walk through the streets past rows of hustlers wearing that orange uniform. But at the time, it seemed like an act of surrender to a world that hated us. I never even considered it as a possibility.

When you've got a nation of hustlers working for a small handful of slots, you learn something that you'll never learn at McDonald's. You learn to compete hard, even when you lose, because you can't settle for second-best as a hustler. It's not worth it. There's no pension and benefits for a scrambler. On the other hand, you might get killed. The only reason to do it is for the top slot, for the number one position. If not just for you, then for you and your crew. If you've got the heart and the brains you can move up quickly and start making enough money to break some off to

THEY'RE WORKING BECAUSE THEY THINK THEY'RE DUE FOR A MIRACLE.

*[The gang leader's] hourly wage was $66 . . . the foot soldiers earned just $3.30 an hour. In other words, a crack gang works pretty much like the standard capitalist enterprise: you have to be near the top of the pyramid to make a big wage . . . so if crack dealing is the most dangerous job in America, and if the salary is only $3.30 an hour, why on earth would anyone take the job?"
—Steven D. Levitt and Stephen J. Dubner, *Freakonomics*

give your moms or your girl a taste—and the ultimate dream seems even closer, worth more and more risks. There's no way to quantify all that on a spreadsheet, but it's that dream of being the exception, the one who gets rich and gets out before he gets got that's the key to a hustler's motivation. Legions of young cats chase after that ghost and die in the streets so a small handful of bosses—the ones who really did catch the miracle—can get richer. Sort of like the music business.

CAUSE I AIN'T SOLD THEM A DREAM, I JUST SHOWED THEM THE CREAM

When I was working out of state, every time I came home to New York I'd link with Jaz. We'd go back and forth to each other's houses and write rhyme for hours. We'd lock ourselves in a room with a pen, a pad, and some Apple Jacks and Häagen-Dazs. We were coming up with new flows, improving our speed, delivery, and composition.

One day in Jersey I got the call I had secretly been hoping for. Jaz got a record deal. EMI advanced him a ridiculous amount of money, nearly half a million. That was huge back then for rappers. That was R&B money. EMI was treating Jaz like the O'Jays, but only because they didn't know any better—they didn't know record labels were signing rappers for cars. The A&R department had convinced Jaz to work with Brian "Chuck" New, a producer who was riding on the success of the Fresh Prince. The label rented Jaz a flat in London to work with Chuck and record his debut.

Jaz invited me along for the ride. Inside I was doing backflips and shit, but when I told my crew, they didn't share my excitement. They thought I was bugging for leaving the block at a time when we were doing so well. "These rappers are hoes," was the general response. "They just record, tour, and get separated from their families, while some white person takes all their money." But it didn't matter to me. Jaz's money was real; I respected that. And even though I didn't go around talking about it to even my closest friends, I believed I could make it as a rapper, too.

Up until that point my life could be mapped with a triangle: Brooklyn, Washington Heights, Trenton. So everything about the trip to London—going to Rockefeller Center to get my passport, packing for a month-long trip, preparing for a trans-Atlantic flight—was new for me. It was a surreal, disorienting experience: two niggas from Marcy in a flat in Notting Hill. But it was fun, too. Once we got out there, I linked up with Monie Love, a cutie and a dope MC who'd recorded with De La.

She'd come through and take us to clubs and to the movies. Irv Gotti was out there, too, DJing for us for a time.

I wasn't really doing anything musical in London, but I was like a sponge when I'd sit in on Jaz's recording sessions and meetings. I never gave my opinion about how his business was being run. I was new and I didn't necessarily know how things worked in the music business. I did notice that even though we were in London more than a month, when the A&R guys from EMI finished Jaz's album, it didn't sound that different than his demo. The only new track they gave him was "Hawaiian Sophie," a poppy song with a ukulele on the hook. That wasn't a song Jaz would've come up with on his own. But we were looking at the plaques on their wall and thinking about the radio play they got Will Smith and we let them convince us that "Hawaiian Sophie" was gonna make this nigga blow.

When we shot the video, we were crazy excited. We were wearing Bermuda shorts and leis, rhyming on a soundstage with sand and palm trees. It looks like a bad joke now, but back then it felt like we were shooting an action movie. Unfortunately, it didn't read that way once the video came out. That single was nearly career suicide for Jaz. He went from being courted at the highest level to not having EMI return his phone calls. The wildest shit about the whole thing was that the executives at EMI and Capitol who'd withdrawn support for Jaz's project were coming to me behind his back trying to holla at me on some solo shit. I thought to myself, "This business sucks." No honor, no integrity; it was disgusting. In some ways it was worse than the streets. Jaz's debut album, something he'd been dreaming about his whole life, did come out, but in the end it was nothing more than a tax write-off for a giant corporation.

IS IT BACK TO CHARGING MOTHERFUCKERS 11 FOR AN O?

After the way EMI handled Jaz, I buried my little rap dreams. If I had any pent-up resentment or anger, I took it out on the block.

We started doing work in Maryland. Once again we had better prices than most kids in town but that didn't make things easy. I remember one night—the coldest night in my memory, bar none—we were hustling in front of the place where we were staying, which was stupid, but anyway, it was part of a development with long buildings facing each other at either end of the block. It created a wind tunnel along the paths between the buildings. We set up shop right in the middle of it. You couldn't really hang in the pathway because people really panicked—they didn't want it too hot. So we had to stand in this hole in the wall so we weren't technically in the pathway. And the nights were freezing. I mean, so cold that your nose couldn't even run. And in that bitter cold, folded into the crevices of a project wall, hundreds of miles from home, I sold crack to addicts who were killing themselves, collecting the wrinkled bills they got from God knows where, and making sure they got their rocks to smoke. I stood there thinking, "What the fuck am I doing?"

This was the flip side of the Life. Here's what I loved about hustling. Forget the money. It may sound strange, but it was usually a fun way to spend time. It was an adventure. I got to hang out on the block with my crew, talking, cracking jokes. You know how people in office jobs talk at the watercooler? This job was almost all watercooler. But when you weren't having fun, it was hell. Maryland ended badly, too—shootouts in clubs, major police investigations, whole crews arrested. I got out of there just in time. Some of my best friends weren't so lucky. It was tragic. I was making money, but winning on the streets, really winning, is hard, nearly impossible.

Maybe that's why boxing is almost a religion to hustlers and the big title fights in Vegas are like pilgrimages. In boxing, you have to impose your will on the situation. You have to make sure the match runs according to your style and rhythm and not get caught up in someone else's game plan. You have to be willing to suffer and to make someone else suffer, because only one of you can win. Once you're winning, you can't let up till the bell rings. And once you've won, you have to be gracious and let your opponent accept his defeat without humiliating him, because it's not personal.

Boxing is a glorious sport to watch and boxers are incredible, heroic athletes, but it's also, to be honest, a stupid game to play. Even the winners can end up with crippling brain damage. In a lot of ways, hustling is the same. But you learn something special from playing the most difficult games, the games where winning is close to impossible and losing is catastrophic: You learn how to compete as if your life depended on it. That's the lesson I brought with me to the so-called "legitimate" world.

A LITTLE BIT OF EVERYTHING, THE NEW IMPROVED RUSSELL

When I was moving off the streets and tried to envision what winning looked like, it was Russell Simmons. Russell was a star, the one who created the model for the hip-hop mogul that so many people—Andre Harrell, Puffy, even Suge Knight—went on to follow.

People in the record business had always made a lot of money. Not the artists, who kept dying broke, but the execs. Still, regular fans had no idea who they were. Russell changed that. His brand as an executive mattered not just within the industry, but among people in the street. And with Def Jam he created one of the most powerful brands in the history of American entertainment.

Russell also made being a CEO seem like a better deal than being an artist. He was living the life like crazy, fucking with models, riding in Bentleys with his sneakers sticking out the windows, and never once rapped a single bar. His gift was curating a whole lifestyle—music, fashion, comedy, film—and then selling it. He didn't just create the hip-hop business model, he changed the business style of a whole generation of Americans.

The whole vibe of start-up companies in Silicon Valley with twenty-five-year-old CEOs wearing shelltoes is Russell's Def Jam style filtered through different industries. The business ideal for a whole generation went from growing up and wearing a suit every day to never growing up and wearing sneakers to the boardroom.

Even as a teenager, I understood what Russell was on to. He'd discovered a way to work in the legit world but to live the dream of the hustler: independence, wealth, and success outside of the mainstream's rules. Coming from the life I was coming from, this was a better story than just being a rapper, especially based on what I now knew about how rappers got jerked.

I first met Russell when Dame, Biggs, and I were negotiating for a label deal for Roc-A-Fella after *Reasonable Doubt* dropped. I remember sitting across the table from him and Lyor Cohen in disbelief that we were negotiating a seven-figure deal with the greatest label in rap history. But I was also feeling a dilemma: I was looking at Russell and thinking, *I want to be this nigga, not his artist.* (In the end, we made a deal with Def Jam that kept us in control of Roc-A-Fella, instead of my just signing up as a solo artist.)

Russell would become a valuable informal mentor for us. He wasn't a gangster by any stretch, but he'd put in his time hustling, selling fake cocaine to college kids in the Village, that sort of thing. He reminded me of a lot of street dudes I'd known: He had a great memory, kept figures in his head, and was a quick judge of character. He also had tremendous integrity and confidence. He knew that the key to success was believing in the quality of your own product enough to make people do business with you on your terms. He knew that great product was the ultimate advantage in competition, not how big your office building is or how deep your pockets are or who you know. In the end it came down to having a great product and the hustle to move it, which was something I learned working the block. Russell was an evangelist for hip-hop. He knew the culture's power and was never shy about leveraging it and making sure that it was the people who were creating the culture who got rich off of it.

That idea was at the heart of Rocawear, the clothing company we founded. In the late nineties I was wearing a lot of clothes from Iceberg, the European sportswear designer. After a while, I'd look out into the audience after my concerts and see hundreds of people rocking Iceberg knits. So it became clear to us that we were directly influencing their sales. Dame set up a meeting with Iceberg and we tried to strike an endorsement deal. I don't even think my second album was out—and my first album hadn't exactly set the world on fire in terms of sales—and the executives at Iceberg looked at us like we were speaking a foreign language. They offered us free clothes, but we wanted millions and the use of their private jet; we walked out of their offices realizing we had to do it ourselves.

In the beginning it was laughable, since we had no idea what we were doing. We had sewing machines up in our office, but not professional ones that can do twelve kinds of stitches; we had the big black ones that old ladies use. We had people sewing shirts that took three weeks each. We actually thought we were going to make the clothes ourselves in our own little sewing shop. Eventually, we got some advice from Russell and did the necessary research, got some partners, and launched Rocawear properly. Once we committed to the fashion industry, we were committed to doing it right. We didn't want a vanity label. We wanted the top slot. I'm lucky that Iceberg didn't give us the bullshit we asked for in the first place, an endorsement contract that would've run out a long time ago, because we might not have ever started a company that's poised to bring in a billion dollars a year in revenue.

I'M A HUSTLER HOMIE, YOU'RE A CUSTOMER CRONY

The spirit of the Iceberg response was replayed years later with another company. From the first time I rapped the line *you like Dom, maybe this Cristal will change your life* on my first album, hip-hop has raised the profile of Cristal. No one denies that. But we were unpaid endorsers of the brand—which we thought was okay, because it was a two-way street. We used their brand as a signifier of luxury and they got free advertising and credibility every time we mentioned it. We were trading cachet. But they didn't see it that way.

A journalist at *The Economist* asked Frederic Rouzaud, the managing director of the company that makes Cristal: "Do you think your brand is hurt by its association with the 'bling lifestyle'?" This was Rouzaud's reply: "That's a good question, but what can we do? We can't forbid people from buying it." He also said that he looked on the association between Cristal and hip-hop with "curiosity and serenity." *The Economist* printed the quote under the heading UNWELCOME ATTENTION.

That was like a slap in the face. You can argue all you want about Rouzaud's statements and try to justify them or whatever, but the tone is clear. When asked about an influential segment of his market, his response was, essentially, well, we can't stop them from drinking it. That was it for me. I released a statement saying that I would never drink Cristal or promote it in any way or serve it at my clubs ever again. I felt like this was the bullshit I'd been dealing with forever, this kind of offhanded, patronizing disrespect for the culture of hip-hop.

Why not just say thank you and keep it moving? You would think the person who runs the company would be most interested in selling his product, not in criticizing—or accepting criticisms—of the people buying it.

The whole situation is probably most interesting for what it says about competition, and the way power can shift without people's being aware of it. It's like in chess, when you've already set up your endgame and your opponent doesn't even realize it. What a lot of people—including, obviously, *The Economist,* Cristal, and Iceberg—think is that rappers define themselves by dropping the names of luxury brands. They can't believe that it might actually work the other way around.

Everything that hip-hop touches is transformed by the encounter, especially things like language and brands, which leave themselves open to constant redefinition. With language, rappers have raided the dictionary and written in new entries to every definition—words with one or two meanings now have twelve. The same thing happens with brands— Cristal meant one thing, but hip-hop gave its definition some new entries. The same goes for other brands: Timberland and Courvoisier, Versace and Maybach. We gave those brands a narrative, which is one of the reasons anyone buys anything: to own not just a product, but to become part of a story.

Cristal, before hip-hop, had a nice story attached to it: It was a quality, premium, luxury brand known to connoisseurs. But hip-hop gave it a deeper meaning. Suddenly, Cristal didn't just signify the good life, but the good life laced with hip-hop's values: subversive, self-made, audacious, even a little dangerous. The word itself—Cristal—took on a new dimension. It wasn't just a premium champagne anymore—it was a prop in an exciting story, a portal into a whole world. Just by drinking it, we infused their product with our story, an ingredient that they could never bottle on their own.

Biggs first put me on to Cristal in the early days of Roc-A-Fella. We were drinking it in the video for "In My Lifetime" in 1994. We didn't have a record deal yet, but back then we'd show up at clubs in Lexuses and buy bottles of Cristal, while most people in the clubs were buying Moët. It was symbolic of our whole game—it was the next shit. It told people that we were elevating our game, not by throwing on a bigger chain, but by showing more refined, and even slightly obscure, taste. We weren't going to stick to whatever everyone else was drinking or what everyone expected us to drink. We were going to impose our sense of what was hot on the world around us.

When people all over started drinking Cristal at clubs—when Cristal became a household name among young consumers—it wasn't because of anything Cristal had done. It was because of what we'd done. If Cristal had understood this dynamic, they never would've been so dismissive. The truth is, we didn't need them to tolerate us with "curiosity and serenity." In fact, we didn't need them at all.

IS THIS WHAT SUCCESS IS ALL ABOUT?

There's a knee-jerk fear in America that someone—especially someone young and black—is coming to take your shit, fuck up your brand, destroy the quality of your life, tarnish the things you love. But in hip-hop, despite all the brand shout-outs, the truth is, we don't want your shit. We came out of the generation of black people who finally got the point: No one's going to help us. So we went for self, for family, for block, for crew—which sounds selfish; it's one of the criticisms hustlers and rappers both get, that we're hypercapitalists, concerned only with the bottom line and enriching ourselves. But it's just a rational response to the reality we faced. No one was going to help us. Not even our fathers stuck around. People who looked just like us were gunning for us. Weakness and dependence made you a mark, like a dope fiend. Success could only mean self-sufficiency, being a boss, not a dependent. The competition wasn't about greed—or not just about greed. It was about survival.

There are times when it gets exhausting, this focus on constant competition. There are times when it gets boring, especially these days when people use beef as a marketing plan. There's something heroic about the winning boxer standing at the center of the ring alone with his opponent sprawled at his feet, roaring "What's my name?" like Ali. But it's tough never being able to let your guard down.

When I described the landscape of hip-hop to Bono that night—a perpetual battlefield with new armies constantly joining in—he just shook his head. It's brutal, but if you step back from it, it's beautiful, too. What you're looking at is a culture of people so in love with life that they can't stop fighting for it—people who've seen death up close, literal death, but also the kind of dormancy and stagnation that kills your spirit. They've seen it all around them and they don't want any part of that shit, not at all. They want to live like they want to live—they want to impose themselves on the world through their art, with their voices. This impulse is what saved us. It's what saved me.

I don't scrap with every comer these days. I've got so many people coming at me that I'd never do anything else. I'm not just competing on records and I'm not just competing with rappers anymore. I look at things a little differently than I used to. The competition isn't always zero sum like it was on the streets of Trenton; I've discovered that there really is such a thing as a win-win situation. And sometimes, I'm only competing with myself, to be a better artist and businessman. To be a better person with a broader vision. But it's still that old sense of competition that motivates me. I'm still that nigga on the corner seven nights straight, trying to get back the money I lost. I'm still the kid who'd fight to be able to walk through a park in Trenton, the MC who'd battle anyone in a project courtyard or back room. This is what the streets have done for us, for me. They've given us our drive, they've made us stronger. Through hip-hop we found a way to redeem those lessons, and use them to change the world.

PORTRAIT OF THE ARTIST

AS A YOUNG STAR

1. MOST KINGS
(Unreleased)

2. SUCCESS
FEATURING NAS
(AMERICAN GANGSTER, 2007)

3. RENEGADE
FEATURING EMINEM
(THE BLUEPRINT, 2001)

4. CAN I LIVE?
(REASONABLE DOUBT, 1996)

Jean-Michel Basquiat was from Brooklyn, like me, although he spent most of his brief adult life in Soho, where he started off living in the streets as a graffiti artist who called himself SAMO. He later became a celebrity in the downtown scene in New York in the seventies and eighties. He was hanging with Madonna before she was famous and collaborated with Andy Warhol. He came onto the scene with a crew of graffiti writers but didn't want to be boxed in with that movement, so when the graffiti scene died, he didn't die with it. He moved in a white art world but flooded his art with black images, attitude, and icons. He wanted to be the most famous artist in the world. He was hip-hop when hip-hop was still in its cradle: If you look at the video for Blondie's "Rapture," the first rap song (using the word rap loosely) to play on MTV, you see Basquiat, young, skinny, standing in front of a set of turntables while Debbie Harry struts by. He played Spoonie Gee records at gallery openings. On the night he died—he was twenty-seven—Basquiat had been planning to see a Run-DMC show. When people asked him what his art was about, he'd hit them with the same three words: "Royalty, heroism, and the streets."

When he died, in 1988, I'm not sure I knew who he was, even though he was a Brooklyn kid like me and not that much older. He was deep in a world that I really didn't have much to do with—I was making money out of state and rhyming in Brooklyn, not hanging out with Andy Warhol at the Mudd Club. New York has a thousand universes in it that don't always connect, but we do all walk the same streets, hear the same sirens, ride the same subways, see the same headlines in the *Post,* read the same writing on the walls. That shared landscape gets inside of all of us and, in some small way, unites us, makes us think we know each other even when we don't.

Basquiat got his wish. He's probably among the most famous artists in the world, two decades after his death. I own a few of his paintings. He's known today, to some degree, as a painter that hip-hop seems to embrace. Part of that comes from his technique, which feels like hip-hop in the way it combined different traditions and techniques to create something new. He brought together elements of street art and European old masters. He combined painting and writing. He combined icons from Christianity and Santería and voodoo. He turned boxers and jazz musicians into kings with golden crowns. And on top of all that mixing and matching he added his own genius, which transformed the work into something completely fresh and original. The paintings don't just sit on my walls, they move like crazy.

LIGHTS IS BLINDING

Basquiat's work often deals with fame and success: the story of what happens when you actually get the thing you'd die for. One Basquiat print I own is called *Charles the First*—it's about Charlie Parker, the jazz pioneer who died young of a heroin overdose, like Basquiat. In the corner of the painting are the words, MOST ~~YOUNG~~ KINGS GET THIER HEAD CUT OFF.

Like a lot of the art Basquiat created, that line has layers of meaning. The head could mean the literal head on your shoulders or it could be referring to your other head—to castration. I read it as a statement about what happens when you achieve a certain position. You become a target. People want to take your head, your crown, your title. They want to emasculate you, make you compromise or sacrifice in a way that no man, or woman, should. And you resist it until one day your albums aren't moving and the shows aren't filling up and it seems like the game might have moved on without you. Then you start to change, you do whatever you need to do to get back into that spotlight. And that's when you're walking dead. One way or another, they get you.

The cliché is, be careful what you wish for, because you might get it. Nearly every rapper who's made it big—or has even been modestly successful—has had to deal with getting one of his heads chopped. Rappers like Pun, Big L, Ol' Dirty Bastard, Pimp C, among many, many others, have literally lost their lives just when they were about to peak. Rappers at the top of their game have been locked up, sometimes for long bids. The stories you hear can really make it seem like success can be a curse: rappers who've been dangled over balconies for their publishing money, driven out of their hometowns, fucked up by drugs, sued by their own families, betrayed by their best friends, sold out by their crews. There are rappers who blow up and blow through whole fortunes, squander every opportunity, and before you know it end up back on the block. The crazy thing is, we don't even question it anymore. We take it for granted.

I remember when Hammer was the biggest star in the world, in the eighties. There were a lot of people who clowned him because of the big pants and the dancing, like he was the rapper from Disney World. But Hammer was from East Oakland. Even when he was spinning around with his pants billowing all around him, you could see in his eyes that

HE SHOULD'VE
BEEN ON
A BOAT
SOMEWHERE
ENJOYING
HIMSELF
WITHOUT A
CARE IN THE
WORLD, NOT
WORRYING
ABOUT GET-
TING SHOT UP
ON HIS WAY
TO WORK.

this was still a nigga from the hood. So when he was in *Forbes* magazine with eight figures after his name, big pants and all, I was impressed. It was a huge moment for hip-hop. For a black rapper to make that kind of transition into the mainstream—and to get that kind of money—was unprecedented. A few years later, Hammer was filing for bankruptcy. Today when you see stars rise and fall like that, you just think, "Yep, he fucked it up." But with Hammer, it was the first time we'd seen that kind of fast movement from the bottom to the top and back again. It's no dis to Hammer to say that it was shocking to watch it happen. I'm sure he was as shocked as anyone.

And of course, two of the greatest rappers to ever do it were both murdered in their prime. The not-so-funny shit is that Pac and Biggie were perfectly safe before they started rapping; they weren't being hunted by killers until they got into music. Biggie was on the streets before he started releasing music, but he never had squads of shooters (or the Feds) coming after him until he was famous. And Pac wasn't even heavy in the street. It wasn't till he was a rapper that he started getting shot at, locked up, stalked by the cops—and eventually murdered.

I was reminded of this when I recorded "Moment of Clarity" with Eminem for *The Black Album.* It was 2003 and he was on top of the music world—three major multiplatinum albums, twenty million sold, a number one film with *8 Mile,* and on and on. He was probably the biggest star in the world. When we met at the studio, I reached over to give him a pound, and when we bumped, I could feel that he had on a bulletproof vest. Here was Eminem, someone who was doing the thing he loved and succeeding at it probably beyond his wildest dreams, and he had to wear a bullet-proof vest. *To the studio.* He should've been on a boat somewhere enjoying himself without a care in the world, not worrying about getting shot up on his way to work.

It's easy to take shots at performers when they seem to self-destruct. But there's another way to look at it. When you reach that top level, there's suddenly so much to deal with on all fronts—you have old friends and distant family who are suddenly close, people who feel like they should be getting rich from your success. You have a target on your back from other people—rappers, hustlers, angry cops—who feel like your success should be theirs. You have to deal with lawyers and accountants, and you have to be able to trust these people you're just meeting with everything you have. There's just more of everything. Women, money, "friends," piles of whatever your vice is. There's enough of whatever you love to kill you. That kind of sudden change can destabilize even the most grounded personality. And that's when you lose yourself—like the Eminem song says, *superstardom's close to a post-mortem.*

IT'S STRONGER THAN HEROIN

I was lucky in a lot of ways to have a body of life experiences already under my belt before I had to deal with a serious level of success. I'd made friends and lost them, made money and lost it and made it back. I'd watched people blow up in both games—music and hustling—and then watched them fuck it up and fall back to earth, hard. I was prepared. All that happened to me in music over the first years of my career mirrored a lot of what I'd seen before, just on a larger scale. Eventually the scale got so large that the comparisons stopped making sense or being as useful, but I'm lucky to have a lot of the same friends and family with me that I had when I was recording my first album, people who keep me grounded. I'm also lucky never to have needed the approval of the gatekeepers in the industry because from the start we came into the game as entrepreneurs. That gave me the freedom to just be myself, which is the secret to any long-term success, but that's hard to see when you're young and desperate just to get put on.

When Basquiat painted *Charles the First* he was only twenty-two. People always wanted to stick Basquiat in some camp or another, to paste on some label that would be stable and make it easy to treat him like a commodity. But he was elusive. His eye was always on a bigger picture, not whatever corner people tried to frame him in. But mostly his eye was probably on himself, on using his art to get what he wanted, to say what he wanted, to communicate his truth. Basquiat shook any easy definition. He wasn't afraid of wanting to succeed, to get rich, to be famous. But just because you want the shit doesn't mean you can handle it.

One critic said about Basquiat that the boys in his paintings didn't grow up to be men, they grew up to be corpses, skeletons, and ghosts. Maybe that's the curse of being young, black, and gifted in America—and if you add sudden success to that, it only makes it more likely that you'll succumb, like Basquiat did in a loft not far from the one I live in now, a loft filled with his art. But I don't think so. I don't accept that falling is inevitable— I think there's a way to avoid it, a way to win, to get success and its spoils, and get away with it without losing your soul or your life or both. I'm trying to rewrite the old script, but Basquiat's painting sits on my wall like a warning.

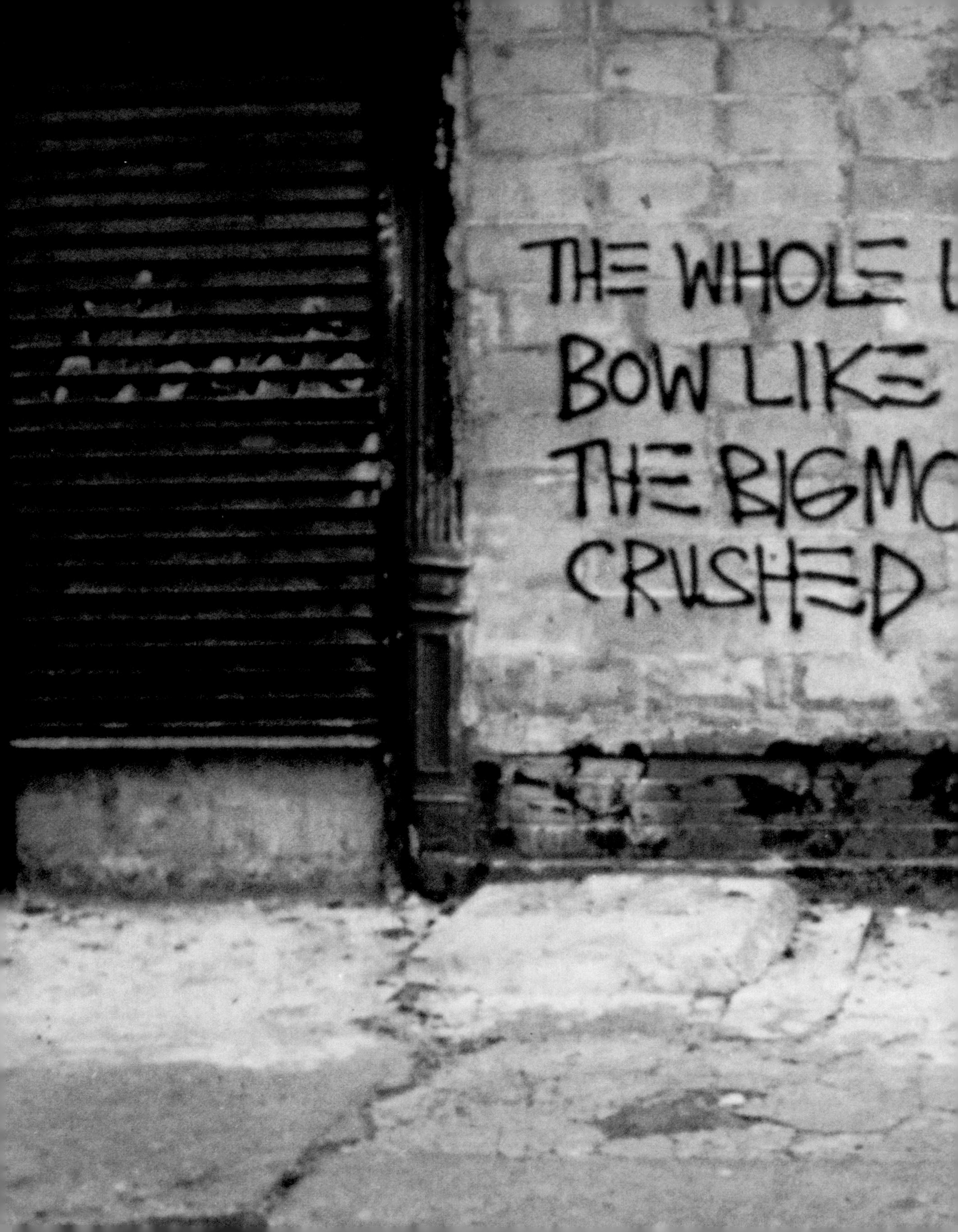

THE WHOLE L
BOW LIKE
THE BIGMO
CRUSHED

Inspired by Basquiat, my chariots of fire / Everybody took shots hit my body up I'm tired / Build me up, break me down, to build me up again / They like Hov we need you back so we can kill your ass again / Hov got flow though he's no Big and Pac but he's close / **How I'm supposed to win they got me fighting ghosts . . .**[1] / **Same sword they knight you they gonna good night you with**[2] / shit that's only half if they like you / That ain't he even the half what they might do / **Don't believe me ask Michael**[3] / See Martin, see Malcolm / You see Biggie, see Pac, see success and its outcome / See Jesus, see Judas / **See Caesar, see Brutus**[4] / See success is like suicide / **Suicide, it's a suicide**[5] / If you succeed prepare to be crucified / Hmm, media meddles, niggas sue you, you settle / Every step you take they remind you, you ghetto / So it's tough being Bobby Brown / **To be Bobby then, you gotta be Bobby now**[6] / **Now the question is, is to have had and lost / Better than not having at all**[7] / **Everybody want to be the**

against him, assuming the worst until they drove him away. When he died, suddenly he was beloved again—people realized that the charges against him might really have been bogus, and that the skin lightening was really caused by a disease, and that his weirdness was part of his artistry. But when he was alive and on top, they couldn't wait to bring him down. (In my opinion sharing sleeping quarters with other people's kids is inappropriate, to keep it real.)

4. Jesus and Caesar were both killed by people close to them, traitors.

5. A reference to KRS-One and Just-Ice's eighties classic "Moshitup." *Buddy-bye-bye!*

6. Bobby then was a young star when he was known for his hit record "Every Little Step"; Bobby now is better known for the hit reality series, *Being Bobby Brown,* a cautionary tale about how it can all slip away.

7. Shout-out to Alfred, Lord Tennyson: "'Tis better to have loved and lost, than to never have loved at all."

1. This is no shot at Big or Pac. The truth is that you can't compare us; Big only did two albums before he was killed, and Pac was still going through metamorphosis; who knows where he would've ended up. So when people make the comparison—as they always do—they're comparing my work not just with the work of Big and Pac, but with what they could've been—should've been—and what their lives and deaths represented to the entire culture. Their shadows still loom over all of us who were their peers.

2. I wanted to conjure an image here: someone kneeling, first to accept the honor of being knighted, and then being beheaded with the same sword, the posture of honor transformed to one of execution.

3. I wrote this before MJ died, and his death only proves my point: When he was alive, the King of Pop, people were tireless in taking him down, accepting as truth every accusation made

king till shots ring[8] / You laying on the balcony with holes in your dream / Or you Malcolm Xed out getting distracted by screams / **Everybody get your hands off my jeans**[9] / Everybody look at you strange, say you changed / Uh, like you work that hard to stay the same / Uh, game stayed the same, the name changed / So it's best for those to not overdose on being famous / Most kings get driven so insane / **That they try to hit the same vein that Kurt Cobain did**[10] / So dangerous, so no strangers invited to the inner sanctum of your chambers / **Load chambers, the enemy's approaching so raise / your drawbridge**[11] and drown him in the moat / The spirit I'm evoking is of those who've been awoken / By shots from those who was most close to them / They won't stop till you a ghost to em / But real kings don't die, they become martyrs, let's toast to em / King Arthur put a robe to em like James Brown / Know the show ain't over till Rome's ruined / Till the republic is overthrowed, till my loyal subjects is over Hov / Long live the king. Know the reign won't stop

8. Here I'm playing with "king" and King—Martin Luther King, who was assassinated on the balcony of the Lorraine Motel.

9. Malcolm was distracted by screams before he was shot—a man shouted, "Nigger get your hands outta my pockets," and then the fatal shots rang out.

10. Kurt Cobain OD'd on heroin before committing suicide, but he also OD'd on fame. Cobain was like Basquiat: They both wanted to be famous, and were brilliant enough to make it happen. But then what? Drug addicts kill themselves trying to get that feeling they got from their first high, looking for an experience they'll never get again. In his suicide note

Cobain asked himself, "Why don't you just enjoy it?" and then answered, "I don't know!" It's amazing how much of a mindfuck success can be.

11. You have to lift the drawbridge of your life once you get famous to keep outsiders outside—whether they're new hangers-on just trying to exploit you, or, like in the streets, they might literally wake you up with a gun to your nose, trying to take your shit. But the "inner sanctum" isn't just your physical home, it's the inner chamber of your life and identity, the place where you protect your essential self. If invaders break in there, you're finished.

SUCCESS / FEATURING NAS

[*Jay-Z*] I got these niggas breezy, don't worry about it / Let that bitch breathe! / I used to give a fuck, now I give a fuck less / What do I think of success / **It sucks too much stress**[1] / I guess I blew up quick, cause friends I grew up with / **See me as a premie,**[2] but I'm not and my nut's big / I don't know what the fuss is / My career is illustrious / My rep is impeccable / I'm not to be fucked with (with) shit / Let that bitch breathe! / I'm way too important to be talking about extorting / Asking me for a portion is like asking me for a coffin / Broad daylight I off ya on switch / Ya not too bright, goodnight, long kiss, / Bye-bye, my reply, blah-blah / Blast burner then pass burner, to Ty-Ty / **Finish my breakfast,**[3] why? / I got an appetite for destruction and you're a small fry / Now where was I / Let that bitch breathe! / I used to give a shit, now I don't give a shit more / Truth be told, I had more fun when I was piss poor / I'm pissed off, is this what success all about / A bunch of niggas acting like bitches with big mouths / All this stress, all I got is this big house / Couple cars, I don't bring half of them shits out / All this Ace of Spade I drank, just to piss out / I mean I like the taste, could have saved myself six hours / How many times can I go to Mr. Chow's, Tao's, Nobu / **Hold up, let me move my bowels**[4] / I'll shit on y'all niggas, OG tell these boys / [*Juan*] Y'all ain't got shit on my nigga / [*Jay-Z*] / I got watches I ain't seen in months / Apartment at the Trump I only slept in once / Nigga said Hova was over, such dummies / Even if I fell I land on a bunch of money / Y'all ain't got nothing for me / Nas, let that bitch breathe!

1. This is a reference to Eminem's "I'm Back": *What do I think of success? It cucks too much pross I'm stressed.*

2. This refers to old friends on the street and in the rap game who still think of me as their sidekick or protégé, or the little nigga they put on. At one point that's maybe who I was—but then my nuts dropped and I became my own man. And that happened a long time ago.

3. Another reference to finishing breakfast, as in "Public Service Announcement," which connects with the "appetite for destruction" and "small fry" in the next line.

4. I went to such a visceral image here because I was trying to make a point: In America—and in hip-hop—success is supposed to be about accumulation and consumption. But the finest meal ends up as shit, which is a great metaphor for the fact that consumption's flip side is decay and waste, and what's left behind is emptiness. Empty apartments, empty stomach, unused objects. Which isn't to say I don't like buying things and eating nice meals as much as the next person (okay, maybe even more), but success has to mean something beyond that.

RENEGADE[1] / FEATURING EMINEM

Motherfuckers— / say that I'm foolish I only talk about jewels (bling bling) / **Do you fools listen to music or do you just skim through it?**[2] / See I'm influenced by the ghetto you ruined / That same dude you gave nothin, I made somethin doin / what I do through and through and / **I give you the news with a twist it's just his ghetto point of view**[3] / The renegade; you been afraid / I penetrate pop culture, bring 'em a lot closer to the block where they / pop toasters, and they live with they moms / **Got dropped roasters, from botched robberies niggaz crouched ove**r[4]/ Mommy's knocked up cause she wasn't watched over / **Knocked down by some clown when child support knocked**[5] / **No he's not around—now how that sound to ya, jot it down**[6] / I bring it through the ghetto without ridin 'round / hidin down duckin strays from frustrated youths stuck in they ways / Just read a magazine that fucked up my day / How you rate music that thugs with nothin relate to it? / **I help them see they way through it—not you**[7] / Can't step in my pants, can't walk in my shoes / **Bet everything you worth; you lose your tie and your shirt**[8] / **I had to hustle, my back to the wall, ashy knuckles**[9] / Pockets filled with a lot of lint, not a cent / Gotta vent, lot of innocent lives lost on the project bench / Whatchu hollerin? Gotta pay rent, bring dollars in / By the bodega, iron under my coat, feelin braver / **Do-rag wrappin my waves up, pockets full of hope**[10] / **Do not step to me—I'm awkward, I box lefty**[11] often / **My pops left me an orphan, my momma wasn't home** / Could not stress to me I wasn't grown; 'specially on nights / **I brought somethin home to quiet the stomach rumblings**[12] / My demeanor—thirty years my senior / **My childhood didn't mean much,**[13] only raising green up / **Raisin' my fingers to critics; raisin' my head to the sky**[14] / **BIG I did it—multi before I die (nigga)**[15] / No lie, just know I chose my own fate / **I drove by the fork in the road and went straight**[16]

1. Eminem produced this song and came up with the concept, which was to attack the mistaken perceptions people had of him. By the time I got my hands on it, he'd already recorded his verse, which is absolutely fucking brilliant, in his lyrical concepts and rhyme schemes—*go to war with the Mormons, take a bath with the Catholics / in holy water it's no wonder they try to hold me under longer*—and in his ridiculous flow—*now I'm debated disputed hated and viewed in America / as a motherfuckin drug addict, like you didn't experiment.* "Renegade" appeared on the *Blueprint* album, which I intended to be spare and personal and soulful; Em's verses here are the only guest appearance on the album.

2. This is directed at critics who only listen to the songs that fulfill their preconceived expectations—the "bling bling" in the background summarizes their usual complaint about my music.

3. This is one of the things that makes me—and all serious rappers—renegades: When we report the news, it doesn't sound the same as when you hear it from CNN. Most of us come from communities where people were just supposed to stay in their corners quietly, live and die without disturbing the master narrative of American society. Simply speaking our truths, which flew in the face of the American myth, made us rebels.

4. The image of niggas "crouched over" is mean to show the other side of the usual street story—what happens when shit goes bad, the gun gets dropped, and you're the one on your knees.

5. Again, I'm talking about the flip side of the "Money, Cash, Hoes" type songs. Sex can knock you up and knock you down.

6. The "jot it down" line is meant to show that I'm talking to a reporter, giving him my "ghetto point of view."

7. Magazines, even hip-hop magazines, would reduce a song to a rating, a number of mics or stars or some other system. But I always wondered how they could try to pin down and attach a rating to music that was really helping people understand their own lives. I always thought that critics should factor in the truthfulness of the rhyme. Truth is a constraint. It's easy to make up a complete fantasy in a song. Trying to rhyme and be clever and witty and tell a coherent story or talk about a coherent concept and stick to something true about life is difficult. But it's that element of truth that makes the songs deeper than just entertainment, that make the music a light that can help people see their way through a hard life.

8. This is meant both literally and figuratively—the critic I'm imagining here is a suit-and-tie sort of guy, who literally doesn't dress like me. But he also can't wear the life I've worn, and if he tried to step in my shoes, walk the streets I walked, he'd lose that tie and shirt, not just his clothes but the smug attitude they represent.

9. Here's the dark side of hustling—actually, not the dark side, which has its own glamour, but the pathetic side of the young hustler's life: ashy knuckles, pockets full of lint, broke, can't pay rent.

10. It's when you take the hustler down a notch that you can start to relate to him, even if it's still complicated. The pocket that was once filled with lint is now filled with "hope"—which is what the crack is to this kid. It's contraband to the law and poisonous salvation to the crackhead, but to the hustler, it's a way out.

11. Southpaw boxers are dangerous because they seem awkward to people used to boxing righthanders. It's a great metaphor for the way those of us from the hood were able to take on the world. We came at shit from a different angle, snuck up on people, surprised them. We turned the thing that made us outcasts into our advantage.

12. Of course, my mother didn't want me on the streets, but it was hard to argue with a young kid who's actually contributing to a household that's stretched thin, even if he's into some dangerous shit to do it.

13. I didn't have much of a childhood. By the time I was a teenager, I was living in another city, far from home, working.

14. After so much of the song is about stripping the life of any sense of glamour and pointing out the real life of the kid in the ghetto, I turn it around to a defiant, triumphant note with this series of raises: raising green up (making money), raising my middle finger to the critics who don't get it, and raising my face to the sky to talk to my nigga Big.

15. This was a conversation Big and I had many times before he died. He wanted for me to see what it was like to be at the multiplatinum level, performing in big arenas. The promise appeared in a song I did with him called "Young G's": *And I told my nigga Big I'd be multi before I die / It's gonna happen whether rappin or clappin have it your way.*

16. I love this concept: Instead of being forced into a fucked up choice where you lose either way, choose your own path. The fork in the road I was presented with was either having those pockets full of lint, or pockets full of dope. I went straight—stopped selling drugs—but I also didn't accept the false choice between poverty and breaking the law. I found my own way through and with my music, I try to help others see their way through it, too.

CAN I LIVE?

Yeah, hah, yeah Roc-A-Fella / We invite you to something epic, y'all know? / Well we hustle out of a sense of hopelessness. Sort of a desperation. / Through that desperation, we 'come addicted, sorta like the fiends we accustomed to servin. / But we feel we have nothin to lose so we offer you, well, we offer our lives, right? / **What do you bring to the table?**[1] / While I'm watchin every nigga watchin me closely / **my shit is butter for the bread they wanna toast me**[2] / I keep my head, both of them where they supposed to be / Hoes'll get you sidetracked then clap from close feet / I don't sleep, I'm tired, I feel wired like codeine, these days / **a brother gotta admire me from four fiends away**[3] / My pain wish it was quick to see, from sellin 'caine / till brains was fried to a fricassee, can't lie. / At the time it never bothered me, at the bar / gettin my thug on properly, my squad and me / lack of respect for authority, laughin hard / Happy to be escapin poverty, however brief / I know this game got valleys and peaks, expectation / **for dips, for precipitation we stack chips, hardly**[4] / The youth I used to be, soon to see a milli'n / No more Big Willie my game has grown prefer you call me William / Illin for revenues, Rayful Edmond like / **Channel 7 news, round seven jewels, head dead in the mic**[5] / Forgettin all I ever knew, convenient amnesia / I suggest you call my lawyer, I know the procedure / Lock my body can't trap my mind, easily / explain why we adapt to crime / **I'd rather die enormous than live dormant that's how we on it**[6] / Live at the main event, I bet a trip to Maui on it / **Presidential suites my residential for the weekend**[7] / Confidentially speakin in codes since I sense you peekin / The NSX rental, don't be fooled my game is mental / We both out of town dog, what you tryin to get into? / Viva, Las Vegas, see ya later at the crap tables / meet me by the one that starts a G up / This way no fraud Willie's present gambling they re-up / And we can have a pleasant time, sippin margaritas / Ge-ge-geyeahhh, can I live? / Can I live? / **My mind is infested with sick thoughts that circle**[8] / like a Lexus, if driven wrong it's sure to hurt you / Dual level like duplexes, in unity my crew and me / commit atrocities like we got immunity / You guessed it, manifest it in tangible goods / Platinum Rolexed it we don't lease / **we buy the whole car, as you should**[9] / my confederation, dead a nation, EXPLODE / on detonation, overload the mind of a said patient / When it boils to steam, it comes to it / we all fiends gotta do it, even righteous minds go through this / True this, streets school us to spend our money foolish / Bond with jewelers and watch for intruders / **I stepped it up another level, meditated like a Buddhist**[10] / Recruited lieutenants with ludicrous dreams of / gettin cream let's do this, it gets tedious / **So I keep one eye open like C-B-S,**[11] ya see me / stressed right. Can I live? / Can I live? / Can I live? Can I live?

1. Hopelessness and desperation is what you're supposed to feel in poverty. The drive to escape that hopelessness is, for the hustler, the same thing that drives a drug addict to get high—a need to escape. So here, and in other rhymes, I'm identifying with addicts. An addict doubles down on his pain, and like the hustler feels death or jail couldn't be much worse than the pain of poverty. So when we come to the table to gamble, it's with our very lives.

2. In this line I turn a noun, *bread* (meaning "money"), into a verb, *toast* (meaning "shoot"), which draws out the relationship between money and danger.

3. Sleeplessness, weariness, and adrenaline are symptoms of paranoia, of engaging in illegal activity in plain sight. "Four fiends away" indicates the distance between me and the street-level action. The implication is that I'm a boss, to some degree buffered from low-level workers who can be easily urged to cooperate with authorities.

4. The pain of a drug addict is visible. You may or may not have sympathy for him, but he's wearing his pain. The hustler has armor—money, ambition—that makes his pain less visible, less "quick to see." But just like a drug addict's "brain on drugs" the hustler's brain is similarly fried, preparing for inevitable rainy days (precipitation), planning takeovers, stacking and climbing. The "hardly" is an admission that while the intention is to stack, the reality is often the spending.

5. Rayful Edmond was a major hustler who appeared on the news coming out of his own helicopter.

6. This line, "I'd rather die enormous than live dormant," resonates deeply with my listeners. It's a take on the "Live Free or Die Trying," "Liberty or Death" spirit that's woven into the fabric of what it means to be American. But it's also about great ambition, and the alternative, which is stagnation. The risk is death, so the reward should have equal gravity, a life lived to the fullest.

7. "The main event" refers to the reward, the spoils, and, literally, a fight in Vegas. But main event could mean life as much as it means a staged fight. Presidential suites is that Big Willy all grown up—call him William.

8. "Sick thoughts that circle" is about the interior of my mind. Constantly checking thoughts, separating what's real from what's fear and paranoia, what's a part of the plan and what's reckless. Before I learned the Law of Attraction I was aware of the power of my thoughts, staying focused, weeding out thoughts that sabotage.

9. "Immunity" is a shot at white-collar criminals who are as outside of the law as my crew, but it's also about taking reckless risks that lead to material acquisitions, which were also reckless. Advising to buy a car rather than lease one speaks to my naïveté at the time. Cars lose value the minute they leave the lot.

10. The Buddhist reference is about stillness, a break from the spending and buying, a retreat to reveal my ultimate goals.

11. The CBS television network's logo is a single open eye.

BALLING AND FALLING

------

(1) FALLIN'

Featuring Bilal
(American Gangster,
2007)

(2) BIG PIMPIN'

Featuring UGK
(Vol. 3 . . .
Life and Times of
S. Carter, 1999)

(3) STREETS IS WATCHING

(In My Lifetime,
Vol. 1, 1997)

NO 398

Back in the 1990s, before file-sharing became the real disrupter in the music industry, bootlegging was the worst threat. There is no analogy between bootlegging and anything that happens in the streets, unless you count niggas going up in stash spots and straight robbing you. As an artist, you're in the position of having to guard your work from everyone. No one can answer you when you demand to know how your album was leaked in the first place.

So you become paranoid. Is it the engineer in the studio, his assistant, the owner of the studio? Is it the label, the processing plant? I always had some sympathy for our die-hard fans, the ones who were just looking for a way to get their hands on records they couldn't otherwise afford. Back when it was really rampant, I always threw away a hundred thousand units in projections to bootlegging, knowing that bootleggers were so resourceful that they could never be completely beaten, no matter how careful you were. It's almost quaint to think about that now, since digital pirating accounts for many times as many copies as any bootlegger ever managed to get out on the streets. And back then, it was rare for the bootleg to dramatically beat the release date for the legit album.

But when *Vol. 3 . . . Life and Times of S. Carter,* my fourth album, hit the streets more than a month before the official release date, I was totally at a loss. This was really too much. I was flipping out on Def Jam staff, accusing people of having something to do with the bootleg copies on the street. I just couldn't believe how flagrant it was, and how much more damaging it could be than the usual low-level bootlegging. I wanted to know how my shit got out.

People kept giving me the same name as the source of the bootlegging. It was someone I knew, someone I never would have suspected. One night I went to Q-Tip's solo album release party and at some point in the night, I ran into the guy everyone's been telling me is behind the bootleg. So I approached him. When I told him what I suspected, to my surprise, he got real loud with me right there in the middle of the club. It was strange. We separated and I went over to the bar. I was sitting there like, "No the fuck this nigga did not . . ." I was talking to people, but I was really talking to myself out loud, just in a state of shock. Before I even realized what I was doing, I headed back over to him, but this time I was blacking out with anger. The next thing I knew, all hell had broken loose in the club. That night the guy went straight to the police and I was charged with assault.

I went to the Trump Hotel on Central Park West and holed up, tracking coverage of the incident in the media. After a couple of days I called my lawyer and turned myself in at the precinct. That's when I realized how serious things were, not because they threw me in the Tombs, but because they started setting up a press conference. The district attorney had his publicist on the phone, the cop that was assigned to do the perp walk with me was combing his hair and fixing his collar; it was a complete show for them. The hilarious thing, if any of this can be considered funny, is that the Rocawear bubble coat I was wearing when they paraded me in front of the cameras started flying off the shelves the last three weeks before Christmas.

AT ANY GIVEN MOMENT SHAWN COULD LOSE IT

When I was holed up in the Trump Hotel, my entertainment lawyer, Michael Guido, came by and taught me an old college game he used to play, Guts. My whole crew learned how to play. It's a high-stakes game, and I like to watch how people react under the game's pressure. It's revealing. Guts is deceptively simple. You're dealt three cards. Aces and pairs are high. Once you're dealt your three cards, you have to decide whether or not to stay in. The best hand wins the pot, so it is essential to do a quick analysis, read your opponents, and, most importantly, be decisive. It's a game that rewards the kind of self-possession and clarity that quiets your fight-or-flight reflexes. Gambling like that makes you aware of how often your immediate emotional impulses are to do something really stupid because it feels good for a moment. Like what I did at the club that night.

There are some lines in "Streets Is Watching," a song off my second album, that capture the situation. The song's first verse starts off:

Look, if I shoot you, I'm brainless

But if you shoot me, then you're famous—what's a nigga to do?

And the second starts:

Now it's hard not to kill niggas

It's like a full-time job not to kill niggas

The streets can start to make you see the logic in violence. If a thing surrounds you and is targeted at you, it can start to seem regular. What may have once seemed like an extreme or unacceptable measure starts to seem like just another tool in your kit. Even after I left the streets, I was still under the kind of pressure that made me sometimes act without thinking. But when you slip and give in to that pressure, in an instant you can throw your whole life away. I had to learn to keep my mind still so I could think clearly and sometimes hold back even when my heart is telling me to go in.

On the other hand, you have to know when you need to step up and act, even when it might seem reckless to someone on the outside. Knowing the difference between recklessness and boldness is the whole art of gambling. But in the end you're just rolling the dice.

As distracting as my indictment had become, I knew that the next single off the album, "Big Pimpin'," was a gem, even if it wasn't a conventional single by any stretch of the imagination. I asked UGK to get on the track with me because I was a huge fan of their music, even though a lot of my East Coast fans didn't really know who they were. I'd always loved Southern hip-hop, and UGK combined great Southern bounce with sneakily complex rhymes and delivery. And they were funny as hell. Timbaland went wild on that track; he used pieces of North African music, horns that sounded damn near like geese. It didn't sound like anything else on the radio at the time, but I knew it was time to double down.

I rallied the troops and I told my staff to get us on MTV's *Making the Video*, which hadn't been on a rap set before. I got Hype Williams to direct it. I'm notoriously tight with video budgets, but for "Big Pimpin'," I put out a million dollars. We headed to Trinidad for carnival, then booked a mansion in Miami, got the biggest yacht we could find, and hired hundreds of girls from the top agencies. We went Vegas with niggas on that one. But to me, it felt like a sure bet. When we released the single for "Big Pimpin'" in the first week of June 2000, it made up for the bootlegging, the indictment, everything. It was my biggest single up to that point.

WITH ENOUGH BAIL MONEY TO FREE A BIG WILLY

The contrast between the million-dollar extravagance of the "Big Pimpin'" video and the potential of being behind bars for years behind a mindless assault wasn't lost on me. Both were about losing control. "Big Pimpin'" is a song that I wrote in the middle of all the madness, a time when I might have been at my most paranoid and hedonistic. It's a song that seems to be about the purity of the hustler's thrill—pleasure cooked down to a crystal. The lyrics are aggressive; they're about getting high off that thrill, fuck sharing it or saving some for tomorrow. Break taboos, live without limitations, spend money like it'll never run out, fuck bitches, and bounce, forget about catching feelings. Jump out the plane and don't think about how you're going to land. But there's a couplet at the end,

I got so many grams if the man find out
it will land me in jail for life

that shows that even when you're out of control, you know that it could end at any moment, which only makes you go harder. If the price is life, then you better get what you paid for. There's an equal and opposite relationship between balling and falling.

The winter before my case, Puff and Shyne caught a case behind that shoot-out at Club New York, and just as I was being indicted, their case was being prepared for trial. The way Puff and Shyne's trial unfolded was unreal. The district attorney's office spent a lot of money on prosecution and it went on for more than a month. Less than a block from where Puff and Shyne were being tried, the guys accused of bombing the World Trade Center in 1993 were on trial. There were barricades in front of their courthouse. It was a major trial, important to the city, the whole country, but no media were there. Meanwhile Puff's courthouse was swarming with cameras and reporters; the local papers were writing about what Puff's mother was wearing to court. It was un-fucking-real. Of course Shyne got convicted, but the D.A. had put on that spectacle to get Puff. When he walked I knew they'd be even more aggressive about getting a conviction in my case, making an example of me where they'd failed with Puff. So I settled and took probation. No way was I going to allow myself to be a sideshow for the state.

But more than that, I realized that I had a choice in life. There was no reason to put my life on the line, and the lives of everyone who depends on me, because of a momentary loss of control. It sometimes feels like complete disaster is always around the corner, waiting to trap us, so we have to live for the moment and fuck the rest. That kind of fatalism—*this game I play ain't no way to fix it, it's inevitable*—feels like realism, but the truth is that you can step back and not play someone else's game. I vowed to never allow myself to be in a situation like that again.

FALLIN' / FEATURING BILAL

[*Chorus: Bilal*] **I know I shouldnt've did that**[1] / I know it's gon' come right back / I know it's gon' destroy everything I made / It's probably gon' get ya boy sent away / But this game I play, ain't no way to fix it / It's inevitable that I'm / Falling / [*Jay-Z*] Said where I would stop before I even started / **When I get to one brick,**[2] then the Game I will depart with / Got to one brick then I looked to the sky, like / **Sorry God, I lied, but give me one more try**[3] / **Got to two bricks, new cars, new whips**[4] / But niggas never learn till they end up in the newsclip / The irony of selling drugs is sort of like I'm using it / Guess it's two sides to what "substance abuse" is / Can't stop, won't stop, addicted to this new shit / **Brand new convertibles, I'm so ruthless**[5] / Front row, fight night—see how big my tube is? / **Fuck HD, nigga see how clear my view is?**[6] / (FALLING) / But there's a price for overdoing it / Doin it this big'll put you on the map / **Stick-up kids is out to tax**[7] / Plus the FBI boys with the cameras in the back, damn! / I know I shouldnt've did that / I know it's gon' come right back / I know it's gon' destroy everything I made / It's probably gon' get ya boy sent away / But this game I play, ain't no way to fix it / It's inevitable— / Now you're / (FALLING) / When you should've fell back, / Now you're / (FALLING) / Right into they lap / **Falling, they applaud and they screamin' at the screen**[8] / "Damn, you fucked up!" like your favorite movie scene / Godfather, Goodfellas, Scarface, Casino / You seen what that last run did to DeNiro / When he can't beat the odds, can't cheat the cards / **Can't blow too hard, life's a deck of cards**[9] / Now you're

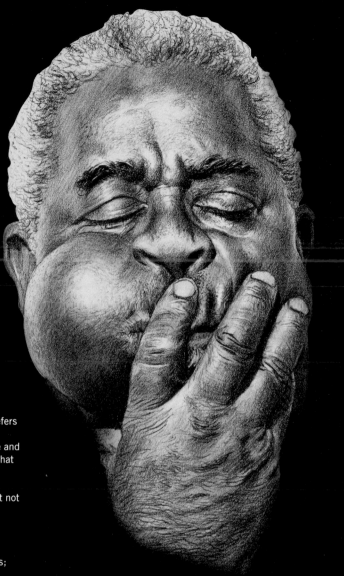

1. "That" is ambiguous here. The context shows that it refers to the drug game, and of course this is on the *American Gangster* album, which was inspired by Frank Lucas's rise and fall as a drug kingpin. But it can refer to anything we do that we know, even while we're doing it, will end badly.

2. A brick is a serious entry-level weight, a nice score, but not necessarily a lifetime commitment to the Game.

3. This is the kind of bogus negotiation people normally associate with drug *addicts,* not drug dealers. The theme of this song is the similarity between the users and sellers; they're on opposite ends of the transaction, but are both addicted to a fix that they know will destroy them.

4. "Whips" are fast, expensive cars. It might seem redundant to say "new cars, new whips" but "whips" adds a layer of meaning and suggestion. For instance, you can make the connection between the word "whip" and the way lust for material items has become almost a slavemaster to the song's narrator, pushing him forward against his own better judgment. Or the way "whip" makes you feel the speed with which the narrator's game is rising.

5. This is a play on the similarity between "ruthless" and "roofless," as in convertible.

6. This is about how clear his view of the fight is, but also about how he sees the larger picture of life much clearer now, or thinks he does.

7. Reference to Nice & Smooth's "Funky for You": *Dizzy Gillespie plays the sax / Me myself I love to max / Redbone booties I'm out to wax / Stick-up kids is out to tax.* Dizzy Gillespie played the trumpet, but fuck it, it's a great rhyme. Premier sampled the line for the chorus of another hip-hop classic, Gang Starr's "Just to Get a Rep."

8. First, this conjures the image of agents in the back of an FBI van looking at their surveillance screen and applauding because you fucked up, and then morphs into the image of a crowd at a movie, yelling at the character on the screen who is about to fuck up.

9. "Can't blow too hard" means you can't show off too much, or your whole life can tumble.

tumbling, it's humbling, you're falling, you're mumbling / Under your breath like you knew this day was coming / (FALLING) / Now let's pray that arm candy / That you left your ex for stay down and come in handy / **Cause come January, it gets cold**[10] / **When the letters start to slow, when your commissary's**[11] low / When your lawyer screams "Appeal!" only thinkin 'bout a bill / When your chances are nil, damn, gravity's ill . . . / [*Bilal*] I know I shouldnt've did that / I know it's gon' come right back / I know it's gon' destroy everything I made / It's probably gon' get ya boy sent away / But this game I play, ain't no way to fix it / It's inevitable— / That you're / (FALLING) / [*Jay-Z*] And you can't get up / **All you do is push-up, pull-up, sit-up**[12] / Locked down, the town now belongs to the Squares / **Who say they won't make the same mistakes**[13] that got you there / And ya arm candy's sweet on 'em / **And the woman that you left for this heffa got a college degree comin**[14] / Bad news keeps coming / Hard to keep something on your stomach / You're sick 'bout what your life is becoming / (FALLING) / Bunch of used to's, has beens bragging bad 'bout all the new dudes / **Talking tough on the YouTube bout what you used to do**[15] / But that's old school to the new crew / They're doing numbers like Sudoku / They're the new you / And its damn near inevitable they'll experience deja vu too / Fight, and you'll never survive / Run, and you'll never escape / So just fall from grace, damn . . . / [*Bilal*] I know I shouldn't've did that / I know it's gon' come right back / I know its gon' destroy everything I made / It's probably gon' get ya boy sent away / But this game I play, ain't no way to fix it / It's inevitable that I'm / FALLING

10. January is the coldest, darkest month of the year, which mirrors the hopeless feeling of being locked down and forgotten by the people on the outside.

11. Commissary is the prison "store" where prisoners can buy basic items using an account that gets filled by people outside of prison.

12. The prisoner's routine is heavy on exercises whose names are like a cruel joke.

13. The cycle continues.

14. The implication is that the narrator dumped a good, self-sufficient woman—now getting a college degree—for "arm candy" that gets sweet on whoever's hot.

15. Now he's out of jail, but all he has to fall back on is empty boasting about his old life—problem is, no one gives a shit. It's like the old ballplayer telling the young boys about how nice he used to be, how he could've been a contender—but if you blew it, no one cares.

BIG PIMPIN' (EXTENDED) / FEATURING UGK

Uhh, uh uh uh / It's big pimpin baby . . . / It's big pimpin, spendin cheese / Feel me . . . uh-huh uhh, uh-huh . . . / Ge-ge-geyeah, geyeah / Ge-ge-geyeah, geyeah . . . / You know I thug em, fuck em, love em, leave em / Cause I don't fuckin need em / Take em out the hood, keep em lookin good / **But I don't fuckin feed em**[1] / First time they fuss I'm breezin / Talkin bout, "What's the reasons?" / I'm a pimp in every sense of the word, bitch / Better trust than believe em / In the cut where I keep em / **till I need a nut, til I need to beat the guts**[2] / Then it's, beep beep and I'm pickin em up / Let em play with the dick in the truck / **Many chicks wanna put Jigga fists in cuffs**[3] / Divorce him and split his bucks / Just because you got good head, I'ma break bread / so you can be livin it up? Shit I / parts with nothin, y'all be frontin / Me give my heart to a woman? / **Not for nothin, never happen**[4] / **I'll be forever mackin**[5] / Heart cold as assassins, I got no passion / I got no patience / And I hate waitin / Hoe get yo' ass in / And let's RI-I-I-I-I-IDE check em out now / RI-I-I-I-I-IDE, yeah / And let's RI-I-I-I-I-IDE check em out now / RI-I-I-I-I-IDE, yeah / [*Chorus: Jay-Z*] / We doin big pimpin, we spendin cheese / Check em out now / Big pimpin, on B.L.A.D.'s / We doin big pimpin up in N.Y.C. / It's just that Jigga Man, Pimp C, and B-U-N B / Yo yo yo big pimpin, spendin cheese / We doin big pimpin, on B.L.A.D.'s / We doin big pimpin up in N.Y.C. / **It's just that Jigga Man, Pimp C, and B-U-N B**[6] / On a canopy my stamina be enough for Pamela Anderson Lee / MTV jam of the week / Made my money too long for gambling with me / **Still sittin on blades,**[7] gettin off treys / **Standin on the corner of my block hustlin**[8] / Still gettin that cane / half what I paid slippin right through customs / It'll sell by night it's eggshell white . . . / I got so many grams if the man find out / it will land me in jail for life / But I'm still big pimpin spendin chesse / with B.U.N. B, Pimp C, and Timothy / **We got bitches in the back of the truck, laughin it up**[9] / Jigga Man that's what's up

1. This is my take on a classic piece of pimpology, Pretty Tony's riff in the movie *The Mack:* "Just like my hoes, I keep 'em broke. They wake up one morning with some money, they subject to go crazy. I keep 'em looking good, pretty and all that, but no dough." These lines have been referred to a lot in hip-hop—they were sampled completely by Ghostface Killah—but it's not meant to endorse actual pimping, that was never my thing. Pretty Tony's delivery is so slick, the slang is so dead-on, the exaggeration so outrageous, and the sentiment so pure and distilled, that as ridiculous as the words are, it still comes off real. It's fucked up and mesmerizing. It's also comedy. I was trying to get some of that feeling in this song.

2. Here are two of the most selfish, least romantic ways to describe sex you can imagine: "need a nut" and "beat the guts." I was intentionally pushing it—the song is meant to be about pimpin, which is, by definition, selfish and unromantic—but this was also where my head was when I recorded the song. The truth is that when you reach a certain level of success, relationships between men and women can get really fucked up and start feeling like a raw transaction, with high levels of suspicion on both sides.

6. I was a longtime fan of UGK, and they killed their verses on this song. After Pimp C died, Bun B and I performed his verse together at a show in Houston, their hometown. His short verse was a perfect eulogy for Pimp C—it was funny, outrageous, defiant, and bouncey, and he didn't waste a single word: *if I wasn't rapping baby / I would still be ridin Mercedes / coming down and sippin daily / no record till whitey pay me.* Leaving aside the racial reference, he was in a contract dispute with Jive.

7. Blades = B.L.A.D.'s = rims.

8. Even in a song about pushing pleasure to the limit, I can't help but make the connection between the "big pimpin" and the work that makes it possible—which takes us from the cars, women, and the alcohol, the sun, the mansion, and Carnival—and brings us back to the streets, the corner of the block, the coke, and the potential for a long prison bid hanging over me like a cloud. The recklessness of the pleasure—the selfish craziness of pimping—matches the recklessness of the work.

9. The girls bring us back from the grim reminder about the work, but not all the way. I've already made it clear that these are not girls that I'll have a relationship with, these are girls that I'll "thug, fuck, love, and leave," and these same girls, "laughin it up," are definitely not going to be holding me down if I do get caught out there. One way or another, in real life, the laughter is going to end. But not in this song. Here, the laughter is the last thing you hear, because this is a song about that moment of pleasure, not about consequences and regrets. But the tension of what comes next also lingers.

3. I like the way "fists in cuffs" sounds like "fisticuffs." It shows exactly how the song's narrator sees commitment, almost as an assault.

4. The irony here, of course, is that like most pimps who throw on the pimp act, I'd eventually give my heart to a woman.

5. Another *The Mack* reference.

STREETS IS WATCHING

Uh-huh uh huh uh / Gee-gee-geyeah / Baby, watchin, streets / Uh-huh uh huh uh / You don't have to look / Uh-huh uh / The streets is watching / Check it, check / Uh-huh uh, check / **Look, if I shoot you, I'm brainless / But if you shoot me, then you're famous**[1]—what's a nigga to do? / When the streets is watching, blocks keep clocking / **Waiting for you to break, make your first mistake**[2] / Can't ignore it, that's the fastest way to get extorted / **But my time is money, and twenty-five, I can't afford it**[3] / Beef is sorted like Godiva chocolates / Niggaz you bought it, I pull the slide back and cock it / Plan aborted, you and your mans get a pass / This rhyme, you're operating on bitch time / Y'all niggaz ain't worth my shells, all y'all niggaz / tryin to do is hurt my sales, and stop trips to John Menielly / The type to start a beef then, run to the cops / **When I see you in the street got, one in the drop**[4] / Would I rather be on tour getting a hundred a pop / Taking pictures with some bitches, in front of the drop / The streets is watching / [*Chorus*] / When the streets is watching / Blocks keep clocking / Waiting for you to break, make your first mistake / Can't ignore it / Now it's hard not to kill niggaz / It's like a full time job not to kill niggaz, **can't chill / the streets is watching you, when you froze your arms**[5] / **Niggaz wanna test you and your gun goes warm**[6] / **Can't get caught with your feet up, gotta keep your heat up / Sweet niggaz running 'round swearing shit is sweeter**[7] / **Once you're tagged lame the game is follow the leader**[8] / Everybody want a piece of your scrilla, so you gotta keep it realer / Kidnap niggaz wanna steal ya / **Broke niggaz want no cash, they just wanna kill ya / for the name,**[9] niggaz don't know the rules / Disrespectin the game, want you to blow your cool / Force your hand, of course that man's plottin / Smarten up, the streets is watching, it's on / [*Chorus*] **My street mentality flip bricks forever,**[10] know me and money / we like armed co-defendants, nigga we stick together / Shit whatever for this cheddar ran my game into the ground /

1. This is one of my most often repeated lines. I'm describing asymmetrical warfare, where one side has much more to lose than the other side and it applies to all kinds of situations.

2. This is a song all about paranoia. To be watched by the streets themselves, clocked by the block, means you're being watched by everyone and everything all the time, all looking for the slightest opening to come at you.

3 To ignore the predatory streets is a quick way to get extorted—but in this case, I mean extorted for your time, your life, with a long prison sentence.

4. "One in the drop" = one in the chamber.

5. Arms are frozen from "ice" (ice = diamonds, in this case, on a watch or bracelet), ironically the ice means I "can't chill."

6. The warm gun follows the frozen arms, and both mean that the gun is no longer being used—"you gotta keep your heat up."

7. A hazard in any successful business is that the one at the top gets relaxed—"feet up"—and becomes addicted to the sweet life, which marks him as weak to all the sharks circling below him. The funny thing about this is that even bullies—the ones who reach the top—can be soft and weak. As soon as they get exposed, it's a wrap.

8. A couple of deadly children's games. Getting tagged here is like a permanent game of freeze tag. And when they play "follow the leader," it's not out of obedience, but more like a predator tracking prey.

9. More dangerous than the cats who want to kidnap you for dough are the killers just trying to make their reputations, because those are the ones you can't negotiate with; it's kill or be killed.

10. The line really means that no matter if I'm actually on the streets or not, my mentality—"hustle harder"—is the same. The narrator of the song is the sort of high-level drug dealer who has to prove that he isn't sweet, even though he's not literally on the streets—he has to prove his street mentality to keep his credibility on the block.

Hustle harder until indictment time came around / Now you can look up and down the streets and I can't be found / Put in twenty-four-hour shifts but, that ain't me now / Got a face too easy to trace, niggaz mouths got slow leaks / Had to hire a team of workers, couldn't play those streets / Stay out in space like Mercury, you jerkin me? Hectic / Had to call upon my wolves to send niggaz the message / I said this: "Let's play fair and we can stay here / I'm trying to transform you boys to men like daycare" / **Hey there's money to be made and niggaz got the picture / Stopped playing with my paper and we got richer**[11] / Then hard times fell upon us, half of my staff / **had warrants, the other half, in the casket lay dormant**[12] / I felt like life was cheating me, for the first time / in my life I was getting money but it was like my conscience was eating me / **Was this a lesson God teaching me? Was he saying that?**[13] / I'm playing the game straight from Hell from which few came back / like bad coke, pimp or die, was my mindframe back / When niggaz thinkin simplify I was turning cocaine crack? / Ain't a whole lot of brain to that, just trying to maintain a stack / and not collide like two trains that's on the same track / But I get my life together like the oils I bring back / In the bottom of the pot when the water gets hot / **Got my transporter take it 'cross the border then stop**[14] / Set up shop with a quarter of rock, here's the plan / For three straight weeks, niggaz slaughtered the block / But you know the game is cruel, fucked up me and my dudes / One drought can wipe a nigga out, faster than the cops / and this unstable way of living just had to stop / **Half of my niggaz got time, we done real things**[15] / By ninety-four became the subject of half of y'all niggaz rhymes / **Public apologies to the families of those caught up in my shit**[16] / But that's the life for us lost souls brought up in this shit / The life and times of a nigga's mind, excited with crime / And the lavish luxuries that just excited my mind / I figured, "Shit why risk myself I just write it in rhymes / **And let you feel me, and if you don't like it then fine"**[17] / The mindstate of a nigga who boosted the crime rate / so high in one city they send National Guards to get me / Ya dig?

11. This is a regular theme in gangster narratives, especially in hood stories. There have always been smart guys in the game who wanted to just focus on making money—to put all the gorilla shit to the side, all the thugging and stupid rivalries, and work together, because all the rest, the violence and animosity, actually hurt your money and create unnecessary collateral damage. These are the guys who thought you could run a criminal operation like a Fortune 500 company on some Stringer Bell shit. When I was in the streets, I was all about making money. I wasn't in it for the violence or making a rep and all that. But in the end, between the cops, the crazies, and the poison product, it's a fucked-up game, and it's hard to play it clean.

12. The language tells the story: Even though I call my crew "staff," like it's a regular company, most staffs aren't made up of criminal defendants and corpses.

13. Even when you find some "success," the paranoia and guilt tighten around you like a noose.

14. I switch up here from a moment of conscience back to the practical details of the work. It's like the work has such a hold on me that it interrupts every other thought.

15. This is based in reality. The last crew I worked with was largely incarcerated in a sweep that happened after I'd started moving into the rap game.

16. It's a small thing, but it's rare that you'll hear a rhyme in the whole "crack rap" genre where the narrator acknowledges the damage to innocent people that occurs in the game.

17. In the end, I make it even more autobiographical by talking about my own transition from someone living the life to someone telling its stories in rhyme, where disagreements don't lead to death.

(1) OPERATION CORPORATE TAKEOVER

(MIX TAPE FREESTYLE, 2006)

BEAT THE SYSTEM

BEFORE IT BEATS YOU

(2) MOMENT OF CLARITY

(*THE BLACK ALBUM*, 2003)

My parents were into every kind of music, including early rap—I remember them playing songs like "King Tim III" by the Fatback Band and, of course, "Rapper's Delight," the first rap song to really break out nationally—and internationally. But while millions of people loved it, including nine-year-old me, it drove the serious rappers of 1979 absolutely crazy.

Rappers had been growing their art for years before this so-called "first rap song" appeared. MCs were tight when they heard it, not just because the lyrics were lightweight, but because the MCs on the record were considered to be wack no-names. Whole chunks of the song were completely bitten: Big Bank Hank not only stole Grandmaster Caz's lyrics for his part in the song, he didn't even bother to change the part where he spells out his name: *Check it out I'm the c-a-s-a-n the –o-v-a* . . .

But it was a major hit and it created the first real crossroads in the story of hip-hop. Some rappers got angry about the commercializing of their culture. Other people saw it as an opportunity: If a group like the Sugar Hill Gang could have a hit, then that meant that there was a real audience out there for hip-hop. Russell Simmons was in a club with some of the pioneers of hip-hop when he first heard "Rapper's Delight" and, like them, was surprised that the first hip-hop hit came from a group of outsiders. But he did his homework on it and went gold with Kurtis Blow, formed Run-DMC, managed the Fat Boys and Whodini, and launched Def Jam, dominating hip-hop for the next two decades. A lot of other people in that room that night never got paid for the art form they helped invent and are still nursing a grudge against the people who did.

It's a recurring story in hip-hop, the tension between art and commerce. Hip-hop is too important as a tool of expression to *just* be reduced to a commercial product. But what some people call "commercializing" really means is that lots of people buy and listen to your records. That was always the point, to me. After my first record got on the radio and on BET, it was wild being at home, feeding my fish, and suddenly seeing myself on TV. But it was satisfying. Hearing it on the radio was even better. There may be some artists who don't believe in radio, especially now, because the radio business is such a shady racket, but radio love puts you in the hood for real. I care if regular people—sisters on their way to work, dudes rolling around in their cars—hear my shit. I'm a music head, so I listen to everything. People around me are passionate about music. We study music, seek it out. I know there are a million music blogs out there and people who are willing to put in the work finding new music on them. But I like to reach people who get their music from clubs and the radio and television, too. I want my music to play where those people live. While there's something intensely personal about what I rap about, I also make choices in technique and style to make sure that it can touch as many people as possible without it losing its basic integrity.

There are sometimes two Jay-Zs when you look at my music. There's the one who can drop a "Big Pimpin'" or "I Just Wanna Love U (Give It 2 Me)," songs that are intended for wide audiences, designed to just get listeners high off the sheer pleasure of them. And then there are the deeper album cuts, which are more complicated. The entire package is what makes an album. I think it's worth it to try to find that balance. It's like life—sometimes you just want to dumb out in the club; other times you want to get real and go deep.

Even then, the idea some people have of "dumbing down" is based on a misperception of what a great rap song can do. A great song can be "dumbed down" in the sense that it appeals to a pretty low common denominator—a big chorus and a great beat and easy-to-follow lyrics can get you a hit (but even then there's an art to combining those elements). But that's not the whole story: A great hit can also give listeners a second layer, and then a third, and more.

The song that's probably the biggest hit in my career so far, "Empire State of Mind," is a great example of how this can work. On the "dumb" side, it's driven by Al Shux's incredible track, Alicia Keys's giant arc of a hook, and my in-the-pocket flow—those are completely universal in their appeal. The next layer down is the storytelling. For a hit song, the narratives are pretty ambiguous: They're about loving a city for all the regular guidebook stuff (the Yankees, the Statue of Liberty, et cetera), but also recognizing it as the place where I used to *cop in Harlem* and have a *stash spot* where I cooked up work like a *pastry*. There's a great tension between the anthemic, even hopeful chorus and the lines about the *gang of niggas rollin with my click* and *corners where we selling rocks* and the story of girls who come to the *city of sin* and get turned out.

And for the hip-hop heads who come looking for technique, it's got all kinds of sneaky Easter eggs if you're a close listener: the way I played with the flow on *and in the winter gets cold in vogue with your skin out* to also make it sound like a reference to Anna Wintour, the editor of *Vogue* (which conjures the image of glossy fashion as a counterpoint to the literal meaning of the line); the way I turn the old cliché about New York being a "melting pot" into a fresh reference to the drug game; the way I use the punchy sonic similarity between "bus trip," "bust out," and "bus route" to amplify a metaphor about getting sexually exploited. Even little shit—the Special Ed shout-out or the line about LeBron James and Dwayne Wade—forces you to keep listening beyond the "dumb" elements. And then there are the bits of snap philosophy—*Jesus can't save you life starts when the church ends*—and punch lines with new slang like *nigga, I be Spiked out, I could trip a referee.* It's a trick I learned from all the greatest emcees: a "dumbed down" record actually forces you to be smarter, to balance art, craft, authenticity, and accessibility.

When I first heard the track for "Empire" I was sure it would be a hit. It was gorgeous. My instinct was to dirty it up, to tell stories of the city's gritty side, to use stories about hustling and getting hustled to add tension to the soaring beauty of the chorus. The same thing happened with another big hit, "A Hard Knock Life." The chorus is a sweet-sounding children's song, but the lyrics are adult: violent and real. Knowing how to complicate a simple song without losing its basic appeal is one of the keys to good songwriting.

LET ME HANDLE MY BUSINESS, DAMN

The other part of "commercialization" is the idea that artists should only be thinking about their art, not about the business side of what we do. There was maybe a time when people in hip-hop made music only because they loved to make music. But the time came when it started to pay off, to the point that even dudes in the street started thinking, "Fuck selling drugs, this rap shit is going to be my hustle!" A lot of people came to hip-hop like that, not out of a pure love of music, but as a legit hustle, another path out of the hood. I've reflected some of that in my music because, to be honest, it was my mentality to some degree—when I committed to a career in rap, I wasn't taking a vow of poverty. I saw it as another hustle, one that happened to coincide with my natural talents and the culture I loved. I was an eager hustler and a reluctant artist. But the irony of it is that to make the hustle work, really work, over the long term, you have to be a true artist, too.

In the streets there aren't written contracts. Instead, you live by certain codes. There are no codes and ethics in music because there are lawyers. People can hide behind their lawyers and contracts and then rob you blind. A lot of street cats come into the music game and expect a certain kind of honor and ethics, even outside of contracts. But in business, like they say, you don't get what you deserve, you get what you negotiate. So I mind my business and I don't apologize for it.

There's this sick fascination with the dead artist, the broke artist, the drugged-out artist, the artist who blows all his money on drugs and big chains and ends up on a VH1 special. Or artists so conflicted about making money from their art—which so often means making money from their pain and confusion and dreams—that they do stupid shit with it, set it on fire or something. This is a game people sometimes play with musicians: that to be real, to be authentic, you have to hate having money or that success has to feel like such a burden you want to kill yourself. But whoever said that artists shouldn't pay attention to their business was probably someone with their hand in some artist's pocket.

OPERATION CORPORATE TAKEOVER

I'm getting courted by the bosses, the Edgars and Doug Morrises-sss / **Jimmy I and Lyor's-ses**[1] / Gotta be more than choruses / They respecting my mind now, just a matter of time now / Operation take over corporate / **Make over offices**[2] / Then take over all of it / Please may these words be recorded / To serve as testimony that I saw it all before it / Came to fruition, sort of a premonition / Uh, uncontrollable hustler's ambition / **Alias superstition / Like Stevie, the writing's on the wall like my lady, right baby?**[3] / **Saw it all before some of y'all thought I was crazy**[4] / Maybe like a fox I'm cagey / Ah, ah, the more successful, the more stressful / The more and more I transform to Gordon Gekko / In the race to a billion, got my face to the ceiling / **Got my knees on the floor, please Lord forgive him**[5] / Has he lost his religion, is the greed gonna get him? / **He's having heaven on Earth, will his wings still fit him?**[6] / I got the *Forbes* on my living room floor / **And I'm so close to the cover, fucker I want more**[7] / *Time*'s most influential was impressive / Especially since I wasn't in the artist's section / Had me with the builders and the titans / Had me right with Rupert Murdoch / **Billionaire boys and some dudes you never heard of**[8] / Word up on Madison Ave is I'm a cash cow / Word down on Wall Street homie you get the cash out / **IPO Hov no need for reverse merger**[9] / The boy money talks no need to converse further / The baby blue Maybach like I own Gerber / **Boardroom I'm lifting your skirt up**[10] / The corporate takeover

1. Edgar Bronfmann is CEO of Warner Music Group, Doug Morris is CEO of Universal Music Group, Jimmy Iovine is head of Interscope, and Lyor Cohen, CEO of Recorded Music at Warner.

2. When I did this freestyle, I was president of Def Jam, a gig I landed after being courted by Universal and Warner. The "makeover" wasn't just about rearranging the chairs. It was about changing the orientation and spirit of the business. That's what hip-hop has tried to do whenever it gets into the boardroom. It's not about sitting behind the same desks and doing work the same way as the people that preceded us. Our goal is to take what we've learned about the world from our lives—and what we've learned about integrity and success and fairness and competition—and use it to remake the corporate world.

3. "Superstition" is the Stevie Wonder classic, of course; *The Writing's on the Wall* was the name of the second album from Destiny's Child.

4. In the song I keep talking about seeing it all before and it's true—not that I was prophetic, but that I always used visualization the way athletes do, to conjure reality.

5. "Face to the ceiling" and "knees on the floor" creates a simultaneous image of straining ambition and humble prayer and forces your mind to reconcile that contradiction.

6. This refers to the biblical verse about the meek inheriting the earth. If I'm Gordon Gekko in this life, do I sacrifice my place in heaven?

7. I'm close to the cover physically—it's on the floor, just out of arm's reach—but also close to the cover in the sense of being nearly successful enough to be on the cover of the magazine.

8. *Time* had me in their "most influential" issue with builders and titans and "people you never heard of," the kind of wealthy industrialists who don't get on the covers of magazines but quietly run the world.

9. Lots of business lingo piles up here. I'm turning the business world's terminology into the raw material for the rhyme.

10. This is an aggressive final image to make the point that I'm like a lot of people that came out of hip-hop—our ambition was never to just fit into the corporate mold, it was to take it over and remake that world in our image.

MOMENT OF CLARITY

(Wooo) (Yeah) / (Turn the music up turn the lights down I'm in my zone) / [*Chorus*] / **Thank God for granting me this moment of clarity**[1] / This moment of honesty / The world'll feel my truths / Through my *Hard Knock Life* time / My *Gift and the Curse* / **I gave you volume after volume**[2] of my work / So you can feel my truths / I built the *Dynasty* by being one of the realest niggas out / Way beyond a *Reasonable Doubt* / (You all can't fill my shoes) / From my *Blueprint* beginnings / To that *Black Album* ending / Listen close you hear what I'm about / Nigga feel my truths / When Pop died / Didn't cry / **Didn't know him that well**[3] / Between him doing heroin / And me doing crack sales / With that in the egg shell / Standing at the tabernacle / Rather the church / Pretending to be hurt / Wouldn't work / So a smirk was all on my face / **Like damn that man's face was just like my face**[4] / So Pop I forgive you / For all the shit that I live through / **It wasn't all your fault**[5] / Homie you got caught / And to the same game I fought / **That Uncle Ray lost**[6] / My big brothers and so many others I saw / I'm just glad we got to see each other / **Talk and re-meet each other**[7]/ Save a place in Heaven / till the next time we meet forever / [*Chorus*] / The music business hate me / **'cause the industry ain't make me**[8] / Hustlers and boosters embrace me / And the music I be making / I dumb

1. The most famous lines in this song are about my philosophy of music and the tension between my commercial instincts and my instincts as an artist. But the first verse is all about my father.

2. After *Reasonable Doubt,* my next three albums were called *Vol. 1, Vol. 2,* and *Vol. 3,* with subtitles—*In My Lifetime, Hard Knock Life,* and *Life and Times of S. Carter.* The *Volume* series was meant to emphasize the connection between the albums, that each was a continuation and expansion of the same basic story.

3. This sounds cold, but the truth is that my father left my family for good when I was young and didn't reenter my life until I was an adult. Three months after we had our first conversation in twenty years, he died. My mother had pushed for the meeting because she knew he didn't have long and she didn't want him to die with our issues still unresolved. So at the funeral I was more intrigued than devastated.

4. When I did finally see my father again and we stood face-to-face, it was like looking in a mirror. It made me wonder how someone could abandon a child who looked just like him.

5. My father and I didn't have a lot of deep conversations before he died, but we did have one important one. When I first reconnected with him, I hit him with questions and he came back with answers until I realized nothing he could ever say would satisfy me or make sense of all the feelings I'd had since he turned his back on us. In the end, he broke down and apologized. And, somewhat to my surprise, I forgave him.

6. The death of my father's brother, my uncle Ray, changed everything for my pops. Ray was murdered outside of a crowded Brooklyn bar and everyone knew who did it, but the police didn't do anything about it. My dad swore revenge and became obsessed with hunting down Uncle Ray's killer. The tragedy—compounded by the injustice—drove him crazy, sent him to the bottle, and ultimately became a factor in the unraveling of my parents' marriage. As a kid, I didn't know all this. I had no idea that it was the death of his brother that undid my dad. When I found this out I realized that yeah, of course every father that bounced had a reason. I didn't excuse him for leaving his kids, but I started to understand.

7. Although this verse starts off on a cold note—I seem indifferent and even smirking about his death—that's only me being honest. I didn't cry. I didn't know him that well. But at the same time, it was so important that we did meet up before he died. It was important for me to hear him say he was sorry and for me to hear myself say, "I forgive you." It changed my life, really. I wish every kid who grew up like me could have the same chance to confront the fathers who left them, not just so they can lay out their anger, but so they can, in the end, let that anger go. That anger still stunts so many of us.

8. I was lucky in some ways to have come into the game on my own two feet—along with my partners Biggs and Dame—and not because the industry wanted to make me the flavor of the month and then throw me away.

down for my audience / And double my dollars / They criticize me for it / **Yet they all yell "Holla"**[9] / If skills sold / Truth be told / I'd probably be / Lyrically / **Talib Kweli**[10] / Truthfully / I wanna rhyme like Common Sense / (But I did five mil) / **I ain't been rhyming like Common since**[11] / When your sense got that much in common / And you been hustling since / Your inception / Fuck perception / Go with what makes sense / **Since**[12] / I know what I'm up against / **We as rappers must decide what's most important**[13] / And I can't help the poor if I'm one of them / So I got rich and gave back / To me that's the win-win / So next time you see the homie and his rims spin / Just know my mind is working just like them / (The rims that is) [*Chorus*] My homie Sigel's on a tier / **Where no tears**[14] should fall / 'cause he was on the block where no squares get off / See in my inner circle all we do is ball / **Till we all got triangles on our wall**[15] / **He ain't just rappin for the platinum**[16] / Y'all record / I recall / 'cause I really been there before / **Four scores and seven years ago**[17] / Prepared to flow / Prepare for war / I shall fear no man / You don't hear me though / These words ain't just paired to go / In one ear out the other ear / NO / YO / **My balls and my word is all I have** / **What you gonna do to me?** / **Nigga scars'll scab** / **What you gonna box me homie?** / **I can dodge and jab** / **Three shots couldn't touch me**[18] / Thank God for that / **I'm strong enough to carry Biggie Smalls on my back**[19] / And the whole BK nigga holla back

9. I love that this has become such a popular line for people to riff off of in hip-hop—Lupe Fiasco did a great song called "Dumb It Down" that brought the whole thing full circle, for example—since the point of the line was to provoke conversation.

10. Kweli is a great MC—as is Common—and they've both carved out impressive careers without big records. They're great technical MCs, but there is a difference between being a great technician and a great songwriter. I deeply respect their craft, but even the most dazzling lyrical display won't translate to a wide audience unless it's matched with a big song.

11. This whole lyric is overstated—and I love Common—but I'm trying to make a point. I didn't come into the rap game just to enjoy my own rhymes; I could've done that by myself in my house with my tape recorder. I came into the music business to reach as many people as possible—and to get paid.

12. I use "sense" or "since" six times in the preceding nine lines, alternating between them, a technical flourish that works as its own commentary.

13. Ultimately, every artist has to make a choice about what makes the most sense for them, and I'm not mad at whatever they decide. To honor the art of lyrical rhyming on one hand, and try to reach a wide audience on the other, is an art form in itself. It's not easy, but that's just another challenge that I love to take on.

14. The homonym of tiers and tears connects prison tiers with crying—but you can't cry in prison (at least not out in the open).

15. This geometric series—block/square, ball/circle, and then triangle—is the kind of unnecessary technical challenge I like to drop into songs just to give the lines extra energy and resonance. The "triangles on our wall" refer to platinum plaques; *Billboard* magazine's symbol for platinum sales is a triangle.

16. Even though earlier I made the point about doubling my dollars, here I'm being clear that the rapping isn't just for sales, because I've already sold millions—so there's still something deeper at work.

17. A play on Abraham Lincoln's Gettysburg Address—except instead of his "four score and seven years ago," my "four scores" are four number one albums, and "seven years ago" goes back to the beginning of my career.

18. This is about not having fear: "Scars'll scab" means that even if you injure me, I'll recover; "I can dodge and jab" means that swinging on me won't stop me; and even "three shots couldn't touch me." The whole point of the "moment of clarity" is that after I confront my own demons, I'm left with nothing but "my balls and my word," which makes me untouchable.

19. Biggie was huge, arguably the greatest of all time. Carrying him on my back means taking the weight of all he represented. But the image of Biggie—who wasn't skinny—on my back reinforces how hard it is to do.

A STERN DISCIPLINE

Breathe Easy (Lyrical Exercise)
(The Blueprint, 2001)

My 1st Song
(The Black Album, 2003)

When I was a kid my family loved sports. I played baseball with a Little League squad out in Brooklyn. My big brother Eric played basketball in junior and summer leagues and was a straight star. When we first moved to Marcy my father set up a little basketball hoop in our apartment—and we would all sweat it out right there in the living room like it was Madison Square Garden.

But we never could fully dedicate ourselves to becoming true athletes. Life intervened. I hit the streets. But I still loved sports. Playing them, watching them. I wasn't one of those cats who was too cool to lose his shit over a game. I cared.

There's always been a connection between sports and the streets. When Biggie rapped in "Things Done Changed" that *either you slangin' crack rock or you got a wicked jump shot,* he was talking about the two paths out that most young black men think are open to them. The irony is that if you're "slangin' crack rock" you'll probably end up in jail, and if you got a "wicked jump shot," you still won't make it to the NBA unless you're extremely lucky, like win-the-lottery lucky.

But even if dreams of the NBA are one of the hoaxes played on young black boys, I also believe that there's a lot to be learned from elite athletes. Sports are one of the great metaphors for life, and watching athletes perform is like watching different ideas about life playing themselves out. Athletes aren't just fascinating for their physical skills, but for what their performances tell us about human potential and character.

I AM THE MIKE JORDAN OF RECORDING

I know I'm not alone when I say this, but I absolutely love Michael Jordan. Kobe is impressive for his dedication to the game, and has an outside chance to eclipse Jordan someday, and I think LeBron is the best of his generation, but as of now Jordan's inarguably the greatest player to ever touch a basketball. What made his game magical is the way it spoke to deeper shit than just wins and losses. His career was a perfectly composed story about will. To see him come out of retirement, after his father was buried, to come back and win championships, there was nothing better in the world. In 1998, when the Bulls were down by three in Game Six of the Finals with seconds left, and Jordan scored, stole the ball from Karl Malone, came down, crossed over Bryon Russell, and hit the winning shot at the buzzer—well, I could have laid down and died after that game. It was perfect.

The first time I met Jordan was at St. John's University, where he was giving the keynote address at their graduation one year. We talked briefly, but didn't really chop it up. A couple of months later, in Chicago, I went to his restaurant at his invitation to have dinner with him. I had Ty-Ty and my friend Juan with me and I told Jordan that if I was going to sit and break bread with him, I'd have to be able to ask him anything. I meant anything.

It was so perfect that I had Juan with me because he's a die-hard Knicks fan, and as much as he respected Jordan, he hated the way Jordan personally sat the Knicks down every year in the Eastern Conference play offs. Juan is a real sports fan; he'd be sick for a week, I'm talking depressed—he wouldn't leave the house—after his team lost. That night he had to sit there and dine with his nemesis. Jordan told Juan the story of how he almost came to the Knicks. He said he was a second away from closing the deal, he was packing his bags to come to New York, when Jerry Krauss called and matched the Knicks' offer at the last minute. Juan looked like he was going to cry.

I asked Jordan who was the hardest nigga that ever guarded him; he told me Joe Dumars. I found out how much Jordan loves Hakeem Olajuwon; he pointed out that he was a leader in steals, which is rare in the center position. I asked him to name his five favorite centers, the best games he ever played, which championship meant the most to him. I got to be an unabashed fan. It was an absolute dream conversation for me.

The thing that distinguished Jordan wasn't just his talent, but his discipline, his laser-like commitment to excellence. That's something I always respect, especially in people who have great natural talents already. Making music requires a lot of that same discipline and commitment. It's true that I'm able to sometimes come up with songs in a matter of minutes after hearing a track, but that's a skill that I've honed over hundreds of hours of practice and work since I was nine. My earliest mentors in rap taught me that making music is work, whether it was Jaz locking himself in a room working on different flows or Big Daddy Kane taking the time to meticulously put together a stage show. There's unquestionably magic involved in great music, songwriting, and performances—like those nights when a star athlete is totally in the zone and can't miss. But there's also work. Without the work, the magic won't come. There are a hundred Harold Miners (no disrespect) for every Michael Jordan.

For instance, tours are the most lucrative aspect of a recording artist's career; you have a lot more control and fewer people are in your pockets as compared to album sales. It can also be stressful beyond belief. Every night you're in a different city, every crowd brings a different vibe, every show is subtly different—but at the same time, you have to hit the same marks night after night, find a new way to get your own energy up when you're performing the same song you did the night before. It becomes less about your innate charisma and talent—although that's still required—and more about being able to meet the mental and physical challenge of it. A tour requires stamina, willpower, and the ability to self-motivate, to hype yourself into game mode night after night. When you're on tours like the ones I've done over the last decade, you're like a professional athlete, except that night after night you're the only one with the bat.

When it comes to signing up new talent, that's what I'm looking for—not just someone who has skill, but someone built for this life. Someone who has the work ethic, the drive. The gift that Jordan had wasn't just that he was willing to do the work, but he loved doing it, because he could feel himself getting stronger, ready for anything. He left the game and came back and worked just as hard as he did when he started. He came into the game as Rookie of the Year, and he finished off the last playoff game of his career with a shot that won the Bulls their sixth championship.

That's the kind of consistency that you can get only by adding dead-serious discipline to whatever talent you have.

BREATHE EASY (LYRICAL EXERCISE)

[*talking*] / So I had to memorize these rhymes until I got home / Ya understand? Once you memorize a sentence / **It's like an exercise**[1] / [*echoes*] / [*heavy breathing*] / [*talking*] / Ya niggas can't be serious right now / I'm the all time heavy weight champion of flows / I'm leading the league in at least six statistical categories right now / Best flow, Most consistent, Realest stories / Most charisma, I set the most trends / And my interviews are hotter / Holla / I jog in the graveyard / Spar in the same ring / Now it's housed by the building / **Where Malcolm X was slain**[2] / **I spring train in the winter**[3] / Round early December / Run suicide drills over and over / With the weight of the world on my shoulder / **That's why they call me "Hova"**[4] / I'm far from being God / But I work goddamn hard / I wake up with the birds when the nerds are asleep / I'm catching my second wind the second the first one end / I am focused man / And I'm not afraid of death / And I'm going all out / I circle the vultures in a van and / I run the block (run) / Pull up in a drop (pull up) / **Push up on my money (push up)**[5] / I'm in great shape dunny / I keep jacks jumping thirty-six sets / Like a personal

1. I developed that habit of holding rhymes in my head from working so hard on the streets. When I was still a teenager I might be on the corner when a rhyme came to me. I would have to run to the corner store, buy something, then find a pen to write it on the back of the brown paper bag till I got home to put it in my notebook. I couldn't keep doing that because I had to concentrate on work, not on scheming to get my hands on brown paper bags. So I created little corners in my head where I stored rhymes. Once I got good at it, I actually preferred it as a technique. I'm not sure it's better than writing shit down, but it's the only way I know. When I was working on the *Kingdom Come* album, I tried to sit down and actually write my rhymes, but it just doesn't work that way for me.

2. "Spar in the ring" referred to performing at the Apollo in Harlem. Malcolm was assassinated at the Audubon Ballroom, a couple miles away.

3. "Spring train in the winter" refers to the fact that most of my albums dropped in the fall or winter. The suicide drills refers to the drilling I get from doing press before the album releases, which I find as tedious and uncomfortable as athletes find suicide drills.

4. Hova is, of course, short for Jay-Hova, which is a play on Jehovah—a piece of wordplay that irritates the fuck out of some religious people. They should just relax and listen to the next line.

5. These exercise metaphors describe the hustler's routine—running, pullups, and pushups.

trainer **I teach coke to stretch**[6] / I pump in Roc sweats / All white trainers / The ghettoes, Billy Blanks / I show you niggas what pain is / Maintain your stamina / Hov will damage ya / Spot you two rhymes y'all niggas is amateurs / The fifth / A dead lift if / Niggas don't want to get shot then y'all niggas better squat / I drop your set for rep / No need to hit the showers / **The spit from the fifth leave you wet**[7] / Lyrical exercise / [*hard breathing*] / Y'all niggas ain't tired right? / One, One / Two, Two / Three, Three / Four, Breathe Easy / Suckers / Get your weight up / Not your hate up / Jigga man is diesel / **When I lift the eight up**[8] / Y'all ain't ready to workout with the boy / Your flow is brain on drugs / Mines is rap on steroids / I lift every voice when I sing / My ability / Make yours look like an exercise in futility / Bring your squad / Biceps, Triceps, and Quads / We don't struggle with undeveloped muscle / Y'all ain't real / That's y'all Achilles' heel / Same routine when you see me you know the drill / I spot ya / I lift the weight of the watch off your arm / Remain nice and calm / Put down your things / **Trinidad of the game know my way around your ring**[9] / No matter how many pounds you bring / It sounds like the same old thing / R-O-C is the strongest team

8. Again, my exercise in the song largely consists of lifting guns (an "eight" is a .38) and quantities of drugs. This also reminds me of a photo of Shaq lifting Kobe after the Lakers won their first championship in the Kobe/Shaq era. (One of Shaq's nicknames is "Diesel" and Kobe wears the number 8.)

9. Felix Trinidad is a boxer who knew his way around the ring, and when your ring joins your watch, so will I.

6. Stretching coke means figuring out ways to cut it with baking soda so you have more than you originally purchased. You can only stretch the work if it's already premium quality.

7. More exercise imagery used to describe a hustler's threats: squats, sets, reps, and showers. This whole rhyme—a bonus track on the *Blueprint* album—is really about technical rhyming, like the rhymes Jaz and I used to come up with just to challenge ourselves. In this case, the challenge is to create as many clever rhymes as possible using the exercise metaphor—I tried to fit one into every line, and nearly succeeded. The whole thing curves in on itself in this final double entendre in the first verse: The "lyrical exercise" is to compose *lyrics* about *exercise*.

MY 1ST SONG

[Intro: Notorious B.I.G. interview] / I'm just, tryin to stay above water y'know / Just stay busy, stay workin / Puff told me like, the key to this joint / The key to staying, on top of things / is treat everything like it's your first project, knahm-sayin? / Like it's your first day like back when you was an intern / Like, that's how you try to treat things like, just stay hungry / *[Jay-Z]* Uhh, uhh, yes, yes / Y'all wanna know, why he don't stop / Y'all wanna know, why he don't flop / Let me tell you pe-eople why / Came from the bottom of the block I / When I was born, it was sworn, I was never gon' be shit / Had to pull the opposite out this bitch / Had to get my ri-ide on / Eyes on the prize, Shawn knew I had to / Had to had **to get these chips** / **Had to make moves like Olajuwon**[1] / Started out sellin dimes and nicks / Graduated to a brick / No exaggeration, my infatuation with the strip / Legendary like a schoolboy / **Crushin merely nearly every every**[2] chick / Heavy shit—that's how schoolboy got whipped / And got left on some "**Just Me, Myself and I**"[3] / On some Trugoy shit / Had to move to a place, a place of no return / **Had to play with fire and get burned** / **Only way the boy ever gon' learn**[4] / Had to lay way in the cut, till I finally got my turn / Now I'm on top in the spot that I earned / It's my life—it's my pain and my struggle / The song that I sing to you it's my ev-ery-thing / Treat my first like my last, and my last like my first / And my thirst is the same as when I came / It's my joy and my tears and the laughter it brings to me / It's my ev-ery-thing / Like I never rode in a limo / Like I just dropped flows to a demo / Like it's ninety-two again and / And I got O's in the rental / Back in the stu' again, no problemo livin was a whole lot simpler / When you think back, you thought that / you would never make it this far, then you / take advantage of the luck you handed / Or the talent you been given / **Ain't no half-steppin,**[5] ain't no, no slippin / Ain't no different from a block that's hittin' / Gotta get it while the getting's good / **Gotta strike while the iron's hot, 'fore you stop**[6] / Then you gotta bid it good riddance / Goodbye, this is my second major breakup / My first was with a pager / With a hooptie, a cookpot, and the GAME / This one's with the studio, with the stage, with the fortune / **Maybe not the fortune, but certainly the FAME**[7]

1. "Chips" is slang for money, and championships, which relates to Hakeem Olajuwon, who won multiple championships in the NBA and in college.

2. The rhyme scheme here is pretty dense. The pace is double-time and the lines are all stuffed with internal rhymes, which gives the song the breathless rhythm of my earliest songs, when I was essentially a speed rapper.

3. "Me, Myself and I" was a song by De La Soul, a trio that featured the rapper Trugoy.

4. Brain scientists are actually starting to discover that this is true: The only way we learn how to take responsibility is to take risks when we're young—which, if you're not under regular adult supervision, usually means fucking up, playing with fire, getting burned. But it's not the kid's fault—it's his nature. The fault is in a society that doesn't protect him from himself.

5. "Ain't No Half-Steppin" was a hit in the eighties by Big Daddy Kane. It sampled "Ain't No Half-Steppin" by Heatwave, a funk group in the 1970s. Kane's version has in turn been sampled a dozen times in other rap songs.

6. This is a song about hunger, and a big part of being hungry is never slipping, never missing a chance to strike. One of the great lessons to me was in 1998, when DMX released two number one albums in the same year. It was crazy. But he was hot, and he proved that the market would support an artist who was willing to supply it while he was at his peak of popularity. It takes a serious work ethic to keep up that kind of production at a high level.

7. I'm doing a bad Prince impersonation with this line, referencing his line in "Adore," *You could burn up my clothes / smash up my ride (well, maybe not the ride).* Of course, my breakup with the music biz wasn't permanent, but the message of the song is still true.

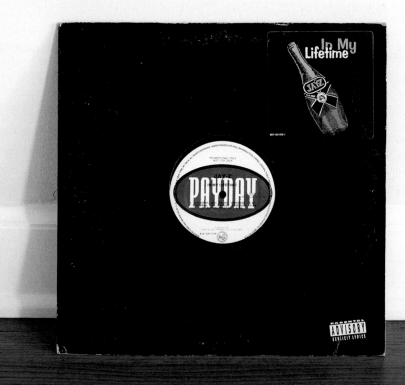

"**I**f you're proud to be an American, put your hands up now!" It was the night after the inauguration and I was in Washington, D.C., playing a free show for ten thousand Obama for America volunteers. It was the cap of a euphoric and surreal few months, when the entire history of the world that I'd known up to that point totally flipped. The words "proud to be an American" were not words I'd ever thought I'd say. I'd written America off, at least politically.

Of course, it's my home, and home to millions of people trying to do the right thing, not to mention the home of hip-hop, Quentin Tarantino flicks, the crossover dribble and lots of other things I couldn't live without. But politically, its history is a travesty. A graveyard. And I knew some of the bodies it buried.

It never seemed as hopeless as it was during the eight years that preceded that night in Washington. I was so over America that if John McCain and Sarah Palin had won that election I was seriously ready to pack up, get some land in some other country, and live as an expat in protest. The idea of starting a show that way would've been, at any other time in my entire life up to that point, completely perverse. Because America, as I understood the concept, hated my black ass.

FUCK GOVERNMENT, NIGGAS POLITIC THEMSELVES

Poor people in general have a twisted relationship with the government. We're aware of the government from the time we're born. We live in government-funded housing and work government jobs. We have family and friends spending time in the ultimate public housing, prison. We grow up knowing people who pay for everything with little plastic cards—Medicare cards for checkups, EBT cards for food. We know what AFDC and WIC stand for and we stand for hours waiting for bricks of government cheese. The first and fifteenth of each month are times of peak economic activity. We get to know all kinds of government agencies not because of civics class, but because they actually visit our houses and sit up on our couches asking questions. From the time we're small children we go to crumbling public schools that tell us all we need to know about what the government thinks of us.

Then there are the cops.

In places like Marcy there are people who know the ins and outs of government bureaucracies, police procedures, and sentencing guidelines, who spend half of their lives in dirty waiting rooms on plastic chairs waiting for someone to call their name. But for all of this involvement, the government might as well be the weather because a lot of us don't think we have anything to do with it—we don't believe we have any control over this thing that controls us. A lot of our heroes, almost by default, were people who tried to dismantle or overthrow the government—Malcolm X or the Black Panthers—or people who tried to make it completely irrelevant, like Marcus Garvey, who wanted black people to sail back to Africa. The government was everywhere we looked, and we hated it.

Housing projects are a great metaphor for the government's relationship to poor folks: these huge islands built mostly in the middle of nowhere, designed to warehouse lives. People are still people, though, so we turned the projects into real communities, poor or not. We played in fire hydrants and had cookouts and partied, music bouncing off concrete walls. But even when we could shake off the full weight of those imposing buildings and try to just live, the truth of our lives and struggle was still invisible to the larger country. The rest of the country was freed of any obligation to claim us. Which was fine, because we weren't really claiming them, either.

CAN'T SEE THE UNSEEABLE, REACH THE UNREACHABLE

Hip-hop, of course, was hugely influential in finally making our slice of America visible through our own lens—not through the lens of outsiders. But it wasn't easy.

There are all the famous incidents of censorship and intimidation: the way politicians attacked rappers, the free-speech cases with groups like Two Live Crew, the dramas surrounding Public Enemy and political rap, the threatening letters from the FBI protesting NWA. But the attempts at censorship only made the targets bigger stars. NWA couldn't have bought the kind of publicity they got from having *the actual fucking FBI* attacking them over a song. This was when you had one prominent Harlem pastor renting a bulldozer and calling news cameras to film him running over a pile of rap CDs in the middle of 125th Street. When WBLS, a legendary black-owned radio station in New York, stripped hip-hop from their playlists in sympathy with the protest, another radio station, Hot 97, came along with an *all-rap* format and went straight to number one. In a few years, WBLS came back to rap. In the end, you can't censor the truth, especially when it comes packaged in hot music.

Those battles were big for all of us in hip-hop and offered an important survival lesson: Politicians—at the highest levels—would try to silence and kill our culture if they could hustle some votes out of it. Even black leaders who were supposed to be representing you would turn on you—would pile your records up and run over them with a fucking bulldozer or try to ban you from radio—if they felt threatened by your story or language. But the thing is, we kept winning.

THey NeVer T

GARVey IN 00

ChRISToPher

TheIR GoLDe

ught MARCUS

& School

COLUMBUS IS

RULE

GUNS WERE EASIER TO GET IN THE HOOD THAN PUBLIC ASSISTANCE. THERE WERE TIMES WHEN THE VIOLENCE JUST SEEMED LIKE BACKGROUND MUSIC, LIKE WE'D ALL GONE NUMB.

The push for censorship only reinforced what most of us already suspected: America doesn't want to hear about it. There was a real tension between the power of the story we wanted to tell and just how desperately some powerful people didn't want to hear it. But the story had to come out sooner or later because it was so dramatic, important, crazy—and just plain compelling.

Back in the eighties and early nineties cities in this country were literally battlegrounds. Kids were as well armed as a paramilitary outfit in a small country. Teenagers had Uzis, German Glocks, and assault rifles—and we had the accessories, too, like scopes and silencers. Guns were easier to get in the hood than public assistance. There were times when the violence just seemed like background music, like we'd all gone numb.

The deeper causes of the crack explosion were in policies concocted by a government that was hostile to us, almost genocidally hostile when you think about how they aided or tolerated the unleashing of guns and drugs on poor communities, while at the same time cutting back on schools, housing, and assistance programs. And to top it all off, they threw in the so-called war on drugs, which was really a war on us. There were racist new laws put on the books, like the drug laws that penalized the possession of crack cocaine with more severe sentences than the possession of powder. Three-strike laws could put young guys in jail for twenty-five years for nonviolent crimes. The disease of addiction was treated as a crime. The rate of incarceration went through the roof. Police abuses and corruption were rampant. Across the country, cops were involved in the drug trade, playing both sides. Young black men in New York in the eighties and nineties were gunned down by cops for the lightest suspected offenses, or died in custody under suspicious circumstances. And meanwhile we were killing ourselves by the thousands.

Almost twenty years after the fact, there are studies that say between 1989 and 1994 more black men were murdered in the streets of America than died in the entire Vietnam War. America did not want to talk about the human damage, or the deeper causes of the carnage. But then here came rap, like the American nightmare come to life. The disturbing shit you thought you locked away for good, buried at the bottom of the ocean, suddenly materialized in your kid's bedroom, laughing it off, cursing loud, and grabbing its nuts, refusing to be ignored anymore. *I'm America's worst nightmare / I'm young black and holding my nuts like shh-yeah.* Hardcore rap wasn't political in an explicit way, but its volume and urgency kept a story alive that a lot of people would have preferred to disappear. Our story. It scared a lot of people.

WE TOTE GUNS TO THE GRAMMYS

Invisibility was the enemy, and the fight had multiple fronts. For instance, 1998 was an important year for hip-hop. It was two years after Pac had been gunned down, and just a year after Biggie was killed. DMX dropped two number one albums that year. Outkast released *Aquemini,* a game-changing album lyrically and sonically, but also for what it meant to Southern rap. (Juvenile's *100 Degreez,* also released in '98, was a major shot in the growing New Orleans movement. I jumped on a remix of his single "Ha," which was a great mix of regional styles.) Mos Def and Talib Kweli had their Black Star album, one of the definitive indie rap records of all time. The prototypical "backpack rappers," A Tribe Called Quest, released their last album, *The Love Movement.* And the biggest album of the year in any genre was *The Miseducation of Lauryn Hill.*

It was a beautiful time all the way around in hip-hop. The album I released that year, *Vol. 2 . . . Hard Knock Life,* was the biggest record of my life. The opening week was unreal for me—we did more than three hundred thousand units, by far the biggest opening number of my career to that point. The album moved Lauryn Hill down to number four, but Outkast's *Aquemini* was right behind me, and *The Love Movement* was number three. Those four albums together told the story of young black America from four dramatically different perspectives—we were bohemians and hustlers and revolutionaries and space-age Southern boys. We were funny and serious, spiritual and ambitous, lovers and gangsters, mothers and brothers. This was the full picture of our generation. Each of these albums was an innovative and honest work of art and wildly popular on the charts. Every kid in the country had at least one of these albums, and a lot of them had all four. The entire world was plugged into the stories that came out of the specific struggles and creative explosion of our generation. And that was just the tip of the iceberg of what was happening in hip-hop that year.

So, in this incredible year for diverse strands of real hip-hop, what happens at the Grammy Awards? First, DMX, with two number one albums and a huge single, "Get at Me Dog," that brought rap back to its grimy roots, was completely snubbed. And then, in this year when rap dominated the charts and provided the most innovative and creative

music you could find on the radio, they decided not to televise any of the rap awards. Rap music was fully coming into its own creatively and commercially, but still being treated as if it wasn't fit to sit in the company of the rest of the music community.

I was nominated three times that year, but when they told us they weren't televising our awards I decided to stay home. It wasn't a big-deal, formal boycott. God knows there were bigger issues in the world. And eventually I started coming to the show and even performing. But not until they started showing rap the respect it deserves. The larger point was, I wasn't going to be a partner to my own invisibility.

CROOKED OFFICER, WHY YOU WANNA SEE ME IN A COFFIN, SIR?

When the politicians can't censor you and the industry can't marginalize you, call the cops. The statistics on the incarceration of black men, particularly of men of my generation, are probably the most objective indication that young black men are seen in this country as a "problem" that can be made to literally disappear. No one in the entire world—not in Russia or China or Iran—is locked up like black men are locked up in this country.

I had to deal with the cops when I was hustling, and that made sense. I had to deal with the cops before that, too, because even before I started running the streets, I was on their radar just because of who I was. But when I was done with the streets, and done with my one major brush with law enforcement after I left the streets, I still wasn't done with five-oh.

One night I was at Bassline with my man Tone from Trackmasters, working on the song that would become "Izzo (H.O.V.A.)" on the *Blueprint* album. I left the studio to run by Club Exit in midtown because I had promised Ja Rule that I'd come by and join him for our big hit "Can I Get A . . ." I went to the club, performed the song, and ten minutes later I left. I hopped in my Suburban with Ty-Ty and my bodyguard and the driver pulls off. We were one block away from the club when an unmarked police van cut us off, like in a movie. Since there's a limo partition in the SUV, it took me a few minutes to see what was happening, but it sounded like a raid—sirens flashing, cops yelling. When I lifted the partition I saw half a dozen squad cars surrounding us. My bodyguard was already out of the car and a detective was showcasing his gun up in the air like he had found something. But my bodyguard claimed the gun and showed them his license. I was in the backseat laughing because they were so overdoing it, but the next thing I knew someone was opening my door and putting their hands on me, trying

RAPPERS
ARE YOUNG
BLACK
MEN TELLING
STORIES
THAT THE
POLICE,
AMONG
OTHERS,
DON'T WANT
TO HEAR.

to drag me out of the car and make me turn around. I tried to talk to them. "You know this isn't necessary; he has a license, he claimed the weapon. What's the problem?" The cop looked back at me with that *shut up, nigger* screwface, but I could tell he was confused. This wasn't going as planned. He asked his partner what he should do. Right in front of me his partner made a call and explained the situation to whoever was on the other end. "I got Jay-Z," he said into the phone, with a sense of accomplishment. Then he told his man to arrest me. I was dumbstruck as they loaded me into the back of the cruiser like a prize catch.

When they got me to the precinct for questioning, I saw a giant Peg-Board, the sort you've seen before in police television shows and movies. On the Peg-Board were organizational charts of rappers, like you'd have for a major crime organization, like the mafia. But for *rappers*. Once they had me, they made me do the perp walk, the police-escorted stroll in public, which meant dragging me in front of all the photographers outside the precinct. The charges were dropped, of course—it clearly wasn't my weapon. But they made sure to humiliate me first. With my other case still pending, this would help paint the picture of me as a menace to society.

If I were just a fan or a casual observer of hip-hop and you told me the NYPD had created a squad or division to deal with rappers, I'd laugh in your face. But it's clear now that the hip-hop police existed—there have been some media investigations and even a public admission by one prominent detective, the so-called hip-hop cop. Dossiers were created on rappers and their associates, cops staked out shows and nightclubs and followed rappers in broad daylight. The hip-hop cop *stayed* outside the clubs I was in. Every time I walked into a club he'd joke with me. *You got a gun?* I would fuck with him right back: *Do you?* For seven years that cop was there, at every club, every show.

But I still have to ask myself why. Rappers, as a class, are not engaged in anything criminal. They're musicians. Some rappers and friends of rappers commit crimes. Some bus drivers commit crimes. Some accountants commit crimes. But there aren't task forces devoted to bus drivers or accountants. Bus drivers don't have to work under the preemptive suspicion of law enforcement. The difference is obvious, of course: Rappers are young black men telling stories that the police, among others, don't want to hear. Rappers tend to come from places where police are accustomed to treating everybody like a suspect. The general style of rappers is offensive to a lot of people. But being offensive is not a crime, at least not one that's on the books. The fact that law enforcement treats rap like organized crime tells you a lot about just how deeply rap offends some people—they'd love for rap *itself* to be a crime, but until they get that law passed, they come after us however they can.

Sometimes it's surprising to find out who's trying to put the invisibility cloak on you. It's one thing when it comes from the government or from the people in the larger music industry who are trying to keep niggas in their place. But it's harder to take coming from other artists.

In 2008 I was invited to play at the Glastonbury Festival in England. I took the gig because it was a chance to knock some doors down for the culture. It's a huge festival, one of the largest outdoor festivals in the world. It started in the seventies and mostly featured rock music, even though the definition of rock music wasn't always clear—what do Massive Attack, Radiohead, the Arctic Monkeys, Björk, and the Pet Shop Boys really have in common? Well, here's one thing: None of them rap. When it was announced that I'd be headlining Glastonbury, Noel Gallagher of Oasis said, "I'm not having hip-hop at Glastonbury. It's wrong." That quote that went around—"I'm not having hip-hop"—said a lot, like he had a veto. But kids today have a mix of songs from all over the place in their iPods, and they take pride in it. There is no rock music with walls around it. It's one of the great shifts that's happened over my lifetime, that popular culture has managed to shake free of the constraints that still limit us in so many other parts of life. It's an open field.

As planned, I played that show in front of 180,000 people. I stood backstage with my crew and we looked out at the crowd. It wasn't like any other crowd I'd played. There were tens of thousands of people staring up at the stage but it might as well have been a million—bodies covered my entire field of vision. We were under a dark, open sky. Their cheers and chants were like a tidal wave of sound crashing over the stage. It was awesome and a little ominous.

Before I came out, we played a video intro reel about the controversy that included Gallagher's quote that I had "fucking no chance" of pulling off Glastonbury. Then I walked out on stage with an electric guitar hanging around my neck and started singing Oasis's biggest hit, "Wonderwall." It went over big. Then I tore through my set, with my band, a band, by the way, that's as "rock" as any band in the world. The show was amazing, one of the highlights of my career. It was one of those moments that taught me that there really is no limit to what hip-hop could do, no place that was closed to its power.

No, I'm not havin hip hop at
Glastonbury

Fuckin *no chance*

My purposefully fucked-up version of "Wonderwall" put it back on the charts a decade after it came out, ironically.

The whole sequence felt familiar to me—that same sense of someone putting their hands and weight on me, trying to push me back to the margins. Telling me to be quiet, not to get into the frame of their pristine picture. It's the story of my life and the story of hip-hop. But the beautiful thing at Glastonbury was that when I opened with "Wonderwall," over a hundred thousand voices rose up into that dark sky to join mine. It was a joke, but it was also kind of beautiful. And then when I segued into "99 Problems," a hundred thousand voices rocked the chorus with me. To the crowd, it wasn't rock and rap or a battle of genres—it was music.

LIKE IT'S '92 AGAIN AND I GOT O'S IN THE RENTALS

Little controversies like Glastonbury felt like the death spasms of an old way of thinking. Even in the world outside of music, things really were changing. For instance, there was Bill Clinton. In 1992, when he was running for president, Clinton made a point of publicly denouncing Sister Souljah at a Rainbow Coalition event—he compared her to David Duke, the white supremacist and former Grand Wizard of the KKK—because of some comments she made after the L.A. riots. At the time, everyone knew he was trying to prove to white America that he could stand up to black people, particularly young black people involved in hip-hop, and especially in the aftermath of the L.A. riots. He knew that demonizing young black people, their politics, and their art was always a winning move in American politics.

In 1992 I was, well, I won't get into details, but I was probably somewhere in the Middle Atlantic region of the United States, doing things that Bill Clinton probably wouldn't have approved of. I wasn't registered to vote back then, and even if I was, I don't know that I would've bothered to vote for Bill. Clinton was known as being comfortable with black folks; he played the sax on Arsenio Hall's show and some people even talked about him as the "first black President." He wasn't, of course. Even if he liked black people, whatever that means, back in '92 he saw people like me as a punching bag he could use to get votes from people nothing like me, people who hated me. In other words, he didn't see people like me at all. I can't say I saw him, either.

By 2008, I actually knew Bill Clinton. I first really sat down with him at the Spotted Pig. Bono brought him in one night and we hung out for a long time in the back room of the restaurant, joking and talking about music. It was so strange for me, sitting across the table from Bill Clinton, swapping stories. It made the distance between 1992 and 2008 seem deeper than just the passage of time. The world had changed around us, like it had been hit by some kind of cultural earthquake that rearranged everything. Like we'd all been launched into the air in 1992, me from the block, him from the White House, and somehow we landed next to each other in the back room of the Spotted Pig on a banquette with Bono.

I like Bill Clinton. He has a quick laugh and genuine curiosity and a big appetite for life. That night at the Spotted Pig he went to the kitchen and posed for photos with the busboys and waiters and signed every autograph he could before he left. He was clearly big-hearted. He'd done a lot of good as president. But he'd also taken the country to war in the Balkans and sat in his office while AIDS ravaged Africa and genocide broke out in Rwanda. And one day in 1992 he looked out at an audience of black people and told them that Sister Souljah was as bad as the Klan.

But I'm not exactly the same person I was in 1992, either. Everyone needs a chance to evolve.

YOU GOT IT, FUCK BUSH

Another Clinton was running for president in 2008, but, as much as I'd come to like the Clintons, I wasn't supporting Hillary. Wasn't even considering it. I'd done some campaign events in 2004 when Kerry was running for president, but in 2008, for the first time in my life, I was committed to a candidate for president in a big way.

A close friend of Barack Obama is a big fan of my music and reached out to someone in my camp to set up a meeting. This was still pretty early in the process, before the primaries had gotten started, and I hadn't really engaged with the whole thing yet or given any money to anyone or anything. All I knew was that I was sick about what had happened with this country since 9/11, the wars and torture, the response to Hurricane Katrina, the arrogance and dishonesty of the Bush administration. I sat down with Barack at a one-on-one meeting set up by that mutual friend and we talked for hours. People always ask me what we talked about, and I wish I could remember some specific moment when it hit me that this guy was special. But it wasn't like that. It was the fact that he sought me

HE COULD,
THROUGH
SHEER
SYMBOLISM,
REGARDLESS
OF ANY OF
HIS ACTUAL
POLITICS,
CHANGE
THE LIVES
OF MILLIONS
OF BLACK
KIDS WHO
SAW SOME-
THING DIF-
FERENT TO
ASPIRE TO.

out and then asked question after question, about music, about where I'm from, about what people in my circle—not the circle of wealthy entertainers, but the wider circle that reaches out to my fans and all the way back to Marcy—were thinking and concerned about politically. He listened. It was extraordinary.

More than anything specific that he said, I was impressed by who he was. Supporters of Barack are sometimes criticized for getting behind him strictly because of his biography rather than his policies. I thought his policies were good, and I liked his approach to solving problems, but I'm not going to lie: Who he was was very important to me. He was my peer, or close to it, like a young uncle or an older brother. His defining experiences were in the nineties in the projects of Chicago, where he lived and worked as a community organizer before going to Harvard Law School. He'd seen me—or some version of me—in those Chicago streets, and we lived around a lot of the same kinds of things over those years, although obviously from very different angles. I could see he wasn't going to be one of those guys who burned hip-hop in effigy to get a few votes. He even had the guts to tell the press that he had my music on his iPod.

And he was black. This was big. This was a chance to go from centuries of invisibility to the most visible position in the entire world. He could, through sheer symbolism, regardless of any of his actual policies, change the lives of millions of black kids who now saw something different to aspire to. That would happen on the day he was elected, regardless of anything else that happened in his term. No other candidate could promise so much.

Early on, there were a lot of influential black people who didn't think he could win and withheld their support. I got into some serious arguments with people I respect over supporting Barack over Hillary. But I could see what Barack in the White House would mean to kids who were coming up the way I came up. And having met the man, I felt like Barack wasn't going to lose. I ran into him again at a fund-raiser at L. A. Reid's house and he pulled my coat: "Man, I'm going to be calling you again."

I was touring at the time for the *American Gangster* album, and when I hit the lyric in "Blue Magic" where I say *fuck Bush,* I'd segue into "Minority Report," my song about Hurricane Katrina from the *Kingdom Come* album. The jumbo screen behind me would go black and then up would come an image of Barack Obama. The crowd would always go wild. I would quickly make the point that Barack was not asking me to do this—and he hadn't. I didn't want him to get caught up in having to defend every one of my lyrics or actions. I've done some stuff even I have trouble explaining—I definitely didn't want him to have to. I didn't want my lyrics to end up in a question at a presidential debate. I knew enough about politics and the media to know that something that trivial could derail him.

I thought a lot about that. There were people like Reverend Jeremiah Wright who caused trouble for Barack because of things they'd said or done in the past but refused to lay low, even when it was clear they were hurting the cause. I was happy to play the back and not draw attention to myself. I didn't need to be onstage or in every picture with him. I just wanted him to win.

But he did eventually call me and ask me to help. It was in the fall of the year and he told me he wanted to close it out like Jordan. So I did a bunch of free shows all over the country before the election to encourage young people to register to vote. I wasn't surprised at the historically low rate of voting among young black people because I'd been there myself. But I had to make it clear to them: If you want shit to get better in your neighborhood, you have to be the one who puts the guy in office. If you vote for him, he owes you. That's the game—it's a hustle. But even aside from all that, I told people, this election is bigger than politics. As cliché as it might sound, it was about hope.

THIS MIGHT OFFEND MY POLITICAL CONNECTS

When I came to Washington for the inauguration—needless to say, the first inauguration of my life—I just wanted to soak it all in, every second of it. As soon as I walked into the lobby of the hotel where I was staying, the vibe was unlike anything I'd ever felt, people of all races and ages just thrilled to see each other. Beyoncé performed at the Lincoln Memorial the day before the inauguration and I decided to watch her from the crowd, so I could feel the energy of everyday people. It was unbelievable to see us—me, Beyoncé, Mary J. Blige, Puff, and other people I've known for so long, who represent people I've known my whole life—sharing in this rite of passage, one of America's grandest displays of pageantry.

On the day of the inauguration, I came down in the elevator of the hotel with Ty-Ty. An older white woman in the elevator with us turned and admired Ty-Ty's suit and gently straightened his tie. It wasn't patronizing at all, it felt as comfortable as if we were family. We had seats for the ceremony, which was an unexpected honor, and from underneath my Russian mink hat (it was two degrees below zero) I watched Air Force II—the president's helicopter, with George Bush in it—take off from the White House while a million people chanted nah-nah-nah-nah, hey, hey, hey, goodbye. And then the moment came when Barack faced the Chief Justice of the Supreme Court and took the oath of office to become the forty-fourth President. That was when it hit me the hardest. We'd started so far outside of it—so far from power and visibility. But here we were.

The first show I played when I got to Washington, two days before the inauguration, was a little different from the official inaugural events I played, where I was keeping it presidential. It was at Club Love and I was dropping in on Jeezy's set to do the remix version of "My President Is Black." It was a real hip-hop show—stage crowded with niggas facing a hot, crowded club. It was the kind of show I've been doing since I was running with Kane. The spirit was familiar, too—the crowd was rocking to the music, arms in the air, getting the rush from being so close to the performers, so close to one another. But it was also different. There were people waving small American flags back at me. And onstage, we were all smiling. Grinning. We couldn't control it. Jeezy had the funniest line of the night: "I know we're thanking a lot of people . . . I want to thank two people: I want to thank the motherfucker overseas who threw two shoes at George Bush. And I want to thank the motherfuckers who helped him move his shit up out the White House."

Those lines—in fact, the whole performance, which someone posted up on the Internet—would get twisted and cause a little stir among the right-wing media in the days that followed, which only validated my initial decision to lay low during the campaign. But it was over now and we'd won; fuck it—it was a celebration. We all had chills.

I remembered when I was still campaigning that fall, doing shows all over for voter registration. At one show in Virginia I was closing out my set and looked out at the audience, full of young black kids, laughing and hopeful. I tried to focus on the individual faces in that crowd, tried to find their eyes. That's why I wanted Barack to win, so those kids could see themselves differently, could see their futures differently than I did when I was a kid in Brooklyn and my eyes were focused on a narrower set of possibilities. People think there's no real distinction between the political parties, and in a lot of ways they're right. America still has a tremendous amount of distance to cover before it's a place that's true to its own values, let alone to deeper human values. Since he's been elected there have been a lot of legitimate criticisms of Obama.

But if he'd lost, it would've been an unbelievable tragedy— to feel so close to transformation and then to get sucked back in to the same old story and watch another generation grow up feeling like strangers in their own country, their culture maligned, their voices squashed. Instead, even with all the distance yet to go, for the first time I felt like we were at least moving in the right direction, away from the shadows.

"All the News That's Fit to Print"

The New York Times

VOL. CLVIII . No. 54,485 +   © 2008 The New York Times

NEW YORK, WEDNESDAY, NOVEMBER 5, 2008

Late Edition

Today, limited sunshine, a shower, high 63. Tonight, cloudy, scattered showers, patchy fog, low 55. Tomorrow, rain ends, remaining cloudy, high 62. Weather map, Page B19.

$5 beyond the greater New York metropolitan area. $1.50

OBAMA

RACIAL BARRIER FALLS IN DECISIVE VICTORY

☐ ONLINE

■ *The latest state-by-state results: the presidential contest and House, Senate and governors' races.*
■ *The Caucus blog: updates from The Times's political staff.*

■ *Interactive graphics: the electoral map, voter profiles and analysis.*
■ *Video, audio and photos: reactions from the voters and the campaigns.*
nytimes.com

PRESIDENT-ELECT

THE LONG CAMPAIGN

Journey to the Top

The story of Senator Barack Obama's journey to the pinnacle of American politics is the story of a campaign that was, even in the view of many rivals, almost flawless. After a somewhat lackluster start, Mr. Obama and his team delivered. They developed a strategy to secure the nomination, and stuck with it even after setbacks. PAGE P1

SENATE

NORTH CAROLINA

Democrats in Congress Strengthen Grip

By ADAM NAGOURNEY

Barack Hussein Obama was elected the 44th president of the United States on Tuesday, sweeping away the last racial barrier in American politics with an ease as the country chose him as its first black chief executive.

The election of Mr. Obama amounted to a national catharsis — a repudiation of a historically unpopular Republican president and his economic and foreign policies, and an embrace of Mr. Obama's call for a change in the direction and the tone of the country.

But it was just as much a strikingly symbolic moment in the evolution of the nation's fraught racial history, a breakthrough that would have seemed unthinkable just two years ago.

Mr. Obama, 47, a first-term senator from Illinois, defeated Senator John McCain of Arizona, 72, a former prisoner of war who was making his second bid for the presidency.

To the very end, Mr. McCain's campaign was eclipsed by an opponent who was nothing short of a phenomenon, drawing huge crowds epitomized by the tens of thousands of people who turned out to hear Mr. Obama's victory speech in Grant Park in Chicago.

Mr. McCain also fought the headwinds of a relentlessly hostile political environment, weighted down with the baggage left to him by President Bush and an economic collapse that took place in the middle of the general election campaign.

"If there is anyone out there who still doubts that America is a place where all things are possible, who still wonders if the dream of our founders is alive in our time, who still questions the power of our democracy, tonight is your answer," said Mr. Obama, standing before a huge wooden lectern with a row of American flags at his back, casting his eyes to a crowd that stretched far into the Chicago night.

WHITE
AMERICA

★★★ ● ★★★

1. **YOUNG GIFTED AND BLACK**
   (*S. Carter Collection, 2003*)

2. **HELL YEAH (PIMP THE SYSTEM)**
   Dead Prez featuring Jay-Z
   (*Revolutionary But Gangsta, 2004*)

There are no white people in Marcy Projects. Bed-Stuy today has been somewhat gentrified, but the projects are like gentrification firewalls. When I was growing up there, it was strictly blacks and Puerto Ricans, maybe some Dominicans, rough Arabs who ran the twenty-four-hour bodegas, pockets of Hasidim who kept to themselves, and the Chinese dudes who stayed behind bullet-proof glass at the corner take-out joint. They supposedly sold Chinese food, but most people went there for the fried wings with duck sauce and the supersweet iced tea.

When I started working in Trenton we would see white people sometimes. There were definitely white crackheads; desperate white people weren't any more immune to it than desperate black or Latino people. They'd leave their neighborhoods and come to ours to buy it. You could tell they were looking for crack because they'd slow down as they drove through the hood instead of speeding up. Sometimes they'd hang around to smoke it up. Make some new friends. But the truth is that in most neighborhoods, the local residents were the main customers. And the local residents tended to be black, maybe Latino.

That didn't mean that white people were a mystery to me. If you're an American, you're surrounded on all sides by images of white people in popular culture. If anything, some black people can become poisoned by it and start hating themselves. A lot of us suffered from it—wanting to be light-skinned with curly hair. I never thought twice about trying to look white, but in little ways I was being poisoned, too, for example, in unconsciously accepting the common wisdom that light-skinned girls were the prettiest—*all wavy light-skinned girls is lovin me now*. It was sick.

CHECK OUT MY HAIR, THESE AIN'T CURLS THESE IS PEAS

Hip-hop has always been a powerful force in changing the way people think about race, for better and worse. First it changed the way black people—especially black boys and men—thought about themselves. When I was a young teenager, the top black pop stars were Michael Jackson and Prince, two musical geniuses who fucked up a lot of black people in the head because of how deliberately they seemed to be running away from looking like black people. Their hair was silky straight, their skin was light, and in Michael's case, getting lighter by the day. We didn't know shit about vitiligo or whatever he had back then; we just saw the big, bouncy afro turn into a doobie and the black boy we loved turn white. But aside from Michael and Prince, who were so special that you could just chalk it up to their mad genius, we were getting hit with a stream of singers who weren't exactly flying the flag of blackness. The Debarges and Apollonias and constant flow of Jheri curls. Male singers were taking the bass and texture out of their voices, trying to cross over and get some of that Lionel Richie money. It wasn't their fault—and there was some good music that came out of that moment (shout-out to Al B. Sure!). But it wasn't exactly affirming.

Until hip-hop came along. Run-DMC said it in one of their early songs, "Rock Box": *I never, ever wore a braid / got the peasiest hair and still get paid.* Public Enemy made it even clearer: *I'm black and I'm proud / I'm ready, I'm hyped, plus I'm amped.* Even the Jheri curl came back hard with hip-hop: Ice Cube did Amerikkka's Most Wanted, one of the hardest albums of all time, with a curl dripping down his neck. He turned it from a symbol of self-hatred to the uniform of a black man at the bottom, which is really what it had become. (He still cut that shit off by the time his next album came around.) MCs were taking it back to the images from our childhoods—the blaxploitation heroes, the black power activists, the black aesthetic movement of the 1970s.

I was never on that nationalist tip as an MC, but MCs I looked up to, like Rakim, Kane, and Cube, whatever their politics, were unambiguously black, with no concession to any other standard of appearance. They didn't hate themselves. They knew how to be strong and stylish but stay black in a way that wasn't self-conscious or contrived. Just by being true to who they were, they obliterated the ideal of the light-skinned singer with the S-curl, which, for a lot of kids of my generation, took the edge off the kind of color consciousness that's always lurking for black people in America. Even when hip-hop aired some of the ongoing colorism among black people—like Biggie rapping that he was black and ugly as ever— the point is that we were airing it out, not sweeping it under the rug and letting it drive us crazy trying to pretend it didn't exist. Just one more way that hip-hop kept us sane.

THE WHITE BOY BLOSSOMED

In 2008 I headlined at another big rock festival, the All Points West show in New York. Unlike Glastonbury, there wasn't any real controversy. I wasn't even supposed to be on the bill. I was filling in at the last minute for the original headliners, the Beastie Boys, because MCA, one of the Boys, had to drop out for cancer treatments. In their honor, I opened my show with a cover of their classic Brooklyn anthem, "No Sleep Till Brooklyn." The crowd—which was standing in inches of mud after a torrential rain earlier in the day—was electrified and maybe a little surprised.

I'd known the Beastie Boys for a while—we had a lot in common. We were all from New York and had a strong connection to the legendary Def Jam label. They were its bestselling act in the early years and I spent three years as its CEO.

We'd both worked closely with Rick Rubin—
Rick produced their first album, *Licensed
To Ill;* he produced "99 Problems" for me
on *The Black Album* (in fact, Mike D of
the Beasties was in the studio for that
recording session).

But before I ever met them, I listened
to their music. They were a different sort
of group from the other
acts of the mid-
1980s, hip-hop's
first golden age.
They started off as
a hardcore band
in the New York
punk scene.

Back then punk mixed easily with hip-hop, and Rick and Russell were like mad scientists, mixing elements of big-beat hip-hop with the crunching guitars of heavy metal. That was an element in the sound of a lot their first big acts, like Run-DMC, LL Cool J, and even some Public Enemy. But when these three Jewish boys from New York worked it, they became the biggest act in America.

The evolution of the Beastie Boys has been very strange to watch. I remember first seeing their bootleg little videos for early songs like "She's on It" on the local New York video shows: They wandered up and down the beach in Coney Island like a trio of sloppy, drunken punks, while a gaggle of Brooklyn girls in bikinis did the classic white-girl bop. The music was grinding guitars and the flow was extremely elementary with long pauses: *there's no confusion / in her conclusion.* It had the kind of smirking, smart-ass style that was very New York and very punk rock, but it also had girls in bikinis and Led Zeppelin riffs that any American boy could get behind. When they started working with Rick Rubin, they perfected that formula.

Hip-hop gave a generation a common ground that didn't require either race to lose anything; everyone gained. Black people never had to debase themselves in hip-hop. A lot have, but it was never obligatory. In fact, the most successful albums from black artists have come from artists who are among the most culturally and politically conscious, whether it's Lauryn and the Fugees or Outkast or Tupac or Public Enemy. And the white acts who were the biggest—Eminem and the Beasties, for example—largely came with respect for the culture and its roots. Rap has been a path between cultures in the best tradition of popular music.

YOUNG GIFTED AND BLACK

[*Intro*] And out of the mercy of Allah and the lord written in our nature / We call an individual into existence and when that individual comes / **I make no apologies for what I'm about to do**[1] / [*Jay-Z*] I'm America's worst nightmare / I'm young black and holding my nuts like shh-yeah / Y'all was in the pub having a light beer / **I was in the club having a fight there**[2] / Y'all can go home / Husband and wife there / **My momma at work trying to buy me the right gear**[3] / Nine years old uncle lost his life there / Grew up thinking life ain't fair / How can I get a real job / China white right there / **Right in front of my sight like here, yeah**[4] / There's your ticket out the ghetto / Take flight right here / **Sell me, you go bye-bye here yeah**[5] / Damn there's a different set of rules we abide by here / You need a gun niggas might drive by here / You're having fun racing all your hot rods there / Downloading all our music on your iPods there / **I'm Chuck D standing in the crosshairs here**[6] / **Y'all straight, chicks got horsehair here**[7] / You ain't gotta be in fear of your bosses there / **Y'all lose your job, your pop's rich, y'all don't care**[8] / So I don't care, y'all acting like y'all don't hear / **Hear all the screams from the ghetto all the teens ducking metal here**[9] / Trying to take they mind to a whole different level here / **Yeah, we're real close to the devil here**[10] / There gotta be a better way. Somebody call the reverend here / Yeah, y'all must really be in Heaven there / Somebody tell God that we got a couple questions here / **My little cuz never got to see his seventh year**[11] / And I'm so used to pain that I ain't even shed a tear

7. I mean straight in the sense of being okay, fine, taken care of, but I'm also referring to hair. Black women wear weaves made out of horsehair, in some cases, trying to emulate the naturally straight hair of white women.

8. Some of what I'm talking about here is the idealized vision that kids in the ghetto have about white people in the suburbs. We assume that their lives are carefree and happy, which is, of course, not necessarily true.

9. The metal can refer to prisons or bullets. Even their screams can't be heard.

1. The song starts with a quotation from Louis Farrakhan.

2. It's become a cliché among comics to do the "white people drive like this, black people drive like this" joke, but I'm trying to go a little deeper into the differences between us and "y'all." And the *y'all* doesn't just refer to race; a lot of these differences happen with people who share a race but differ in economic class.

3. My mom is at work trying to buy me the right gear, but that means she can't be at home checking up on me. The value of two parents isn't just sentimental, it's practical. My real mom worked her ass off trying to make ends meet, but since she was doing it alone, no one was ever really there for me to come home to when I was a kid.

4. Straight jobs are scarce; crooked ones are much easier to find. It's "right there" in front of my sight, unavoidable. Certain kids never think about not going to college because college graduates are everywhere they look. It doesn't make them smarter or more moral, they're just followers, like most people. For other kids, everywhere they look they see the drug game. They're not stupid or immoral, they're just following what they see.

5. And, of course, the dream is that selling the drugs will get you out of the hood. But more times than not, you get out by going to jail. Damn.

6. Outside of the ghetto, comfortable kids download music about our lives; but in the ghetto, we're living in those crosshairs.

10. "A block away from hell" is how I put it in "Where I'm From."

11. My cousin fell out of a project window. The bars on the window weren't on right. It's the kind of tragedy that makes you question God about the disparities in the way people live. When niggas in the game get shot, it's tragic in its way, but you can maybe argue that they knew what was up when they got into that life. But when it happens to a kid, you realize that there's something even more troubling going on in the universe, and you start wanting an answer. Or worse, you get used to it.

HELL YEAH (PIMP THE SYSTEM) / DEAD PREZ,[1] FEATURING JAY-Z

[*Jay-Z*] As long as there's drugs to be sold / I ain't waiting for the system to plug up these holes / **I ain't slipping through the cracks[2] / So I'm at Portland, Oregon tryin to slip you these raps / The first black in the suburbs[3]** / You'd think I had Ecstasy, Percocet, and plus syrup / **The way the cops converged,[4]** they fucked up my swerve / The first young buck that I served / I thought back to the block / I never seen a cop when I was out there / They never came out there / **And out there, I was slingin crack to live[5]** / I'm only slingin raps to your kids / I'm only tryin to show you how black niggaz live/ But you don't want your little ones acting like this / Lil Amy told Becky, Becky told Jenny / **And now they all know the skinny[6]** / Lil Joey got his do-rag on / **Driving down the street blasting Tupac's song (Thug Life baby!)[7]** / But Billy like Snoop, got his blue rag on / **Now before you know it, you back in 'Nam[8]** / Now the police got me in the middle of the street / Trying to beat me blue, black and orange / I'm like hold up, who you smacking on? / **I'm only trying to eat what you snacking on[9]** / [*Chorus: Jay-Z*] / Hell yeah (y'all don't like that do you?) / Hell yeah (you fucked up the hood nigga right back to you) / Hell yeah (you know we tired of starving my nigga) / Hell yeah (let's ride) hell yeahhh (let's ride) / [*Bridge with Jay-Z ad-libs*] / If you claiming gangsta / Then bang on the system / And show that you ready to ride / Till we get our freedom / We got to get over / We steady on the grind

This is a surprising collaboration to both our fan bases, because we're often thought of as representing entirely different aspects of hip-hop—which is true, in a way. But for all the beefs and rivalries, I've always seen hip-hop as a collective and never let anyone, even the fans, get me to believe that I'm doing something different, or more (or less) acceptable, than a group like Dead Prez.

The line "slipping through the cracks" connects the "drugs to be sold" and the "holes" that need to be plugged up. And the "drug to be sold" is, of course, crack.

I chose Portland because it's the whitest place I could think of. I'm the "first black in the suburbs," but the idea is that I get there through my music, not by actually living there. The music gets everywhere.

This is based on the way the cops, even today, stalk rappers like they're criminals.

The media, in particular, has probably devoted as much time to complaining about rap music as they ever have over the real shit that goes on in the hood. The hypocrisy is stunning.

Becky is considered a classic white-girl name among black folks (and is also slang for a sexual act that is associated with white girls, for some reason). And no matter how much her parents want her to stay sheltered, popular music, of all things, teaches her about how the rest of the country lives.

The so-called "wigger" is ridiculed and stigmatized, in part because he scares the shit out of the powers that be, who see their next generation being influenced by a culture they despise.

Vietnam is obviously a metaphor for a place of warfare and violence, like the gang violence implied by the blue rag. Vietnam is also one of the many nicknames for my hometown of Brooklyn—they call it Brooknam—because it could feel like a war zone.

Hip-hop and hustling both represent ways of making money that pale in comparison to the crooked history of American power and wealth. What rappers and hustlers have made is a fraction of the real wealth generated by so-called legitimate businesses that have been a thousand times more harmful to society. Behind every great fortune, they say, is a great crime. Our fortunes—and our crimes—are not even in the same league as the real wealth in this country.

EARS WIDE
OPEN

**BEWARE
(JAY-Z REMIX)**
Panjabi MC, featuring Jay-Z
(Beware, 2003)

BLUE MAGIC
Featuring Pharrell
(American Gangster, 2007)

FULL FREQUENCY RANGE RECORDING

I've never been good at sitting still, and even when I'm sitting still, my mind is racing. I've built my life around my own restlessness in a lot of ways. School was always easy for me; I never once remember feeling challenged. I have a photographic memory, so if I glanced at something once, I could recall it for a test. I was reading on a twelfth-grade level in the sixth, I could do math in my head, but I had no interest in sitting in a classroom all day. When I was hustling, I wasn't the kid who worked his home corner, in eyeshot of his own bedroom window. I stayed on the road.

I love New York more than probably anything else in the world, but I'm thankful that I got away at a young age to see some of the world outside of Marcy. It opened my perspective on a lot of things, including my taste in music. People in other parts of the country think New Yorkers are snobs about hip-hop and defensive about their position as the birth-place of the art. That's unfair, but being outside of the city so much definitely helped me avoid having any kind of narrow sense of what rap music could sound like.

For instance, the famous East Coast–West Coast beef in hip-hop in the 1990s was based on a lot of things: personal animosities, unsolved shootings, disrespect at awards shows, women, and other assorted bullshit. But as far as I was concerned, one thing it wasn't about was the quality of the music. I was spending a lot of time in Washington, D.C., and Maryland when West Coast hip-hop, led by NWA and then Cube, Dre, and Snoop, started to sweep the entire country. I was a Brooklyn MC to the bone—I wasn't trying to pretend otherwise. But I also got why people loved NWA. I started listening to all kinds of rappers from all over the country, including the Southern rappers and West Coast MCs like Too Short, whose lazy-seeming flows were the opposite of my fast-rapping style at the time and completely contrary to what most New York MCs were doing. I loved the variety that was developing outside of the world of New York hip-hop and absorbed elements of all of it, which helped me enrich my own style.

When you step outside of school and have to teach yourself about life, you develop a different relationship to information. I've never been a purely linear thinker. You can see it in my rhymes. My mind is always jumping around, restless, making connections, mixing and matching ideas, rather than marching in a straight line. That's why I'm always stressing focus. My thoughts chase each other from room to room in my head if I let them, so sometimes I have to slow myself down. I've never been one to write perfect little short stories in my rhymes, like some other MCs. It's not out of a sense of preference, just that the rhymes come to me in a different way, as a series of connecting verbal ideas, rather than full-fledged stories.

But that's a good match for the way I've always approached life. I've always believed in motion and action, in following connections wherever they take me, and in not getting entrenched. My life has been more poetry than prose, more about unpredictable leaps and links than simple steady movement, or worse, stagnation. It's allowed me to stay open to the next thing without feeling held back by a preconceived notion of what I'm supposed to be doing next. Stories have ups and downs and moments of development followed by moments of climax; the storyteller has to keep it all together, which is an incredible skill. But poetry is all climax, every word and line pops with the same energy as the whole; even the spaces between the words can feel charged with potential energy. It fits my style to rhyme with high stakes riding on every word and to fill every pause with pressure and possibility. And maybe I just have ADD, but I also like my rhymes to stay loose enough to follow whatever ideas hijack my train of thought, just like I like my mind to stay loose enough to absorb everything around me.

YOU WANT WAR THEN IT'S WAR'S GONNA BE

I was in a London club when I first heard Panjabi MC's "Mundian To Bach Ke." It wasn't like anything else playing. The bass line was propulsive and familiar, but it took me a second to realize it was from the theme song of *Knight Rider,* a bass line Busta Rhymes had also recently used. On top of the crazy, driving bass line were fluttering drums and this urgent, high-pitched, rhythmic strumming, which came, as it turns out, from a tumbi, a traditional South Asian instrument. I didn't know all that when I heard it in the club. All I knew was it was something totally fresh. It felt like world music in the best sense, like a bunch of sounds from different parts of the globe joined up like an all-star team. People in the club heard it and went crazy. I did, too.

I tracked down the artist and called the next day to see if I could do a remix of the song. It was 2003, early in the Iraq invasion, early enough that people in America still mostly supported the war. Bush had flown onto the aircraft carrier with the big MISSION ACCOMPLISHED banner and people were thinking it was an easy win for Team America. But I'd been traveling all over the world and knew that there was a different perception outside of the United States. Whatever sympathy we had after 9/11 was vanishing. I was able to pick up on some of the arguments that weren't being made on American television. I was one of the people who thought 9/11 was an opportunity to rethink our character as a nation. With the war in Iraq it felt like we were squandering a window of goodwill. It wasn't just that it was a war; as Barack Obama said, it was clearly a dumb war.

When I started working on my remix of "Mundian To Bach Ke"—we called it "Beware of the Boys," which was the Punjabi title translated into English—I wanted to make it a party song, which was the mind-set I was in when I first heard it. But the international feeling of the track—which some people thought was Arabic—moved me into a different direction. So I dropped in a line against the Iraq War. That got me thinking about the recent history of America in the Middle East, so I added something about the Iran-Contra scandal in the eighties—which brought me back to that whole era of big drug kingpins and my own life back then, copping and selling just like Ollie North. I compared Osama Bin Laden to Ronald Reagan in their indifference to the destruction each of them brought to the city I lived in.

I was wading into deeper waters with every connection. So I stopped myself and took it back to the club: But for now mami turn it around and let your boy play.

BEWARE (JAY-Z REMIX)

As soon as the beat drop / We got the streets locked / Overseas at Panjabi MC and the ROC / I came to see the mamis in the spot / On the count of three, drop your body like its hot / One Young / Two you / Want to, three / Young Hov's a snake charmer / Move your body lika snake mama / **Make me wanna put tha snake on ya**[1] / I'm on my 8th summer / **still hot** / **Young's the 8th wonder** / **All I do is get bread**[2] / Yeah, I take wonder / I take one of ya chics straight from under ya arm pit / The black Brad Pitt / I mack till 6 in the AM / **All day I'm P-I-M-P**[3] / I am simply / **Attached to tha track**[4] **like SMPTE**[5] / It's sinfully good young Hov in-finitely hood / [*Chorus*] / R.O.C. and ya don't stop / Panjabi MC and ya don't stop / Nigga NYC and ya don't stop / It's the ROC, it's the

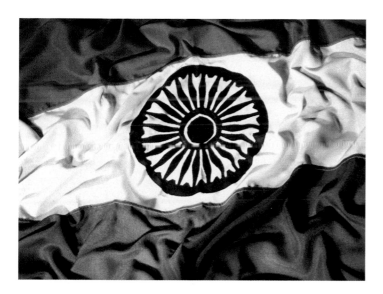

1. Not my cleverest image, but it gets the point across and connects back to the Indian roots of the song (snake charmers are an Indian phenomenon). This opening was done in the spirit of a party song—fun, with a simple and catchy rhyme structure (one/young/two/you) and lyrics that evoke a crowded club.

2. I recorded this eight years after *Reasonable Doubt*. I was also planning on calling my next album *8th Wonder* at the time—it ended up being *The Black Album*. And of course, Wonder is also bread.

3. A couple of subtle Snoop references in these lines, from "6 in the A.M." and "P.I.M.P."

4. The "track" connects back to the P-I-M-P line—pimps run their hoes on "tracks," urban strips where clients come to find prostitutes.

5. SMPTE is a timecode attached to recordings so that they can be edited.

ROC / R.O.C. and we don't stop / Panjabi MC and we don't stop / It's your boy Jay-Z and we don't stop / Nigga, ROC and we won't stop / Ma, I ain't gotta tell ya / But it's your boy Hov from the U.S. / **You just lay down slow**[6] / Catch your boy mingling in England meddling in the Netherlands / Checkin in daily under aliases / We rebellious we back home / screamin leave Iraq alone / But all my soldiers in the field / **I will wish you safe return**[7] / **But only love kills war, when will they learn?**[8] / It's international Hov, been havin the flow / Before bin Laden got Manhattan to blow, / **Before Ronald Reagan got Manhattan to blow,**[9] / Before I was cabbin it there back before / raw we had it all day, Papi in the hallway, cop one on consignment / to give you more yay / Yeah, but that's another story / **But for now, mami,**[10] turn it around and let the boy play.

6. A play off of Biggie's line from "Going Back to Cali": *it's the N-O, T-O, R-I, O /-U-S, / you just lay down slow.*

7. I was against the war, but wanted to be clear that I felt for the soldiers out there fighting it. I know people who joined the military, sometimes just because they didn't have a better option, sometimes because they genuinely thought they were doing something for the good of the country. But soldiers in an army are like soldiers in the hood, to some degree—they're really all fighting someone else's war; they're cannon fodder for men richer and more powerful than them. So I'm not going to attack the soldiers as a group, even if I think their leaders are idiots.

8. This is a weird line coming from me, given that I don't usually rhyme about love being the answer. But I do sometimes get clear about the pointlessness of aggression, and this was one of those days. You have to be a special person—a Gandhi—to really live by that sort of ethic, and I know that if I'm provoked, I'm almost always going to strike back. But deep down, I know it's true that love is what kills hate.

9. Ronald Reagan got Manhattan to "blow"—slang for cocaine—through the whole Iran-Contra scandal, which got the United States involved in the drug trade that brought crack to the hood so they could finance the Contras in Central America. In the worst years of the crack epidemic—the late eighties and early nineties—there were literally thousands of homicides annually in New York. So juxtaposing Reagan and bin Laden isn't as crazy as it may seem. This is a piece of our recent history that people like to forget or pretend never happened so they can maintain some fantasy of American purity—which is why I thought it was important to include it in this rhyme. It's that same sort of historical amnesia and myth of America's innocence that led us into the war in Iraq. In my little way, I'm trying to kill that myth by reminding people of the truth—because that myth is a dangerous thing for the whole world.

10. "Mami" here flows from its opposite, "Papi," a few lines before, and connects the end of the song to the opening when I say "I came to see the mamis in the spot."

BLUE MAGIC / FEATURING PHARRELL

Roc-A-Fella records / The imperial Skateboard P / Great Hova / Y'all already know what it is (Oh shit!) / C'mon! / Yeah / So what if you flip a couple words / I could triple that in birds/ open your mind you see the circus in the sky / **I'm Ringling brothers Barnum and Bailey with the pies**[1] / No matter how you slice it I'm your motherfucking guy / Just like a b-boy with 360 waves **Do the same with the pot, still come back beige**[2] / Whether right or south paw, whether powdered or jar / Whip it around, it still comes back hard. / So easily do I w-h-i-p / **My repetition with wrists will bring you kilo bitches**[3] / I got creole C.O. bitches for my niggas who slipped, became prisoners / Treats taped to the visitors / You already know what the business is / **Unnecessary commissary,**[4] boy we live this shit / Niggas wanna bring the eighties back / **It's OK with me, that's where they made me at**[5] / Except I don't write on the wall / **I write my name in the history books, hustling in the hall (hustling in the hall)**[6] / Nah, I don't spin on my head / I spin work in the pots so I can spend my bread / [*Chorus: Pharrell*] And I'm getting it, I'm getting it / I ain't talking about it, I'm living it / I'm getting it, straight getting it / Ge-ge-ge-get get get it boy / [*Jay-Z*] **(Don't waste you time fighting the life stay your course, and you'll understand)**[7] / Get it boy / It's '87 state of mind that I'm in (mind that I'm in) / **In my prime, so for that time, I'm Rakim (I'm Rakim)**[8] / If it wasn't for the crime that I was in / But I wouldn't be the guy whose rhymes it is that I'm in (that I'm in) / No pain, no profit, P I repeat if you show me where the pot is (pot is) / Cherry M3s with the top back (top back) / Red and green G's all on my hat / North beach leathers, matching Gucci sweater / Gucci sneaks on to keep my outfit together / Whatever, hundred for the diamond chain / Can't you tell that I came from the dope game / Blame Reagan for making me into a monster / Blame Oliver North and Iran-Contra / I ran contraband that they sponsored / **Before this rhyming stuff we was in concert**[9] /[*Chorus: Pharrell*] **Push (push) money over broads, you got it, fuck Bush**[10] / Chef (chef), guess what I cooked / Baked a lot of bread and kept it off the books / Rockstar, look, way before the bars my picture was getting took / **Feds, they like wack rappers, try as they may, couldn't get me on the hook**[11] / D.A. wanna indict me / Cause fishscales in my veins like a pisces / The Pyrex pot, rolled up my sleeves / Turn one into two like a Siamese / **Twin when it end, I'ma stand as a man never dying on my knees**[12] / Last of a dying breed, so let the champagne pop / I partied for a while now I'm back to the block

1. The collision of two figures of speech—"flip," meaning first to speak, and then to sell something for more than you bought it, and "birds," meaning a kilo of coke—creates a third strangely poetic image of birds doing flips in the sky like some kind of hallucinogenic circus act.

2. 360 waves form a circular pattern, like stirring a pot, which is how you turn cocaine into off-white crack rocks (which is why it "comes back hard").

3. In this line I pronounce wrists "wristses" to rhyme it with bitches. Twisting pronunciation to create rhymes works when the distortion feels witty, not desperate.

4. Commissary, the prison's own system for doling out extras, is unnecessary for our crew because we have connections— "creole C.O. bitches" (C.O. = corrections officer)—who will bring them whatever "treats" they need.

5. This was the first single off of my *American Gangster* album, which was inspired by the movie about Frank Lucas and the rise of the drug game in the seventies and eighties in New York.

6. These next lines connect back to the lines about the eighties, which is when hip-hop culture first exploded, with b-boys breaking (spinning on their heads) and writers covering the cities in graffiti. But the eighties were also when hustling exploded, too, and I literally "hustled in the halls" of buildings, even though I never made history—for better or worse—like Frank Lucas.

7. P's singing the hook he borrowed from En Vogue's "Hold On" (*don't waste your time / fighting blind / minded thoughts / of despair*), another eighties reference (okay, it was 1990, but very close).

8. 1987 was the year Eric B and Rakim released *Paid in Full,* a contender for the most influential hip-hop record of all time. This links up to the subtle Rakim reference at the end of the previous verse—*I don't write on the wall / write my name in the history books / hustling in the hall*—which plays off of Rakim's line from "My Melody" (off *Paid in Full*): *whether playin ball / bobbing in the hall / or just writin my name / in graffiti on the wall.*

9. This song is full of homonyms and synonyms—*fishscale, contra, concert.* I love the following quote because I made a conscious effort to use homonyms in this way, and someone actually noticed: "It testifies to Jay-Z's lyrical ingenuity that even though we fully experience these poetic lines by ear rather than by eye, looking at them on the page calls attention to their individual effects, not just their cumulative impact. Equally as impressive as the homonym is that he delivers it while making a fairly complicated point, all while rhyming four lines together." —Adam Bradley, *The Book of Rhymes*

10. Just like in the previous verse, the last line of one verse connects to the first line of this one—the previous verse's last line was about how Reagan and Ollie North were hypocritically working hand-in-hand with hustlers to move drugs, the first line in this verse ends with "fuck Bush," Reagan's crooked-ass Republican heir. There's also another homonym here—Bush as in George and bush as in pussy.

11. Hook/hook is another homonym—*hook* in the sense of getting caught, and *hook* in the sense of a chorus in a song. I wasn't down with either.

12. I like the internal rhymes here. You're waiting for me to finish the rhyme for Siamese, but I throw in *twin/end* and *stand/man* before I get there with *knees.* This is an unusual track—a minimalist beat with drum rolls and synthesizer chords—and I came up with a flow that could weave through it, which meant sometimes the lines breathed and other times the rhymes were more tightly wrapped.

CAUTIONARY TALES

(1) THIS LIFE FOREVER
(BLACK GANGSTER, 1999)
(2) MEET THE PARENTS
(THE BLUEPRINT² : THE LIFT AND CURSE, 2002)
(3) WHERE I'M FROM
(IN MY LIFETIME, VOL. 1, 1997)

My father was crazy for detail. I get that from him. Even though we didn't live together after I was nine, there are some things he instilled in me early that I never lost. He'd walk my cousin B-High and me through Times Square—this is when it was still known as Forty Deuce—and we'd people watch. Back then, Times Square was crazy grimy. Pimps, prostitutes, dealers, addicts, gangs, all the shit from the seventies that other people saw in blaxploitation flicks, Manhattan had in living color. Kids from Harlem and Hell's Kitchen used Times Square as their back-yard—they'd be out there deep, running in and out of karate flicks, break-dancing—but for Brooklyn kids, like me and B-High, midtown Manhattan might as well have been a plane ride away.

My father would take us to Lindy's and we'd get these big-ass steak fries. We would sit in the restaurant looking out the window onto the streets, and play games that exercised our observational skills. Like my pops would make us guess a woman's dress size. There was nothing he missed about a person. He was really good about taking in all the nonver-bal clues people give you to their character, how to listen to the matrix of a conversation, to what a person doesn't say.

For my pops it was just as important to take in places as people. He wanted me to know my own neighborhood inside out. When we'd go to visit my aunt and uncle and cousins my father would give me the respon-sibility of leading, even though I was the youngest. When I was walking with him, he always walked real fast (he said that way if someone's following you, they'll lose you) and he expected me to not only keep up with him but to remember the details of the things I was passing. I had to know which bodega sold laundry detergent and who only stocked candy and chips, which bodega was owned by Puerto Ricans and which one was run by Arabs, who taped pictures of themselves holding AKs to the Plexiglas where they kept the loose candy.

He was teaching me to be confident and aware of my surroundings. There's no better survival skill you could teach a boy in the ghetto, and he did it demonstratively, not by sitting me down and saying, "Yo, always look around at where you are," but by showing me. Without necessarily meaning to, he taught me how to be an artist.

I GIVE YOU THE NEWS WITH A TWIST, IT'S JUST HIS GHETTO POINT OF VIEW

That same kind of close observation is at the heart of rap. Great rappers from the earliest days distinguished themselves by looking closely at the world around them and describing it in a clever, artful way. And then they went further than just describing it. They started commenting on it in a critical way. Rap's first great subjects were ego-tripping and partying, but before long it turned into a tool for social commentary.

It was kind of a natural move, really. The 1970s were a time when black art in general was being used as a tool for social change, whether it was in the poetry of people like the Last Poets or in the R&B of Marvin Gaye or Donny Hathaway or in movies like *Shaft*. And politics had a real cultural angle, too. The Black Panthers weren't just about revolution and Marxism, they were also about changing style and language. Jesse Jackson recited poems like "I Am Somebody" to schoolchildren of my generation. Art and politics and culture were all mixed up together. So it was almost obligatory that any popular art include some kind of political message. Some early rap was explicitly political, like Afrika Bambaataa's Zulu Nation movement. But other rappers played it safe and nonspecific: They'd throw in a line about peace, or supporting your brotherman, or staying in school, or whatever. It took a while before rappers as a whole really sharpened their commentary, but, again, it was hard not to—there was so much to comment about if your eyes were open to what was going on around you.

There was the general squalor of the ghetto, which got aired out in early songs like Run-DMC's first hit, "It's Like That," or "The Message" by Melle Mel. But over time, rappers started really going in on specific issues. Crooked cops were attacked by groups like NWA. Drug dealers were targeted by KRS-One. Drug addicts were mocked by Brand Nubian. Ice Cube called out Uncle Toms. Groups like Poor Righteous Teachers denounced shady churches with bootleg preachers. Queen Latifah was pushing back against misogyny. Salt 'N' Pepa were rallying around safe sex. Public Enemy recorded manifestos on their albums addressing a dozen different issues. You could name practically any problem in the hood and there'd be a rap song for you.

The hip-hop generation never gets credit for it, but those songs changed things in the hood. They were political commentary, but they weren't based on theory or books. They were based on reality, on close observation of the world we grew up in. The songs weren't moralistic, but they created a

stigma around certain kinds of behavior, just by describing them truthfully and with clarity. One of the things we corrected was the absent-father karma our fathers' generation's created. We made it some real bitch shit to bounce on your kids. Whether it was Ed O.G. & Da Bulldogs with "Be a Father to Your Child," or Big mixing rage with double entendre (*pop duke left ma duke, the faggot took the back way*), we as a generation made it shameful to not be there for your kids.

I'M TALKING BOUT REAL SHIT, THEM PEOPLE'S PLAYIN'

Artists of all kinds have a platform and, if they're any good, have a clearer vision of what's going on in the world around them. In my career I've never set out to make songs that function as public service announcements (not even the song "Public Service Announcement") with a few exceptions, one of which is the song "Meet the Parents." But in honoring the lesson of my father—to pay attention—and the lesson of hip-hop—which is to tell the truth—I've been able to create my own kind of social commentary. Artists can have greater access to reality; they can see patterns and details and connections that other people, distracted by the blur of life, might miss. Just sharing that truth can be a very powerful thing.

THIS LIFE FOREVER[1]

I ride through the ghetto windows down halfway[2] / Halfway out of my mind music on 9, blasting **Donny Hathaway**[3] / Me and my niggas spending half the day / Plotting, how we gon get this math today without getting blast away / I wake up to the same problems after today / **Life is harsh, niggas gotta right to spark**[4] / Right from the start they place me in the ghetto tender age of nine / my tender mind had to surrender to crime / Wouldn't wish this on nobody life to end up like mine / Ever since I was quite young a nigga been in a bind / Had to scratch for every plaque, even rap aint even all it's cracked up to be / Niggas dont stack up to me / Had to hustle in a world of trouble / **trapped in, claustrophobic the only way out was rapping**[5] / **America don't understand it, the demographics I tapped in**[6] / I'm the truest nigga to do this nigga and anything else is foolish / Like those who stay high, under God's gray skies / My lyrics is like the Bible, made to save lives / In the midst of all your misery nigga, stay fly / Never let em see you frown, even smile when you down / Shit, I floss on my off days, fuck what they all say / Niggas cant stop me with rumors, I'm too strong / **All day**[7] / **Socks explode and sweatpants pockets is bulging**[8] / Holding it down on the corner with my block frozen / My spot is rollin, drop the price of the coke and / Drove the competition out and let the dough flow in / The cops is closing in, I can do the time /

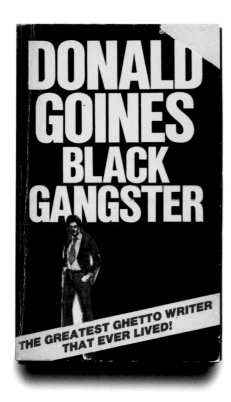

4. "Spark" has a double meaning: It can refer to lighting up a gun or lighting up a blunt. Either way, it's an attempt to escape the harsh life.

5. The music was like a trapdoor from that claustrophobic life. Working in the streets could make you money, but as long as you were in that game, you were in those streets, connected to that life like you were chained.

6. I'm convinced that one of the reasons I struggled to get a record deal is that no one in the business really understood the core audience I reached.

7. These lyrics are in the first person but really they're directed to other people. When I talk about myself here—flossing on off days and being unstoppable—it's really meant as a boost to the cats who feel lost and depressed, "under God's gray skies," to understand that the only way out is to stay up and keep strong.

8. Socks and sweatpants are where you keep the money and the work when you're hustling.

1, I recorded this for the soundtrack of a film that never got made called *Black Gangster,* based on the Donald Goines novel.

2. This song is based on a real moment in my life. It was probably 1994 or 1995, the years before I released *Reasonable Doubt,* before I'd fully made a transition from one life to the next. I was riding in my white Lexus 300, a car that always caught people's eyes when I'd park it outside of shows back then. Everyone at the club might have thought of me as an up-and-coming rapper who didn't even have a deal yet, but the 300 made them think twice about who I really was.

3. That day, I was in the car with my nephews, who were teenagers then. I was listening to Donny Hathaway and moving slow, like ten miles an hour, just rolling around Fort Greene, Brooklyn. I was totally sober, but I felt my consciousness shifting. I looked around and suddenly everything was clear: girls younger than my nephews pushing babies in strollers, boys working the corners, old women wheeling wobbly shopping carts over cracked sidewalks. It was like a movie unfurling on my windshield with Donny Hathaway on the soundtrack. But it wasn't a movie, it was my world. It fucked me up.

But what's really on my mind aint no hoes in the pen / I play the low and try and make it hard to find me / Feds still tryna build a case since '93 / I told them, I'm retired but they like whatever / **You know them pigs don't wanna see you get your life together**[9] / I'm stuck in this life forever / The more things change the more they stay the same / Who am I to change the game? / You gotta move quick like her-o-in and cocaine / The block's hotter than it's ever been / Once again / Hold the gun at eye level, I ain't afraid of conflict / I let the nine rip, nigga say "hi" to the devil / I blind with the bezel, **I'm in line with the ghetto**[10] / What y'all niggas afraid of my mind or the metal / Niggas tryna subtract my life, my mathematics is precise / **I carry the nine, so fucking with me just ain't the answer**[11] / I just can't lose when I was young I was like Fresh / Poppa raised me with chess moves / **And though you're gone I'm not bitter you left me prepared**[12] / We got divided by the years, but I got it from here / Don't sweat that, sounds bump from Marcy to Lefrak / **To that pocket in DC where my man caught his death at**[13] / Over my years I've seen rooks get tooken by the knight / Lose they crown by tryna defend a queen / **Checkmate in four moves the Bobby Fischer of rap**[14] / with raw moves in a time where we all move / Let's face it either you're dough chasin, or basing / Lacing, crack's gotcha feeling strong like Mason / Careful, any infiltration I'm leaving niggas / Leaking more than just information

9. So many times people get caught up by the cops just when they're about to get out of the game, or even after they've left it behind. Think about the movie *Heat*. It could've happened to me—it almost did.

10. The name of this song is "This Life Forever" and this is what it means to be "stuck in this life forever," getting your weight up so you're always ready for conflict, to kill or be killed, to be armed not just with a nine, but with a quicker mind than the people coming for you.

11. Wordplay around the concept of math: "subtract my life," "mathematics is precise," "carry the nine," "just ain't the answer," "divided" by the years. Math is more than just numbers and equations, it's a metaphor for knowledge of the deepest kind.

12. My pop taught me chess, but more than that, he taught me that life was like a giant chessboard where you had to be completely aware in the moment, but also thinking a few moves ahead. By the time he left, he'd already given me a lot of what I'd need to survive.

13. There were a lot of Brooklyn kids heading down to Maryland, Virginia, and D.C. in the mid-nineties, chasing new markets for crack. And a lot of them died.

14. These lines offer a series of double entendres related to chess: Rooks—or rookies—taken by the knight, meaning the long night of death; they lose their crown—or heads, their lives—trying to defend the queen, which could mean fighting over a woman, or defending someone more powerful, someone higher on the chain of command.

MEET THE PARENTS

Woo! Uhh, uhh / It's "The Gift & the Curse"[1] / Uhh, uhh yea / First they love me then they hate me then they love me again / . . . they love me again / Let's take a trip down . . . I gotcha / **Let's take a trip down memory lane at the cemetery**[2] / Rain gray skies, seems at the end of every / young black life is this line, "Damn—him already? / Such a good kid," got us pourin Henn' already **/ Liquor to the curb for my niggaz up above / When it cracks through the pavement that's my way of sendin love**[3] / So, give Big a hug, tell Aa-liyah I said hi / 'Til the next time I see her, on the other side / He was just some thug that caught some slugs / And we loved him cause in him we saw some of us / He walked like ussss, talked like ussss **/ His back against the wall, nigga fought like us—damn**[4] **/ Poor Isis, that's his momma name**[5] / Momma ain't strong enough to raise no boy, what's his father name? / Shorty never knew him, though he had his blood in him / **Hot temper, momma said he act just like her husband**[6] / Daddy never fucked with him, so the streets raised him / Isis blamin herself, she wish she coulda saved him / Damn near impossible, only men can raise men / He was his own man, not even him can save him / He put his faith in, uh, thirty-eight in his waist / But when you live by the gun you die by the same fate / End up dead before thirty-eight and umm / **That's the life of us raised by winter, it's a cold world**[7] / Old girl turned to coke, tried to smoke her pain away / Isis, life just ended on that rainy day / When she got the news her boy body could be viewed / down at the City Morgue, opened the drawer, saw him nude / Her addiction grew, prescription drugs, sipping brew / **Angel dust, dipped in** *woo*!**[8] / She slipped into her own fantasy world**[9] / Had herself pregnant by a different dude / But reality bites and this is her life / He wasn't really her husband, though he called her wife / It was just this night when moon was full / **And the stars were just right, and the dress was real tight**[10] / Had her soundin like Lisa Lisa[11]—*I wonder if I take you home / will you still love me after this night?* / Mike was the hardhead from the around the way / that she wanted all her life, shit she wanted all the hype / Used to hold on tight when he wheelied on the bike / He was a Willie all her life he wasn't really the one to like / It was a dude named Sha who would really treat her right / He wanted to run to the country to escape the city life / **But I-sis, like this, Broadway life**[12] / She loved the Gucci sneakers, the red green and whites / Hangin out the window when she first seen him fight / **She was so turned on that she had to shower twice**[13] / How ironic, it would be some fight that / turned into a homicide that'll alter their life / See Mike at thirty-two was still on the scene / Had a son fifteen that he never saw twice / Sure he saw him as an infant, but he disowned him like / "If that was my son, he would look much different. / See I'm light-skinnded and that baby there's dark." / **So it's momma's baby; poppa's maybe.**[14] / Mike was still crazy out there runnin the streets (fuck niggaz want?) / had his old reliable thirty-eight gun in his reach / It's been fourteen years, him and Isis ain't speak / He runnin around like life's a peach, 'til one day / he approached this thug that had a mean mug / **And it looked so familiar that he called him "Young Cuz"**[15] / Told him, get off the strip but the boy ain't budge (fuck you) / **Instead he pulled out a newer thirty-eight snub**[16] / He clearly had the drop but the boy just paused (hold up) / There was somethin in this man's face he knew he seen before / It's like lookin in the mirror seein hisself more mature / **And he took it as a sign from the almighty Lord**[17] / You know what they say about he who hesitates in war / (What's that?) He who hesitates is lost / He can't explain what he saw before his picture went blank / **The old man didn't think he just followed his instinct**[18] / Six shots into his kin, out of the gun / Niggaz be a father, you're killin your son / Six shots into his kin, out of the gun **/ Niggaz be a father, you killin your sons**[19] **/ Meet the parents. . .**[20]

1. This song was on the *Blueprint²: The Gift & the Curse* album. But it's also a song about the gift and the curse that lies at the heart of the parent-child relationship.

2. Structurally, I was influenced by the nonlinear way Tarantino laid out the story in *Pulp Fiction*. So the song begins with a send-off, a burial.

3. I made his afterlife the prologue to turn the story on its head in narrative terms but also to emphasize the consequences of abandonment, that by walking out on your babies, you're burying them.

4. The kid who died was a "thug" but everything else in these lines tells you he was the kind of person who maintained his honor and was loved by the brothers he left behind.

5. At the graveside I introduce the single mother, Isis. I gave her an Egyptian goddess's name because there's a way we put black mothers on pedestals while at the same time saying they're incapable of raising boys to men, which I basically say in this song. Even if I believed it when I recorded it, I can say I don't believe it now. There are too many men, myself included, whose lives are counterevidence to that idea.

6. Even when the men weren't around us, their blood was pumping inside of us, their DNA programming our moves. No matter how far away we were from our fathers physically, we were biologically inseparable, genetically intertwined. And to the degree that biology and genes determine your fate, our destinies were irreversibly linked.

7. This is a recurring image in my songs, winter as a symbol of a desolate, difficult life. Maybe if I'd hustled in Southern California or Miami the image would have less of a hold on me, but when you hit the streets in the literal darkness and cold of winters on the East Coast, it reinforces your sense that the universe doesn't care about you, that you're on your own in a harsh world.

8. Marijuana dipped in angel dust or PCP.

9. Her inability to deal with his death turns her into an addict.

10. I flash back to her meeting the father of her son, her son's murderer, when she was basically her son's age. And this feeling is real, too: Just because shit is hard doesn't mean that there isn't real romance in the hood! The moon shines, the stars come out. Isis is just like anyone else; she wanted to indulge herself and get lost in the fantasy of love for one night.

11. "I Wonder if I Take You Home" was a hit for Lisa Lisa & Cult Jam.

12. In the flash back you see her as a young girl thrilled by the fast life, rejecting a good dude who wanted to escape the city, for Mike, a guy who turned her on by being a thug.

13. Romance in the hood is a funny thing. All around the world, women fall for the bad guy, the strong, aggressive one who offers a sense of excitement or danger. It's a cliché, practically. But in the hood, the bad guy is a different character with a different fate from the guy in a romance novel. The bad guy in the hood doesn't always have a way to channel that aggression. His strength is frustrated by a system that rejects him, and his aggression is channeled into illegal acts. The excitement isn't controlled—there's no safety net when he falls off that highwire. The bad boy might grow up to be a hard man, if he grows up at all. The street fight that turns the girls on when he's sixteen is less sexy when he's a grown-ass man. And god help the girl that's got his child.

14. The flashback ends abruptly. Like a fake pass, you think I'm going to quarterback Isis's story, but now we pick up Mike's story: Like a lot of immature boys suddenly faced with fatherhood, he squirms free with a weak denial. Fifteen years later he's still in the same streets.

15. I fast-forward to the near past in the song, the night father and son meet in the street. Their confrontation is between father and son, but the subtext is the intergenerational schism. These are fearless, fatherless young boys feeling they owe no respect to the generation of men above them.

16. Mike, who hasn't seen his own son since he denied him fourteen years before, is not only faced with a familiar face when he sees his son, but with a newer, presumably more expensive gun, implying that his son's hustle is a higher risk, higher benefit hustle. Father and son carry the same gun, a .38; it's just that the son's cost more.

17. It's in this pause that I establish the son's humanity, but also his vulnerability. I also show my partiality: I'm on the son's side. Not only does he have the drop and the better gun, but he's also got the moral high ground. He pauses when he sees the man's face. You get the sense that he's studied every face he's seen his whole life, looking for the face of his father. And now here it is. It freezes him.

18. The older man has spent a life in the streets honing his survival skills. Where the son instinctively pauses, the father's only reflex is to act, quickly, in the name of self-preservation. It's the same instinct he exercised when he was still a kid and left his son behind. All he knows is war and survival, and you can't teach an old dog new tricks.

19. The last two phrases are just slight plays on each other. In the first refrain it refers to this specific story, but in the second, it becomes more general, more generational. I never intended "Meet the Parents" to be subtle. In my mind it was a morality play, a PSA for that generation of men who may as well have emptied their guns on their sons when they left their lives. The streets where Mike left his son to be raised are the same streets where he buries him.

20. And the title to the song has dual meanings, too. The song is about a son meeting one of his parents, but it's also a more general introduction to the listener: It's impossible to understand this generation of kids, the hip-hop generation, till you meet the parents.

WHERE I'M FROM

I'm from where the **hammers rung,**[1] **news cameras never come**[2] / You and your man hung in every verse in your rhyme / where the grams is slung, **niggas vanish every summer**[3] / Where the blue vans would come, **we throw the work in the can and run**[4] / Where the plans was to get funds and **skate off the set**[5] / To achieve this goal quicker, **sold all my weight wet**[6] / Faced with immeasurable odds still I gave straight bets / So I felt I'm owed something and you nothing, check / **I'm from the other side with other guys don't walk too much**[7] / And girls in the projects wouldn't fuck us if we talked too much / So they ran up to Tompkins and sought them dudes to trust / **I don't know what the fuck they thought, those niggas is foul just like us**[8] / **I'm from where the beef is inevitable,**[9] summertime's unforgettable / **Boosters in abundance, buy a half-price sweater new**[10] / Your word was everything, so everything you said you'd do / **You did it, couldn't talk about it if you ain't lived it**[11] / I from where niggas pull your card, and argue all day about / **Who's the best MC, Biggie, Jay-Z, and Nas**[12]/ Where the **drugs czars evolve,**[13] and thugs are at odds / At each other's throats for the love of foreign cars / Where cats catch cases, **hoping the judge R-and-R's**[14] / But most times find themselves locked up behind bars / **I'm from where they ball and breed rhyme stars**[15] / I'm from Marcy son, just thought I'd remind y'all / Cough up a lung, where I'm from, Marcy son, ain't nothing nice / **Mentally been many places but I'm Brooklyn's own**[16]/ I'm from the place where the **church is the flakiest**[17] / **And niggas is praying to god so long that they atheist**[18] / Where you can't put your vest away and say you'll wear it tomorrow /

1. I start the song with an image that's visual and aural, solid and ethereal. "Hammer" is a hard word for guns, but here the hammers ring. This sets up the listener's perspective as an observer, not a participant, which is the perspective of most folks in the projects, like the women and kids who hear gunshots as echoes bouncing off concrete walls, ringing like wind chimes through their kitchen windows. The song's first image is like my first experience of violence, not as the trigger man but as the kid in his apartment playing with his toys, hearing that distinctive pounding ring out in the background.

2. "Two young men who admitted that they had raped and sodomized a 39-year-old woman and then thrown her from the roof of a four-story building in Brooklyn last year were sentenced yesterday to terms of 6 to 18 years in prison. . . . Her case, whose shocking brutality was comparable to that of the Central Park jogger, which occurred only a few days earlier, prompted some harsh criticism of the news media, which did not devote comparable attention to it, in part, critics said, because the Central Park jogger was white and the Brooklyn victim was black."—*The New York Times,* October 2, 1990.

3. It could feel like the rapture sometimes, the way someone would be there one minute, and gone the next, bagged by the cops or the coroner, or off to another state to set up business.

4. When cops showed up it was dump and run time.

5. The ambition of a drug-seller was a paradox: to stop selling drugs. To make enough loot to skate—graceful, easy—away from the whole scene.

6. Selling weight "wet" meant to sell the crack so fast it didn't even have time to dry from the cooking. It's cheating, but I justify it in the next line.

7. There's a saying, "the narcissism of small differences," that applies exactly to the way we divvied up the hood: It was projects versus projects, and then building versus building, clique versus clique, brother versus brother.

8. Well, exactly: Tompkins niggas might've seemed somehow different from Marcy niggas, but we were all in the same game, after the same shit, using the same techniques.

9. Hammers are ringing, drugs are being sold, cops are rolling up, girls are being fought over, fast money's being made. And no one's over thirty. It's a recipe for conflict.

10. "Boosters" are shoplifters who'd slide into department stores, stuff a pile of sweaters under their worn-out goose downs, and then sell them for half price back on the streets.

11. Where I'm from, on the streets I'm describing, all you had was your word—it was everything. If you pretended to be something you weren't, your card would get pulled quick. The legit world has a million ways to slip out of the truth; ironically, the underworld depends on a kind of integrity.

12. When I was a kid the debate was LL versus Run-DMC, or, later, Kane versus Rakim. Next year it might be Drake versus J. Cole. It's a tribute to how deeply felt hip-hop is that people don't just sit back and listen to the music—they have to break it down, pick the lyrics apart, and debate the shit with other fans who are doing the same thing. When people talk about forms of media, sometimes they compare lean-forward media (which are interactive, like video games or the Internet) and lean-back media (which are passive, like television or magazines). Music can be lean-back sort of media, it can just wash over you or play in the background—but hip-hop is different. It forces people to lean forward—lean right out of their chairs—and take a position.

13. The "drug czar" here obviously isn't the one that works for the government.

14. "R-and-R" stands for "reverse and remand," an order from a court to reverse a decision or refer it back to a lower court.

15. "Ball" has three meanings: to fuck, to spend money, and to play basketball. I'm talking about playing ball here, but I'm nodding to the other meanings, too. "Breeding" rhyme stars connects back directly to the rest of this verse: The drugs and guns, the fun and the risk, and, most of all, the survival-of-the-fittest competition, is enough pressure to crush coal into diamonds. It's an idealized, almost romantic, way to look at this life, a sudden reverse after the song's bleak beginning.

16. This is a line from a remix I did with Puff Daddy (as he was then known) and Biggie for a song called "Young G's."

17. The churches really were the flakiest, whether they were storefronts or big old-school churches with vaulted ceilings and steeples. They were kept alive with the donations of poor folks and hadn't seen a paint job in a minute. But more than that, they were full of fake prophets and money-snatching preachers.

18. When your prayers aren't answered, you start to think that maybe there's no one there to answer them. Day after day, year after year, generation after generation, the response seems to be silence—it tests your faith.

'Cause the day after we'll be saying, damn I was just with him yesterday / I'm a block away from hell, not enough shots away from stray shells / **An ounce away from a triple beam still using a handheld weight scale**[19] / You're laughing, you know the place well / Where the liquor stores and the base dwell / **And government, fuck government, niggas politic themselves**[20] / Where we call the cops the A-Team / Cause they hop out of vans and spray things / **And life expectancy so low we making out wills at eighteen**[21] / Where how you get rid of guys who step out of line, your rep solidifies / **So tell me when I rap you think I give a fuck who criticize?**[22] / If the shit is lies, god strike me / And I got a question, are you forgiving guys who live just like me? / **We'll never know**[23] / One day I pray to you and said if I ever blow, I'd let 'em know / Mistakes and exactly what takes place in the ghetto / **Promise fulfilled, but still I feel my job ain't done**[24] / Cough up a lung, where I'm from, Marcy son, ain't nothing nice / I'm from where they cross over and **clap boards**[25] / **Lost Jehovah in place of rap lords, listen**[26] / I'm up the block, round the corner, and down the street / From where the pimps, prostitutes, and the drug lords meet / **We make a million off of beats, cause our stories is deep**[27] / **And fuck tomorrow, as long as the night before was sweet**[28] / Niggas get lost for weeks in the streets, **twisted off leek**[29] / And no matter the weather, niggas know how to draw heat / Whether you're four feet or Manute-size, it always starts out with / Three dice and shoot the five / Niggas thought they deuce was live, until I hit 'em with trips / **And I reached down for their money, pa forget about this**[30] / This time around it's platinum, like the shit on my wrist / And this Glock on my waist, y'all can't do shit about this / Niggas will show you love, that's how they fool thugs / **Before you know it you're lying in a pool of blood**[31]

19. I'm triangulating my location. The block from hell is a double entendre: my block is in close proximity to the worst of the worst, but it's also "the block from hell," like it emerged from a flaming pit. "Not enough shots from stray shells," means that where I'm from no one is really safe from a stray bullet. The last line—"an ounce away from a triple beam"—is a drug-game detail that niggas in the streets picked up on immediately. That ounce away is the difference between struggling and making real money, and a lot of hustlers stay an ounce away and never graduate. But the aspiration to move up to the triple-beam is real, and the handheld weight scale is symbolic of that street-level hustler's hunger—you can hold his weight in your hand, but his hunger is enormous.

20. I wrote this at a time when I felt the government was irrelevant to the ways we organized, resolved conflict, and took care of ourselves. "Politic" is slang for the kind of talk that works things out.

21. "In 2001, the life expectancy in New York City's poorest neighborhoods was 8 years shorter than in its wealthiest neighborhoods." —"Health Disparities in New York," New York City Department of Health.

22. The stakes are relatively low once you leave the streets. A bad review might hurt your feelings, but really who gives a fuck compared to the equivalent on the streets.

23. This is not the only time I interrogate God; in songs like "D'Evils" (p. 50), "Lucifer" (p. 286), and "Beach Chair" (p. 282) I do something similar, sometimes in a confrontational way, sometimes in a more plaintive way. But these lines aren't about God in the traditional sense, they're almost questions back to myself. Do I forgive guys who live just like me? It's a question that haunts a lot of us—and the song is a defense, a case that in some ways we're just products of our environment. But I'm not convinced that it's that simple.

24. The "promise fulfilled" is the promise I made to God—or to myself—in the earlier line, that if I got successful, I'd let them know "exactly what takes place in the ghetto." This song is the promise's partial fulfillment, but the job wasn't done—I kept trying to get deeper and deeper into the story from song to song.

25. "Clap boards" is more basketball talk—the image catches a player in the air, slapping the backboard while he grabs a rebound, the sound ricocheting through the project courtyards like a gunclap.

26. More blasphemy! Comparing the silent god Jehovah with the rap lords whose voices never left us.

27. This line feels kind of thrown off, but it's maybe the strangest line on the whole record. I've been describing a place that's full of violence, where the scramblers on the corner are trying to make enough money to move, where even God doesn't visit, but the irony is that the stories that came out of this place—*a block from hell*—would make millions for the storytellers.

28. It's hard to argue with this sentiment once you get the context. In the life I'm describing, a night's sweetness is a treasure and worrying about the cost of it is a waste of time.

29. "Leek" is embalming fluid mixed with PCP. On the West Coast, where it's probably more popular, they call it "sherm." It's famous for making people lose their minds, jump off roofs, strip themselves naked in the street and start running. It's a suicidal high.

30. I'm describing a game of Cee-Lo—deuce, "three dice and shoot the five," "hit 'em with trips"—a game played with three dice. On the corner we'd kill time with Cee-Lo—all you need is some dice—but the money is real, so sometimes the stakes expand.

31. The song climaxes with the narrator winning a dice game, stepping his game up to platinum, and keeping guard with a nine, while "niggas show love." Before you get too happy, though, it brings us back to an image of paranoia and death, the cloud that hangs over a hustler's head forever.

FUNERAL PARADE

MINORITY REPORT
(*Kingdom Come*, 2006)

DYNASTY (INTRO)
(*The Dynasty: Roc La Familia*, 2000)

MY PRESIDENT IS BLACK (REMIX)
(unreleased)

THE BURDEN
OF POVERTY
ISN'T JUST
THAT YOU
DON'T
ALWAYS
HAVE THE
THINGS YOU
NEED, IT'S
THE FEELING
OF BEING
EMBARRASSED
EVERY DAY
OF YOUR LIFE

I don't remember exactly where I was in August 2005, but at the end of that month I was mostly in front of the television, like most other people, transfixed and upset by the story of Hurricane Katrina. Most Americans were horrified by what was happening down there, but I think for black people, we took it a little more personally. I've been to shantytowns in Angola that taught me that what we consider to be crushing poverty in the United States has nothing to do with what we have materially—even in the projects, we're rich compared to some people in other parts of the world. I met people in those shantytowns who lived in one-room houses with no running water who had to pay a neighbor to get water to go to the bathroom. Those kids in Angola played ball on a court surrounded by open sewage, and while they knew it was bad, they didn't realize just how fucked up it was. It was shocking. And I know there are parts of the world even worse off than that.

The worst thing about being poor in America isn't the deprivation. In fact, I never associated Marcy with poverty when I was a kid. I just figured we lived in an apartment, that my brother and I shared a room and that we were close—whether we wanted to be or not—with our neighbors. It wasn't until sixth grade, at P.S. 168, when my teacher took us on a field trip to her house that I realized we were poor. I have no idea what my teacher's intentions were—whether she was trying to inspire us or if she actually thought visiting her Manhattan brownstone with her view of Central Park qualified as a school trip. But that's when it registered to me that my family didn't have as much. We definitely didn't have the same refrigerator she had in her kitchen, one that had two levers on the outer door, one for water and the other for ice cubes. Poverty is relative.

One of the reasons inequality gets so deep in this country is that everyone wants to be rich. That's the American ideal. Poor people don't like talking about poverty because even though they might live in the projects surrounded by other poor people and have, like, ten dollars in the bank, they don't like to think of themselves as poor. It's embarrassing. When you're a kid, even in the projects, one kid will mercilessly snap on another kid over minor material differences, even though by the American standard, they're both broke as shit.

The burden of poverty isn't just that you don't always have the things you need, it's the feeling of being embarrassed every day of your life, and you'd do anything to lift that burden. As kids we didn't complain about being poor; we talked about how rich we were going to be and made moves to get the lifestyle we aspired to by any means we could. And as soon as we had a little money, we were eager to show it.

I remember coming back home from doing work out of state with my boys in a caravan of Lexuses that we parked right in the middle of Marcy. I ran up to my mom's apartment to get something and looked out the window and saw those three new Lexuses gleaming in the sun, and thought, "Man, we doin' it." In retrospect, yeah, that was kind of ignorant, but at the time I could just feel that stink and shame of being broke lifting off of me, and it felt beautiful. The sad shit is that you never really shake it all the way off, no matter how much money you get.

SOME GET LEFT BEHIND, SOME GET CHOSEN

I watched the coverage of the hurricane, but it was painful. Helicopters swooping over rooftops with people begging to be rescued—the helicopters would leave with a dramatic photo, but didn't bother to pick up the person on the roof. George Bush doing his flyby and declaring that the head of FEMA was doing a heckuva job. The news media would show a man running down the street, arms piled high with diapers or bottles of water, and call him a looter, with no context for why he was doing what he was doing. I'm sure there were a few idiots stealing plasma TVs, but even that has a context—anger, trauma. It wasn't like they were stealing TVs so they could go home and watch the game. I mean, where were they going to plug them shits in? As the days dragged on and the images got worse and worse—old ladies in wheelchairs dying in front of the Superdome—I kept thinking to myself, *This can't be happening in a wealthy country. Why isn't anyone doing anything?*

Kanye caught a lot of heat for coming on that telethon and saying, "George Bush doesn't care about black people," but I backed him one hundred percent on it, if only because he was expressing a feeling that was bottled up in a lot of our hearts. It didn't feel like Katrina was just a natural disaster that arbitrarily swept through a corner of the United States. Katrina felt like something that was happening to black people, specifically.

I know all sorts of people in Louisiana and Mississippi got washed out, too, and saw their lives destroyed—but in America, we process that sort of thing as a tragedy. When it happens to black people, it feels like something else, like history rerunning its favorite loop. It wasn't just me.

People saw that Katrina shit, heard the newscasters describing the victims as "refugees" in their own country, waited in vain for the government to step in and rescue those people who were dying right in front of our eyes, and we took it personally. I got angry. But more than that, I just felt hurt. In moments like that, it all starts coming back to you: slavery, images of black people in suits and dresses getting beaten on the bridge to Selma, the whole ugly story you sometimes want to think is over. And then it's back, like it never left. I felt hurt in a personal way for those people floating on cars and waving on the roofs of their shotgun houses, crying into the cameras for help, being left on their porches. Maybe I felt some sense of shame that we'd let this happen to our brothers and sisters. Eventually I hit the off button on the remote control. I went numb.

SO I GOT RICH AND GAVE BACK, TO ME THAT'S THE WIN-WIN

It's crazy when people think that just because you have some money and white people start to like you that you transcend race. People try this shit all the time with successful black people, even with someone like me who was plenty black when I was on the corner. It's like they're trying to separate you from the pack—make you feel like you're the good one. It's the old house nigger–field nigger tactic.

But even if you do get it into your head that somehow you're exceptional, that you've created some distance between where you are and where you're from, things like Hurricane Katrina snap you right out of it. I couldn't forget that those were my kin out there in New Orleans, and that, forget the government, I was supposed to do something to help them. I got together with Puffy and we donated a million dollars to the relief effort, but we donated it to the Red Cross, which is barely different from donating to the government itself, the same government that failed those people the first time. Who knows how much of that money actually made it to the people on the ground?

It also made me think of the bigger picture. New Orleans was fucked up before Katrina. This was not a secret. The shame and stigma of poverty means that we turn away from it, even those of us living through it, but turning away from it doesn't make it disappear. Sooner or later it gets revealed, like it was in New Orleans. The work we have to do is deeper than just putting Band-Aids on the problems when they become full-blown disasters.

To some degree charity is a racket in a capitalist system, a way of making our obligations to one another optional, and of keeping poor people feeling a sense of indebtedness to the rich, even if the rich spend every other day exploiting those same people. But here we are. Lyor Cohen, who I consider my mentor, once told me something that he was told by a rabbi about the eight degrees of giving in Judaism. The seventh degree is giving anonymously, so you don't know who you're giving to, and the person on the receiving end doesn't know who gave. The value of that is that the person receiving doesn't have to feel some kind of obligation to the giver and the person giving isn't doing it with an ulterior motive. It's a way of putting the giver and receiver on the same level. It's a tough ideal to reach out for, but it does take away some of the patronizing and showboating that can go on with philanthropy in a capitalist system. The highest level of giving, the eighth, is giving in a way that makes the receiver self-sufficient.

Of course, I do sometimes like to see where the money I give goes. When I went to Angola for the water project I was working on and got to see the new water pump and how it changed the lives of the people in that village, I wasn't happy because I felt like I'd done something so great. I was happy to know that whatever money I'd given was actually being put to work and not just paying a seven-figure salary for the head of the Red Cross. And I did a documentary about it, not to glorify myself, but to spread the word about the problem and the possible solutions.

That's what I tried to do with my Katrina donations, and with my work for Haiti in the aftermath of their earthquake and with other causes I get involved with. I also like to make a point about hip-hop by showing how so many of us give back, even when the news media would rather focus on the things we buy for ourselves. But whether it's public or private, we can't run away from our brothers and sisters as if poverty is a contagious disease. That shit will catch up to us sooner or later, even if it's just the way we die a little when we turn on the television and watch someone's grandmother, who looks like our grandmother, dying in the heat of a flooded city while the president flies twenty thousand feet over her head.

MINORITY REPORT

[*Intro: news excerpts*] The damage here along the Gulf Coast is catastrophic. / There's a frantic effort underway tonight to find / survivors. There are an uncounted number of the dead tonight . . . / People are being forced to live like animals . . . / We are desperate . . . / No one says the federal government is doing a good job . . . / And hundreds and hundreds and hundreds of people . . . / No water, I fought my country for years . . . / We need help, we really need help . . . / In Baghdad, they drop, they air drop water, food to people. Why can't they do that to their own people? / **The same idiots that can't get water into a major American city in less than three days are trying to win a war . . .**[1] / [*Jay-Z*] **People was poor before the hurricane came**[2] / Before the downpour poured is like when Mary J. sang / Every day it rains, so every day the pain / Went ignored, and I'm sure ignorance was to blame / but life is a chain, cause and effected / Niggas off the chain because they affected / It's a dirty game so whatever is effective / **From weed to selling kane, gotta put that in effect, shit**[3] / Wouldn't you loot, if you didn't have the loot? / and your baby needed food and you were stuck on the roof / and a helicopter swooped down just to get a scoop / **Through his telescopic lens but he didn't scoop you**[4] / and the next five

1. These are all actual clips from the news coverage of Hurricane Katrina.

2. "Long before the storm, New Orleans was by almost any metric the worst city in the United States—the deepest poverty, the most murders, the worst schools, the sickest economy, the most corrupt and brutal cops." —Dan Baum, *Nine Lives: Life and Death in New Orleans*.

3. I wanted to do a song about Katrina, but I also wanted the song to be about how what we saw during the hurricane was just an extreme example of the shit that was already happening in New Orleans. The young guys there were motivated by the same desperation as the guy

who loots the store after the hurricane for diapers and formula. Both are just trying to survive in a storm. If you focus only on the criminal act and lose sight of the whole chain of cause and effect, you get a distorted, unfair picture. People are often pushed into desperate acts and bad choices by circumstances.

4. I had to wonder about all those dramatic photos shot from helicopters swooping over people stranded on roofs. I have no idea if those journalists could've picked up the people on the roofs after they'd taken their photo, but it seemed like a metaphor for what was happening all over the country: We were all watching the story unfold but doing nothing.

days, no help ensued / They called you a refugee because you seek refuge / and the commander-in-chief just flew by / Didn't stop, I know he had a couple seats / Just rude, Jet-Blue he's not / Jet flew by the spot / What if he ran out of jet fuel and just dropped / huh, that woulda been something to watch / Helicopters doing fly-bys to take a couple of shots / Couple of portraits then ignored 'em / **He'd be just another bush surrounded by a couple orchids**[5] / Poor kids just 'cause they were poor kids / Left 'em on they porches same old story in New Orleans / Silly rappers, because we got a couple Porsches / MTV stopped by to film our fortresses / We forget the unfortunate / Sure I ponied up a mill, but I didn't give my time / **So in reality I didn't give a dime, or a damn**[6] / I just put my monies in the hands of the same people / that left my people stranded / Nothin but a bandit / Left them folks abandoned / Damn, that money that we gave was just a Band-Aid / Can't say we better off than we was before / In synopsis this is my minority report / **Can't say we better off than we was before**[7] / In synopsis this is my minority report / [*Outro: news excerpts*] . . . *Buses are on the way to take those people from New Orleans to Houston . . .* / They lyin'. . . / People are dying at the convention center / . . . Their government has failed them / . . . George Bush doesn't care about black people

5. This was a fantasy: What would happen if the situation was reversed and Bush was on the ground, surrounded by the folks of the Ninth Ward, as beautiful and fragile as orchids? And how fast would they have gotten him out?

6. Giving money is important, I think, but the people who got down there to help and put their feet in that water were heroic.

7. I repeat this line because it has two meanings. The first time it refers to the money that I donated: I can't say that the money has made anything better. The second time, I'm referring to even further "before," to life before the Civil Rights Movement.

DYNASTY (INTRO)

The theme song to The Sopranos[1] **/ plays in the key of life on my mental piano**[2] / Got a strange way of seein life like / **I'm Stevie Wonder with beads under the do-rag**[3] / Intuition is there even when my vision's impaired, yeah / Knowin I can go just switchin a spare / On the highway of life, nigga it's sharp in my sight / OOh! Keen senses ever since I was a teen on the benches / **everytime somebody like Ennis**[4] was mentioned / **I would turn green, me, bein in the trenches**[5] / Him, livin adventurous not worryin about expenditures / I'm bravin temperatures below zero, no hero / No father figure, you gotta pardon a nigga / But I'm starvin my niggaz, and the weight loss in my figure / **is startin to darken my heart, 'bout to get to my liver**[6] / Watch it my nigga, I'm tryin to be calm but I'm gon' get richer / **through any means,**[7] with that thing that Malcolm palmed in the picture / Never read the Qu'ran or Islamic scriptures / Only psalms I read was on the arms of my niggaz / Tattooed so I carry on like I'm non-religious / Clap whoever stand between Shawn and figures / Niggaz, say it's the dawn but I'm superstitious / Shit is as dark as it's been, nothin is goin as you predicted / I move with biscuits, stop the hearts of niggaz actin too suspicious / **This is food for thought, you do the dishes**[8]

1. "Woke up this morning / got yourself a gun . . ."

2. The opening of the song establishes the feeling that a lot of us had: We didn't worship the Mafia like a lot of people thought, but we completely related to the "us vs. the establishment" mentality. That was the "key of life" for us, the thing that united us, even when we weren't in perfect harmony.

3. Stevie Wonder connects back to the "key of life" metaphor. He famously wore beads—and "beeds" are also what folks used to call nappy hair. My mom used to call them "biddy beeds" and rub my head, which I sometimes covered with a wave cap, also called a do-rag. I'm trying to create a parallel between me and Stevie Wonder. He's blind, obviously, and relies on his other senses to navigate the world. That's how it is on the streets, too, where you have to rely on your instincts to survive and anticipate what's going to happen before you actually see it.

4. "Ennis Cosby, Bill Cosby's only son and an inspiration for some of the comedian's most rollicking television humor and family antics, was shot to death early Thursday after he pulled over to the side of a Los Angeles freeway to change a flat tire." —*The New York Times,* January 19, 1997.

5. Ennis was the kind of kid that a lot of us were envious of: He came from a fortune and seemed to have it all, including his dad, Bill Cosby—the ultimate American dad—while most of us came up with nothing and had never even met our fathers, much less lived with them. (I'm not sure if I was lucky or not to have gotten the chance to know my dad before he bounced.) But Ennis's death was one of those things that sharpens your sight (which continues the blindness/sight metaphor I introduced with Stevie Wonder). It reminded us of life's frailty even for people with money and status. Money can't protect you from fate.

6. Here I'm outside hustling, sometimes in freezing-cold weather. "Below zero" refers to my money situation as well—I'm not starving literally, but I'm hungry for success. I'm willing to do whatever to improve my situation, with no sympathy for anyone else— a survival-of-the-fittest mentality takes over, "darkens my heart." The stress might drive me to drink, too—"'bout to get my liver."

7. Another reference to Malcolm X's by any means necessary— a phrase he coined to talk about political revolution and racial liberation—which is used in hip-hop as a description of getting paid by any means when your back is against the wall. We knew Malcolm was a righteous man fighting for a just cause. But we were a step beyond him in our desperation.

8. From time to time people with sense would tell us to leave "the life" alone, that there was a better way. At this point I'm becoming cynical and "suspicious" of anybody saying anything other than what I can see in front of me. So like Malcolm I was going to get it by any means and protect myself with "biscuits," a word we used for guns, I don't even know why. Now all of this—contradictions included—is to be ingested by the listener. I left a mess of thoughts for you to sort through. I prepared the "food"; it's up to you to clean it up.

MY PRESIDENT IS BLACK (REMIX)

My president is black / My Maybach too / and I'll be god-damn if my diamonds ain't blue / my money dark green / and my Porsche is light gray / **I'm headin for D.C. anybody feel me**[1] / My president is black / My Maybach too / and I'll be goddamn if my diamonds aint blue / **my money dark green**[2] / and my Porsche is light gray / I'm headin for D.C. anybody feel me / My president is black / in fact he's half white / so even in a racist mind / he's half right / if you have a racist mind / **you be aight**[3] / my president is black / but his house is all WHITE / Rosa Parks sat so Martin Luther could walk / Martin Luther walked so Barack Obama could run / **Barack Obama ran so all the children could fly**[4] / So I'ma spread my wings and / you can meet me in the sky / I already got my own clothes / already got my own shoes / I was hot before Barack imagine what I'm gonna do / Hello Ms. America / Hey pretty lady / that red white and blue flag / **wave for me baby**[5] / never thought I'd say this shit baby I'm good / you can keep your puss I don't want no more bush / no more war / no more Iraq / **no more white lies**[6] / the president is BLACK

1. Progress is the theme of this song, but the cool thing is that I'm not president, so I could have a completely politically incorrect chorus.

2. "My least favorite color is light green" is a line from one of my songs, meaning, I don't like my money to get light, in the sense of being scarce. So "dark green" money isn't a reference to the color, but the amount, of the money.

3. This is a joke, but it's true, too: Even though he identifies himself as black, the fact that he is also half white would make it easier to a racist, which I find very funny.

4. This was a little poem that was spread through e-mails during the election.

5. After Barack was elected, I realized that the same thing hip-hop had been doing for years with language and brands—that is, reinventing them to mean something different from what they originally meant—we could now do to American icons like the flag. Things that had once symbolized slavery, oppression, militarism, and hypocrisy might now begin to legitimately represent us. We're not there yet, but Barack's election offered a tantalizing hint of what that might look like, including things like having the American "first lady" be a beautiful black woman who could trace her ancestry to American slaves.

6. By "white lies" I didn't mean race—I was referring to the deceptions, large and small, of the previous administration. The point of the song is that we were progressing beyond simplistic talk about race and could start being honest about it so that we could, eventually, move on.

PART IV

GET ME

When I first started working on this book, I told my editor that I wanted it to do three important things. The first thing was to make the case that hip-hop lyrics—not just my lyrics, but those of every great MC—are poetry if you look at them closely enough. The second was I wanted the book to tell a little bit of the story of my generation, to show the context for the choices we made at a violent and chaotic crossroads in recent history.

And the third piece was that I wanted the book to show how hip-hop created a way to take a very specific and powerful experience and turn it into a story that everyone in the world could feel and relate to.

All of those threads came together at a pivotal moment for me, the moment when I fully crossed from one life to another.

CLARK SOUGHT ME OUT, DAME BELIEVED

I hadn't been to Manhattan in a minute; in fact, I probably hadn't seen any of the five boroughs in months. There's a line in a song I did with Scarface, *guess who's back, still smell the crack in my clothes,* and that's real after you've been putting in work for a while. No one else can actually smell the coke, of course, but you still feel it coming off you, like your pores are bleeding a haze of work into the air around you—especially if you're sitting still for the first time in weeks, ass on a hard chair in a carpeted room with the door closed and windows sealed and a man in a suit staring you down. I could practically see the shit floating off of me.

I was sitting across a table from Ruben Rodriguez, a music business vet wearing the uniform: a double-breasted silk suit, a pinky ring, and a tie knotted like a small fist under his chin. The room, the table, the view outside the window of a pinstriped skyscraper—the whole scene was surreal to me. I'd been living like a vampire. The only people I'd seen in weeks were the people in my crew down south and my girl in Virginia. And, of course, the customers, the endless nighttime tide of fiends who kept us busy. My hands were raw from handling work and handling money; my nerves were shot from the pressure. Now I was in this office, sitting quietly, waiting to hear something worth my time from this dude, who was looking back at me like he was waiting for the same thing. Luckily the silence was filled by the third guy in the room. Sitting next to me was Dame Dash.

Clark Kent, the producer/DJ/sneakerhead, is the one who introduced me to Dame. I knew Clark through Mister Cee, Big Daddy Kane's DJ. Clark was pivotal at this stage in my life. In the mirror, all I saw was a hustler—a hustler who wrote rhymes on corner-store paper bags and memorized them in hotel rooms far away from home—but still, first a hustler. It's who I'd been since I was sixteen years old on my own in Trenton, New Jersey. I couldn't even think about wanting to be something else; I wouldn't let myself visualize another life. But I wrote because I couldn't stop. It was a release, a mental exercise, a way of keeping sane.

When I'd leave Brooklyn for long stretches and come back a hundred years later, Clark would find me and say, "Let's do this music." I don't know if he smelled the blow on my clothes, but if he did, it didn't matter. He kept on me when I was halfway gone.

I appreciated him—and Ty-Ty and B-High—when they'd encourage me, but I was so skeptical about the business that I would also get annoyed. B-High used to really come down hard on me. He's real honest and direct, and he told me straight up he thought I was throwing my life away hustling. He may have had a job, a gig at Chemical Bank with a jacket and tie, but he wasn't exactly in a position to judge. He'd see me on the street after I'd been away for six months and give me a look of absolute disgust. There were whole years when B-High, my own cousin, didn't even speak to me.

But Clark wasn't family like Ty-Ty and B-High. He had no reason to come after me, except that he thought I had something new to offer this world he loved. Clark would call me if there were open mics at a party, and if I wasn't too far away, I'd come home, get on at the party, then head back, sometimes in the middle of the night, to get back to my business. The beats would still be ringing in my ears.

Clark had been passing Dame groups to manage and splitting a signing fee with him. He knew Dame was hungry for talent to represent so he could break into the music industry and thought we'd be a good match. So he arranged a meeting at an office somewhere. Dame walked into the room talking and didn't stop. He would later tell me he was impressed because I had on Nike Airs and dudes from Brooklyn didn't wear Airs, but I didn't say much at that first meeting. I could barely get a word in edgewise. He was a Harlem dude through and through—flashy, loud, animated. Harlem cats enter every room like it's a movie set and they're the star of the flick. Dame was entertaining, but I could see that he was serious and had a real vision. His constant talking was like a release of all the ambition boiling in him, like a pot whistling steam. He was a few years younger than I was, just barely in his twenties, but he projected bulletproof confidence. And in the end, underneath all the performance, what he said made sense. I believed him.

Dame knew I needed convincing to leave hustling alone, so right away he offered to put me on a record, "Can I Get Open," with Original Flavor, a group he was managing. I went to the studio, said my verse, and as soon as we finished the song and video, I skated back out of town and out of

HE HAD NO REASON TO COME AFTER ME, EXCEPT THAT HE THOUGHT I HAD SOMETHING NEW TO OFFER THIS WORLD HE LOVED.

touch. When Dame could catch me, he would set up these meetings with record labels and drag me to them, but none of them were fucking with us. Not Columbia, not Def Jam, not Uptown. Sometimes there was talk of a single deal, but whenever it got to the point where it was supposed to be real, the label would renege.

THE WORLD DON'T LIKE US, IS THAT NOT CLEAR

So one more time here we were, again, in this office with Ruben Rodriguez. I didn't know Rodriguez, but I knew this wasn't like taking a meeting with Andre Harrell or Sylvia Rhone, both of whom had already shut us down. We were working our way down the industry depth chart. I didn't have my hopes up, but I respected Dame's hustle enough to keep coming to these meetings. Dame made his pitch and then Rodriguez sat back in his chair and leveled his eyes at me. "Yo, give me a rhyme right now," he said.

I'm not against rhyming for people when they ask. I'd rapped for free at open mics all over the tri-state area, battling other MCs, spitting on underground radio shows, getting on mix tapes, hopping on pool tables in crowded back rooms. So I wasn't too arrogant to break out into a rhyme. Maybe it was the drive into the city still wearing on me or maybe I was anxious about some loose end in Virginia. Or maybe I was just disoriented by the whiplash of my life. But when he asked me to rhyme, it felt like he was asking a nigger to tap-dance for him in his fancy suit and pinky ring. So I bounced. Well, first I said, "I ain't giving no free shows," and then I walked. It wasn't arrogant, but I did expect a level of respect, not just for me personally, but for the art.

It's hard to explain the feeling in the air in the early and mid-nineties. MCs were taking leaps and bounds. You had Big getting established. You had underground battle legends like Big L creating dense metaphorical landscapes, inventing slang so perfect you'd swear it was already in the dictionary. You had Nas doing *Illmatic*. Wu-Tang starting to buzz. There was some creative, mind-blowing shit going on. Every MC with a mic was competing to push the art further than the last one, flipping all kinds of new content, new ways of telling stories, new slang, new rhyme schemes, new characters, new sources of inspiration. When I would come back to New York and get into the music, that was the world I was walking in, competing in. For all of my disgust with the industry, I never stopped caring about the craft or my standing in it. When I was in the presence of another true MC, I'd spit for days; I never said no. I'd put all the money and hustling to the side and be just like a traveling bluesman or something, ready to put my guitar case down and start playing. I wasn't so thirsty for rap to pay my bills. It wasn't just about money.

Every time Dame left these meetings he'd get so heated. He couldn't believe they didn't "get" me. But I wasn't surprised. I expected nothing from the industry. I just tried to shrug it off and get back to my real life. Dame was getting frustrated trying to keep up with me, so he put together a makeshift tour to keep me focused on music. At the time, Dame was trying to do business with Kareem "Biggs" Burke, his man from the Bronx. Biggs and I clicked right away. We had a similar outlook and disposition. He came on and acted as a kind of road manager to help Dame with the tour dates, if you could call it a tour. Sometimes Dame and his group Original Flavor—Suave Lover, Tone, and Ski—and I would just pile up in a Pathfinder and do shows up and down the East Coast. I was being a team player; I piled in the truck, stayed in the double rooms with the rest of them. In some ways, those were like my college days, taking road trips, bunked up with friends, learning my profession, except that I still had a full-time job. It was a schizoid life, but it was all I knew.

THE SAME PLACE WHERE THE RHYME'S INVENTED

In some ways, rap was the ideal way for me to make sense of a life that was doubled, split into contradictory halves. This is one of the most powerful aspects of hip-hop as it evolved over the years. Rap is built to handle contradictions. To this day people look at me and assume that I must not be serious on some level, that I must be playing some kind of joke on the world: How can he be rapping about selling drugs on one album and then get on *Oprah* talking about making lemon pie the next day? How can he say that *police were al-Qaeda to black men* on one album and then do a benefit concert for the police who died on 9/11 to launch another? How can a song about the election of a black president and the dreams of Martin Luther King have a chorus about the color of his Maybach? When I was on the streets, my team would wonder why I was fucking with the rap shit. And when I was out doing shows, music cats would shake their heads at the fact that I was still hustling. How can he do both unless he's some kind of hypocrite?

But this is one of the things that makes rap at its best so human. It doesn't force you to pretend to be only one thing or another, to be a saint

HIP-HOP
CREATED A
SPACE WHERE
ALL KINDS OF
MUSIC COULD
MEET, WITH-
OUT CONTRA-
DICTION.

or sinner. It recognizes that you can be true to yourself and still have unexpected dimensions and opposing ideas. Having a devil on one shoulder and an angel on the other is the most common thing in the world. The real bullshit is when you act like you *don't* have contradictions inside you, that you're so dull and unimaginative that your mind never changes or wanders into strange, unexpected places.

Part of how contradictions are reconciled in rap comes from the nature of the music. I've rapped over bhangra, electronica, soul samples, classic rock, alternative rock, indie rock, the blues, doo-wop, bolero, jazz, Afrobeat, gypsy ballads, Luciano Pavarotti, and the theme song of a Broadway musical. That's hip-hop: Anything can work—there are no laws, no rules. Hip-hop created a space where all kinds of music could meet, without contradiction.

When I recorded "Hard Knock Life (Ghetto Anthem)" over a mix of the theme song from *Annie*—a brilliant track put together by Mark the 45 King that I found through Kid Capri—I wasn't worried about the clash between the hard lyrics (*where all my niggas with the rubber grips, buck shots*) and the image of redheaded Annie. Instead, I found the mirror between the two stories—that Annie's story was mine, and mine was hers, and the song was the place where our experiences weren't contradictions, just different dimensions of the same reality.

To use that song from *Annie* we had to get clearance from the copyright holder. I wasn't surprised when the company that owned the rights sent our lawyers a letter turning us down. Lord knows what they thought I was going to rap about over that track. Can you imagine "Fuck the Police" over "It's a Hard Knock Life"? Actually, it would've been genius.

But I felt like the chorus to that song perfectly captured what little kids in the ghetto felt every day: "'Stead of kisses, we get kicked." We might not all have literally been orphans, but a whole generation of us had basically raised ourselves in the streets. So I decided to write the company a letter myself. I made up this story about how when I was a seventh-grader in Bed-Stuy, our teacher held an essay contest and the three best papers won the writers a trip to the city to see *Annie*. A lie. I wrote that as kids in Brooklyn we hardly ever came into the city. True. I wrote that from the moment the curtain came up I felt like I understood honey's story. Of course, I'd never been to see *Annie* on Broadway. But I had seen the movie on TV. Anyway, they bought it, cleared it, and I had one of my biggest hits. During my live shows I always stop the music and throw it to the crowd during the chorus. I stare out as a sea of people—

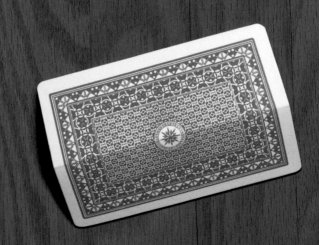

old heads, teenagers, black, white, whatever—throw their hands up and heads back and sing like it's the story of their own lives.

But it's not just the music that allows hip-hop to contain contradictions. It's in the act of rhyming itself. It's simple: Rhymes can make sense of the world in a way that regular speech can't. Take my song "Can I Live," from *Reasonable Doubt*. The song opens with a spoken intro, just me talking:

We hustle out of a sense of hopelessness, sort of a desperation, through that desperation, we become addicted, sorta like the fiends we accustomed to serving. But we feel we have nothin' to lose so we offer you, well, we offer our lives, right. What do you bring to the table?

That's some real shit! But it's a statement that raises questions. It's sort of like the beginning of an argument. You can agree or disagree. Now here's a line from the body of the song:

I'd rather die enormous than live dormant / that's how we on it

That's it. No argument, it is what it is. Why? The rhyme convinces you. The words connect. That simple couplet takes the idea of the spoken intro and makes it feel powerful, almost unassailable. Think about it: O. J. Simpson might be a free man today because "glove don't fit" rhymed with "acquit." It was a great sound bite for the media, but it was also as persuasive as the hook on a hit song. That's the power of rhymes.

But while it seems like rhymes are tricking you into making connections that don't really exist—*wait a minute, what about the DNA evidence, dammit!*—the truth is that rhymes are just reminding you that everything's connected. Take the first verse of Rakim's classic "In the Ghetto." If you just made a list of the rhyming words in that first verse, here's what it would look like:

Earth, birth, universe / Soul, controller / First, worst / Going, flowing / Rough, bust / State, shake, generate, earthquakes / Hard, boulevard, God, scarred, / Hell, fell / Trip, slip, grip, equip / Seen on, fiend on, lean on / Go, flow, slow / Back, at

First of all, when you look at a list like this, you realize how brilliant Rakim in his prime was. The rhyming words alone tell stories: *Rough / bust. Go / slow / flow.* The combination of *earth / birth / universe* is a creation epic in three words. But what's really dope is when you look at words that seem to have nothing to do with each other, like *seen on / fiend on / lean on.* What's *that* story? Here's the couplet:

any stage I'm seen on, a mic I fiend on
I stand alone and need nothing to lean on

Fantastic. Rakim chose the words because they rhymed, but it was his genius to combine them in a way that made it feel like those words were *always* meant to be connected.

So maybe it's not an accident that rhyming kept me sane in those years when I was straddling so many different worlds. The rhymes brought me back to something basic in me, even if they were just technical rhymes, just rhyming for rhyming, with no real, deep subject. And when I started writing about my life and the lives of the people around me, the rhymes helped me twist some sense out of those stories. And eventually the rhymes created a path for me to move from one life to another. Because I never had to reject Shawn Carter to become Jay-Z. Shawn Carter's life lives in Jay's rhymes—transformed, of course: Flesh and blood became words, ideas, metaphors, fantasies, and jokes. But those two characters come together through the rhymes, become whole again. The multitude is contained. It's a powerful magic. No wonder so many MCs lose their minds.

BLACK ENTREPRENEUR, NOBODY DID US NO FAVORS

After every label in the industry turned us down, and I do mean every label in town, Dame, Biggs and I decided, Fuck it, why be workers anyway? Being a recording artist on a major label is the most contractually exploitative relationship you can have in America, and it's legal. All three of us had read *Hit Men,* the industry bible, and we knew what kind of gangsters had established record companies. And the truth is, even if we were willing to be exploited workers, these dudes were not fucking with us, at all.

Dame had taken the rejection personally; he wanted to win for the same reasons we all did, but he also looked forward to the day when the same people who'd turned us down would be calling us for hits. I never do things to get a reaction from other people, good or otherwise. My personal breakthroughs came in stages.

First, I had to let go of some of the past. My girlfriend in Virginia would sometimes come with me on my trips to New York. She knew what I was doing in Virginia—her brother was down with my crew—but she didn't really know about my dreams of being an MC. On one road trip I told her about what happened in London with EMI and Jaz and how disappointed I had been. It was my first time really talking about it with anyone—not just the facts, but the feeling of a dream being crushed. When I said it to her, I realized I was actually scared of it happening again. When I heard myself telling her about Jaz, I realized that I was holding on to disappointment over failure that didn't even belong to me. I was standing in my own way.

It still took me a while to let it go, even as things were getting darker for me on the streets. I was doing well in that world, but the irony is that the more success you have in the life, the deeper the costs become and the clearer it becomes that you can't keep doing it. That it's killing you and hurting everyone you know. One of the ways the streets kept ahold on me was that I lived the independence of that life. One of the benefits of me and my crew working out of town was that I never had to be under the thumb of one of the big Brooklyn bosses. We were like pioneers on the frontier, staking out new territory where we could run things ourselves. I didn't want to give that up to become someone's contracted employee. I'd been on my own since I was a kid. But when I could really see myself not just rapping but being part of a partnership that would run the whole show, I knew I was ready to take that step.

So in 1994, Dame, Biggs, and I pooled our resources to form Roc-A-Fella Records. Tone came up with the name, which was aspirational and confrontational.

The first record we made was the single "I Can't Get With That." We recorded it in Clark Kent's basement studio, and my man Abdul Malik Abbott shot the video for five thousand dollars. The song was a showcase for my variety of flows: fast rhyming, slow rhyming, stacked, spare. The video was pretty basic, but our only goal was to get it in on Ralph McDaniels' Video Music Box, a New York institution that aired on a local UHF station. We pressed up our own vinyl. B-High made champagne baskets and sent them to DJs. We made sure that the mix-tape DJs—like Ron G, S&S, and Kid Capri—had it. We sent the record to mainstream stations, too, although getting it played on the big stations was a long shot.

We didn't know the business yet, but we knew how to hustle. Like a lot of underground crews on a mission, we were on some real trunk-of-the-car shit. The difference with us was that we didn't want to get stalled at low-level hustling. We had a plan. We did more than talk about it, we wrote it down. Coming up with a business plan was the first thing the three of us did. We made short and long-term projections, we kept it realistic, but the key thing is that we wrote it down, which is as important as visualization in realizing success.

The early Roc team was kids like Lenny Santiago, Biggs's little brother Hip-Hop, Gee Roberson, and other soldiers—all of whom have gone on to tremendous success in the industry. Back then they'd go to record stores—this is when New York record stores like Fat Beats and the spot on 125th and Broadway still sold singles on consignment. They'd drop the single off and come back every couple of days to collect half the proceeds of what had been sold. They'd show up and collect 150 dollars, an amount that would've been toll money in a former life. Ty, B-High, and I were right in there, too, in the stores, politicking with retailers, and personally building relationships with DJs. It was do or die.

I RAP AND I'M REAL, I'M ONE OF THE FEW HERE

"In My Lifetime" was the first song that really connected all the dots for me. It featured a distinctive flow, but subtly. It wasn't a song *about* flow. It was a song about the Life. It wasn't a brand-new subject—a million other rappers had already talked about selling drugs—but I knew niggas knew the difference.

BUT THEN HE
BUILDS IT,
TAKES YOU
ALONG STEP
BY STEP, TILL
YOU DON'T
EVEN REALIZE
WHEN YOU'VE
LEFT REALITY
AND ENTERED
A FEROCIOUS
FANTASY OF
THREATS AND
REVENGE

I know the phrase *keeping it real* has been killed to the point where it doesn't even mean anything anymore in rap but to me it's essential. The realness comes from how an MC shapes whatever their experience is into a rhyme. It's in the logic the lyrics follow, the emotional truth that supports it, the human motivations the MC fills in, and the commitment to getting even the smallest details right. That's probably true for all stories, whether they're in books or movies or songs. When I first watched *Menace II Society,* I had no idea whether or not the Hughes brothers had lived the life they described—or, to be honest, if anyone did—but when I saw the opening scene, I immediately believed the story was real. It was because of the details, the way the smoke filled that red-lit room, the little pistol homeboy's dad whipped out, Marvin Gaye soul spinning on the turntable. The look on the kid's face when his pop started blazing. You can't fake that kind of emotional truth. You might say, "Well, it *was* a fictional story, and those weren't real people, they were actors." But the film was executed in a way that made it real—everybody, the writers, the actors, the set designers, tapped into something true.

Big's records were like that. They could be about the most outrageous things—hijacking a subway, pulling off an armed heist, robbing one of the New York Knicks—but he'd ground them in details that made them feel completely real, even when you knew he was just fucking with you. Like he begins his song "Warning" with completely humble, relatable details—*now I'm yawning, wipe the cold out my eye*—so that from the beginning you trust him. But then he builds it, takes you along step by step, till you don't even realize when you've left reality and entered a ferocious fantasy of threats and revenge—*c4 to your door no beef no more, nigga.* And even there, he doesn't just say, I'll blow up your house. He specifies the explosive by its technical name. He gets the details right—the homey ones and the fantastical ones—and gets the emotion right, too, which is that familiar feeling of *I can't believe this shit, but I really wish a nigga would.* We've all been there at some point, although probably without the dynamite. It all stays real, whether he's kind of shaking his head in sad disbelief in the chorus—*damn, niggas want to stick me for my papers*—or on some next-level violent braggadocio—*got the rottweilers by the door, and I feed 'em gunpowder.* And then you get to the end and he suddenly catches himself in the middle of his crazy, escalating threats and becomes regular-guy Big again: *Hold on, I hear somebody coming.* Which starts the story again.

When Big got into it with Tupac, some hip-hop journalists were like, *Hey, isn't this the same nigga who said c4 at your door? Why hasn't he planted a bomb in Pac's house yet?* which is just the kind of dumb shit that rap always gets subjected to. Not to say there wasn't real beef there, lethal beef, maybe, but *Entertainment Weekly* isn't outraged that Matt Damon isn't really assassinating rogue CIA agents between movies. It goes to show that even when he was narrating a fantasy with all the crazy, blood-rushing violence of a Tarantino flick packed into three minutes, Big was real enough that some people thought he was just describing a day in his life.

Even some of our greatest MCs sometimes strayed away from their own emotional truth. You'll hear a conscious MC do an ignorant joint and you'll feel a little sick because it's so wrong. Or a classic party starter like MC Hammer suddenly becomes a gangsta and you go, *Really? Please don't. You don't have to!* When I was the CEO at Def Jam, one of my initial signings was the Roots. When I sat down with ?uestlove to talk about their new album, I told him, "Don't try to give me a hot radio single. That's not who you are. Worry about making a great album, from the first cut to the last, a great Roots album." You can't fake whatever the current trend is if it's not you, because it might work for a second, but it's a house of sand.

I remember in the 1980s, when rock music started losing ground, which created a lane for hip-hop to become the dominant pop music. Once MTV launched, rock started to change. Style started trumping substance, which culminated in the rise of the big hair bands. There were probably some great hair bands—I wouldn't really know—but I do know that most of them were terrible; even they'll admit that now. And what's worse is that the thing that made rock great, its rawness, whether it was Little Richard screaming at the top of his lungs or the Clash smashing their guitars, disappeared in all that hairspray. It was pure decadence. It crippled rock for a long time. I wasn't mad, because rap was more than ready to step in.

A couple years ago when Auto-Tune started to really blow up in black music, I got the sinking feeling that I'd seen this story before. There were people who used Auto-Tune technology cleverly, to make great pop music, the kind of music that gives you a sudden sugar high and then disappears without a trace. Kanye made a great, original Auto-Tune album, *808s & Heartbreak,* which was entirely his own sound. Kanye's a genuine talent, so he did it right. But then rappers across the board started fucking with

YOU'LL HEAR A CONSCIOUS MC DO AN IGNORANT JOINT AND YOU'LL FEEL A LITTLE SICK BECAUSE IT'S SO WRONG.

it. It was disturbing. It felt almost like a conspiracy. Instead of aspiring to explore their humanity—their brains and hearts and guts—these rappers were aspiring to *sound like machines*. And it worked for some rappers; they made quick money with it. But they were cashing in at the expense of a whole culture that had been built over two decades by people like Rakim and Kane, by legends like Big and Tupac. And in the end, these Auto-Tune rappers were going to fuck up everybody's money; I also saw developments in indie rock that made me think they were ready to take rap's mantle, because they were experimenting with different paths to that same authentic, raw place that rap used to inhabit.

So I recorded a song called "D.O.A. (Death of Auto-Tune)." It wasn't because I was trying to destroy the career of anyone in particular. I wanted to kill Auto-Tune like Kurt Cobain killed the hair bands. It's not a game. Musical genres have been known to die, mostly because they lose their signature and their vitality, and let other genres steal their fire. Where's disco? Where's the blues, for that matter?

What's hip-hop's greatness? It's a cliché, but its greatness is that it keeps it real, in the most complicated sense of reality. And that realness lives in the voice of the MC. That will never change.

IN MY LIFETIME, NIGGA, THAT WAS ME FIRST

To get "In My Lifetime" out there, we negotiated a single deal with Payday that guaranteed wider distribution than we'd been able to get on our own. Once we secured that deal, we rented an office in the financial district, on John Street, around the corner from the World Trade Center. In our minds, we were staying close to the money, to Wall Street. Our girls, who to this day still work with me on some level, were holding us down. Tiny, funny-ass Chaka Pilgrim, who's like my little sister, was in the office, complaining about the mice and the dirty watercoolers. Dara and Omoyole McIntosh started our fan club, Fan Fam, before we even had any fans. Our office felt more like an apartment, with a big-screen TV, a leather couch, and dice games jumping off in the corner. We didn't have desks, computers, air-conditioning, or any of the shit we really needed; we had a business plan, but we were still wild, rough around the edges. When Chaka and Omye would go to leave the office at noon, Ty and I would be like, "Where ya'll going?" and Chaka's smart ass would be like, "Hello? We're going to lunch—ever heard of it? People with real jobs in offices go on them." I started ordering food in, like, "Sit your little ass down."

There was so much love back then; everyone who started out with the Roc believed in us and wanted to see us win.

When we went to Payday to promote the song they gave us a box of flyers. Can you imagine that shit? Their budget could fit on a Kinko's receipt. Shit was so laughable. Some cats would've been derailed by lack of support from their label, but we had that plan. So we just hired Abdul Malik Abbott again and got on a plane to St. Thomas to shoot our own video for the song.

We shot "In My Lifetime" in the Caribbean, when other rappers were making videos at Coney Island (no disrespect to Nice & Smooth). We were filming on boats while dudes were dancing in alleys. The video wasn't aspirational. This was really the life we were living, before we'd even released a single. We'd always had pool parties, but this one was even more of a celebration. When I looked on the monitor and saw Ty-Ty and B-High having the time of their lives, I knew it was because they were proud that I was doing the music thing, and doing it right.

The next record I did was "Dead Presidents." It was a strong single and we knew it, and we wanted it to pop in the biggest rap radio market, New York, which meant we had to get spins from Funkmaster Flex at Hot 97. Flex had become New York's hottest hip-hop DJ, with prime-time airspace on Hot 97 on the weekends and a huge Sunday night gig at the Tunnel, a megaclub in Manhattan. We tried everything we could do to get Flex to play "Dead Presidents," but this nigga was not seeing us. Irv Gotti, who I've known since I was in London with Jaz, was working with artists like Mic Geronimo. He had Flex's ear and just stalked him until he finally broke the record. Irv also met DJ Clue at a gas station and gave him the single like it was a drug deal or something. It was the first time we got an "add" on the radio. That was a major. Irv also gave us a great piece of advice. He told us "Dead Presidents" was a great record but too hard for a hit. He said the record on the flip side, "Ain't No Nigga," was the one that was going to get played in the clubs and on radio. He was right.

Still, on the strength of the heat from "Dead Presidents," Dame and I were in a position to finally negotiate a distribution deal that could support a national album release, which we did with Priority, an indie label. We had a small window of opportunity from the time Flex started playing it, in the beginning of 1996. I figured I had until that summer to complete an entire album, about three to four months from studio to pack-aged product with a marketing plan, and then we would be in a position to launch the label proper.

We locked out D&D studios and I would be in the lab by noon, going from one room to another working with producers. I was lucky to work with some remarkable producers for my first album. Clark and Ski from Original Flavor did a lot of the work. Ron G, Harlem's mix-tape king, had switched his format from cassette to CD, and he named his first CD release of the year "Dead Presidents." Being hot on mix tapes made it easier to work with a legendary producer like Premiere for "Friend or Foe." Talented people were coming out to help me with my debut, and I appreciated the love. I don't think I slept for weeks at a time back then. I was living off pure adrenaline.

When Big came through one of my sessions to see Clark, Clark played him the beat for "Brooklyn's Finest." He told Clark he *had* to get on it. I remembered Big from Westinghouse; he was quiet like me, but I can distinctly recall passing him in the hallway and giving him the universal black-man-half-nod of recognition. This time around we clicked right away. More than anything, I love sharp people; men or women, nothing makes me like someone more than intelligence. Big was shy, but when he said something it was usually witty. I'm talkative when I get to know you, but before that I can be pretty economical with words. I'm more of a listener.

When Big said he wanted to get on the track, I went into the booth and started laying down vocals. Big was in the back of the room smoking and nodding. He didn't get on that night, though; he said he wanted to go home and think about his verses. In that moment, I gave his coming back to be on the song a fifty-percent chance of actually happening. There was a fifty-percent chance he was just talking shit like an industry nigga. We went to see Bernie Mack later that night and really clicked. He sent the song a couple weeks later.

Another collaboration on the album was with Foxy Brown. I knew Inga Marchand from before she did LL's "I Shot Ya" in the fall of 1995. She was a tough, pretty girl I knew from downtown Brooklyn and perfect for the concept I had for the song "Ain't No Nigga." One night I took a break from D&D to go to the Palladium—and when "Ain't No Nigga" came on, it seemed like every single person on every level of the club went to the dance floor. That night the phrase *put your drinks down and report to the dance floor* floated through my mind for the first time. [I'd later use it as an ad-lib on the single "Do It Again (Throw Your Hands Up)"]. I had never seen anything like the response to that record. They played it seven times in a row and the audience went wild every time.

BURNT IT ALL, THIS MUSIC IS WHERE I BURY THE ASHES AT

When I was a kid, my parents had, like, a million records stacked to the ceiling in metal milk crates. They both loved music so much. When they did break up and get a divorce, sorting the records out was probably the biggest deal. I remember "Walking in Rhythm," by the Blackbyrds, "Love's Theme," by the Love Unlimited Orchestra, "Dancing Machine," by the Jackson 5, "Tell Me Something Good," by Rufus, "The Hustle," by Van McCoy and the Soul City Symphony, "Slippery When Wet," by the Commodores, "Pick Up the Pieces," by the Average White Band, "It Only Takes a Minute," by Tavares, "(TSOP) The Sound of Philadelphia," by MFSB (Mother Father Sister Brother), the *Superfly* soundtrack by Curtis Mayfield, James Brown, Billy Paul, Honeycomb, Candi Staton, Rose Royce, the Staple Singers, the Sylvers, the O'Jays, Blue Magic, Main Ingredient, the Emotions, Chic, Heatwave, A Taste of Honey, Slave, Evelyn "Champagne" King, Con Funk Shun. If it was hot in the seventies my parents had it. They had a turntable, but they also had a reel-to-reel. My parents would blast those classics when we did our Saturday cleanup and when they came home from work. We'd be dancing in the living room, making our own *Soul Train* line with B-High, his sisters, and my sisters. I loved all music, but Michael Jackson more than anyone. My mother would play "Enjoy Yourself," by the Jacksons, and I would dance and sing and spin around. I'd make my sisters my backup singers. I remember those early days as the time that shaped my musical vocabulary. I remember the music making me feel good, bringing my family together, and more importantly, being a common passion my parents shared.

That music from my childhood still lives in my music. From my very first album, a lot of the tracks I rapped over were built on a foundation of classic seventies soul. On *Reasonable,* we sampled the Ohio Players, the Stylistics, Isaac Hayes, and the Four Tops.

The music from that era was incredible, full of emotion. It could be exuberant like the Jackson 5 (who I would sample on songs like "Izzo (H.O.V.A.)" later in my career) or passionate like Marvin Gaye records (whose "Soon I'll Be Loving You Again" I sampled on my *American Gangster* album) or troubled and transcendent like Curtis Mayfield (I rapped over a snatch of his beautiful, mournful "Man, Oh Man" on "Go Crazy" with Jeezy). The songs carried in them the tension and energy of the era. The seventies were a strange time, especially in black America. The music was beautiful in part because it was keeping a kind of torch lit in a dark time.

I feel like we—rappers, DJs, producers—were able to smuggle some of the magic of that dying civilization out in our music and use it to build a new world. We were kids without fathers, so we found our fathers on wax and on the streets and in history, and in a way, that was a gift: We got to pick and choose the ancestors who would inspire the world we were going to make for ourselves. That was part of the ethos of that time and place, and it got built in to the culture we created. Rap took the remnants of a dying society and created something new. Our fathers were gone, usually because they just bounced, but we took their old records and used them to build something fresh.

I remember that when I was a kid in the eighties every song I heard had some kind of innovation. From Run-DMC to LL to Slick Rick to Rakim to BDP to PE to Tribe, everything was fresh, even though it was all built on ruins—dusted-off soul and jazz samples, vocal samples from old Malcolm X speeches, the dissonant noise of urban life that genius producers like the Bomb Squad turned into music.

It wasn't just another youth culture; it was something new and transcendent, the kind of art that changes the paths of people's lives. I know that sounds overblown, but ask any kid of my generation—and this applies to black kids and white kids and kids in Indonesia and South Africa and Amsterdam—whether hip-hop changed their lives, and you'll see what I'm talking about. I'm not saying that these kids grew up to be rappers. I'm talking about kids who discovered politics from listening to Chuck D and were never the same. Or who felt connected to other eccentrics because of Tribe. Or whose love of language came directly from their first experience with Rakim. Or who got their sense of humor from Prince Paul skits or Biz Markie's rhyming about picking boogers. There's a whole generation who hear "Reminisce," by Pete Rock and CL Smooth, or Bone Thugs' "Crossroads," and connect it to their own personal tragedies. There are cats who felt like Cube was saying all the shit they'd get arrested for thinking; some felt like Scarface was telling their story. I know for a fact that there are kids who learned about and got real cozy with the Cali behind "The Chronic." Or who lost their virginity to *don't stop, get it, get it* and learned to respect women (or themselves as women) from Queen Latifah and Lauryn Hill.

Rap started off so lawless, not giving a fuck about any rules or limits, that it was like a new frontier. We knew we were opening up new territory even if we left behind a whole country, or sometimes our own families. But we struck oil.

I FEEL LIKE WE—RAPPERS, DJS, PRODUCERS—WERE ABLE TO SMUGGLE SOME OF THE MAGIC OF THAT DYING CIVILIZATION OUT IN OUR MUSIC AND USE IT TO BUILD A NEW WORLD.

And it's not over. The beauty of hip-hop is that, as I said at the beginning, it found its story in the story of the hustler. But that's not its only story. At this point, it's a tool that can be used to find the truth in anything. I'm still rhyming—not about hustling in the same way I rhymed about it on my first album, but about the same underlying quest. The hook to that first single, "In My Lifetime," was sampled from Soul II Soul's "Get a Life," just these words repeated over and over and over again: *What's the meaning? What's the meaning of life?* That's the question rap was built on from the beginning and, through a million different paths, that's still its ultimate subject.

WE ARE REALLY HIGH, REALLY HIGH TONIGHT

I hadn't been on vacation since I'd gotten serious about music, so I was happy to go to Miami to shoot the video for "Ain't No Nigga" with Foxy. Big was touring, but he took time out to fly down and make a cameo. Big loved to smoke, but I could count the number of times I'd smoked trees. Champagne and the occasional Malibu rum were my thing back then, but mostly I liked to stay sober, the better to stay focused on making money. I come from that class of hustlers who looked at smoking as counterproductive. We used to judge niggas who smoked as slackers, or workers. When I did smoke it was on vacation, in the islands.

But when Big asked me to smoke with him, I told myself, "Relax, you're not on the streets anymore." It was happening and I had to admit it. I was out of the Life. So I smoked with Big—and he smoked blunts. The last time I smoked, whenever that was, I'm sure I was hitting a joint. A couple hits later and I was high as shit, sitting there, feeling outside of time, slightly stuck, and laughing uncontrollably.

Big leans in so only I can hear him.

"I got ya."

That fucked me up. Big was a friend, but also a competitor. He gave me an important lesson at that moment. They call it the game, but it's not—you can want success all you want, but to get it, you can't falter. You can't slip. You can't sleep. One eye open, for real, and forever.

Big's joke was such a small thing, but I was like, fuck that. The director was setting up shots and all that, but I went to my room and sobered up for twenty minutes before I came downstairs.

When I came down Big was laughing— his laughter was a beautiful thing, even when the joke was on me. This time I leaned in close to him. "Never again, my nigga."

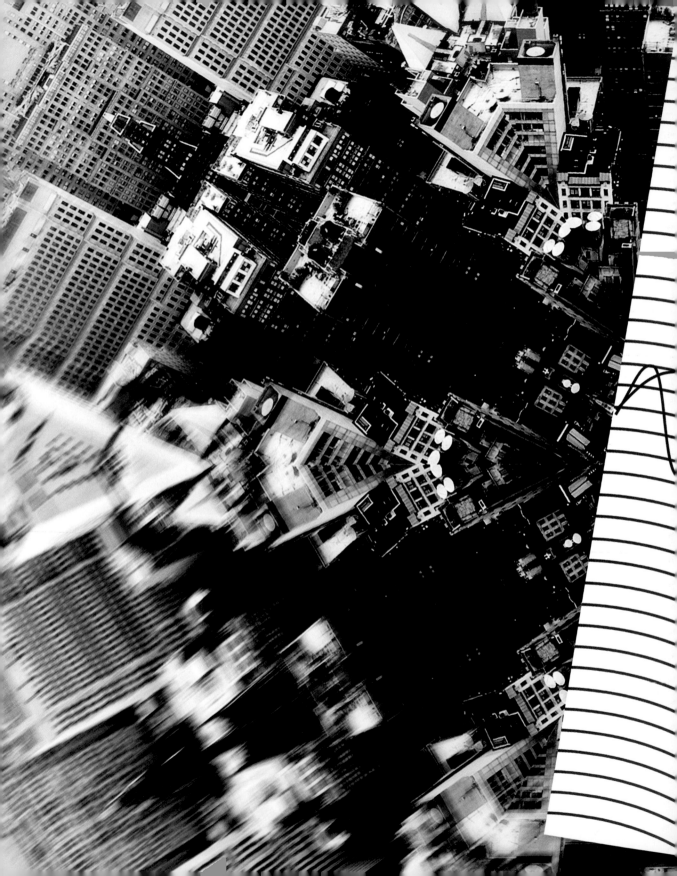

THE VOICE IN YOUR HEAD IS RIGHT

REGRETS
(*REASONABLE DOUBT*, 1996)

THIS CAN'T BE LIFE
FEATURING BEANIE SIGEL AND SCARFACE
(*THE DYNASTY: ROC LA FAMILIA*, 2000)

SOON YOU'LL UNDERSTAND
(*THE DYNASTY: ROC LA FAMILIA*, 2000)

When I was a teenager, I spent a lot of time in my ride, speeding back and forth between Brooklyn and New Jersey, where I lived (and worked) part of the time. I-95 in New Jersey runs along the New Jersey Turnpike, a famously boring stretch of highway, but we'd keep it live by blasting Slick Rick till the speakers bled. Slick Rick was the wittiest shit out back then, but his sense of humor was like Eddie Murphy's or Richard Pryor's, dark and subversive. Maybe his eye patch and English accent had something to do with it, but he could make the rawest rhymes sound like *Masterpiece Theatre,* just through the elegance of his style and his story-telling talent. He had the pimp's gift for talking shit but making it sound like a seduction. And he had the kind of style that hustlers aspired to: at ease with the culture and language of the streets, but with the style and swagger of a prince. He never hit a wrong note. Today people associate the whole gold jewelry and gold teeth thing with a kind of down-south country style, but when Rick first rocked it back in the eighties—complete with a cape and a Kangol—it was the essence of sophisticated street fashion.

Back then I loved his song "Treat Her Like a Prostitute." It's a great, totally ignorant song (and I mean "ignorant" in the best possible sense). But Slick Rick also wrote some of the first rap songs that were genuinely sad—which sounds like a strange thing to say about Slick Rick. His songs were always energetic and hilarious but could also feel bluesy or even haunted, like his classic "Mona Lisa," which is a conversation between the rapper and a young girl he meets at a pizza shop. The two characters flirt with each other through clever disses (*she said, "Great Scott, are you a thief / seems like you have a mouth full of gold teeth"*) but then Slick Rick's boy comes along, calls her a snake, and drags him away. The song ends with the narrator's wistful memory of the girl singing the chorus of "Walk On By" as he leaves. As the voice trails off, the beat goes on for a few bars. It forces you to sit with that sadness for a few seconds longer than you're comfortable.

Slick Rick was too much of an artist to come out with straight-up tearjerkers, but like all great comics he knew how to hide deeper emotions between the punch lines, emotions like regret and loss, the kind of feelings that could make you pause even while you were speeding down the New Jersey Turnpike on the way to your hustling spot. And he never lost his cool, never got weepy and sentimental; the emotion was real, but not a big production. He kept it clean and honest and respected his listeners enough not to manipulate them. In another of his classic songs,

"A Children's Story," he tells a bedtime story to his nieces and nephews, a comic fable about a kid who becomes a thief. The song is kind of a slapstick caper, but then it takes a sudden turn: *This ain't funny so don't you dare laugh / just another case 'bout the wrong path.* Then the final word in the song changes the tone again: *Goodnight!* Uncle Ricky chirps. Is it a joke? Maybe. But those previous lines stick with you, and the laughter dies in your throat.

NOT ONLY MONEY BUT ALL THE EMOTIONS GOING THROUGH US

Slick Rick taught me that not only can rap be emotionally expressive, it can even express those feelings that you can't really name—which was important for me, and for lots of kids like me, who couldn't always find the language to make sense of our feelings. As an instrument for expressing emotion, rap is as good as the writer. If you're willing to put something into a song, the song can usually hold it.

Scarface is one of my favorite rappers and maybe the first truly great lyricist to come out of the South. He's known as a "rapper's rapper," and it's true, he gets respect across the board and his influence is enormous. His music is an extended autobiography and his ability to weave complicated emotions into his songs is uncanny. But where Slick Rick specialized in crisp rhyming that creates spaces where the listener can fill in emotions, Scarface's voice itself always seems filled to the top with feeling. Slick Rick keeps a certain distance from the listener; his songs are playful and witty. But Scarface always feels like he's rapping right in your ear, like the guy on the next bar stool unburdening himself of a story that keeps him up nights or a nightmare that comes back to him all day.

The power of his stories comes in part from his willingness to pull the covers off of taboos, to get into the shit that people pretend isn't really happening, whether he's rhyming about street life or about being in a mental institution.

His most famous verse—on the Geto Boys' "Mind Playing Tricks on Me"—is a great example. He's starts the song in the middle of a nightmare: *At night I can't sleep, I toss and turn / candlesticks in the dark, visions of bodies being burned.* As the song progresses, you realize he's writing about an all-consuming paranoia, the kind that comes from a guilty conscience or even from a kind of raw self-hatred. (In the song he's being stalked by someone who *wears a black hat like I own / a black suit and a cane like my own,* lines that are both beautifully structured and cinematic.)

Even though the two are probably opposites in a lot of ways, Slick Rick and Scarface share that ability to get under your skin by dredging up the kinds of emotions that young men don't normally talk about with each other: regret, longing, fear, and even self-reproach. It's always been my ambition to do the same, because you don't spend every moment of every day as a fucking killing machine. That's the stereotype of young black men, of course. And sometimes we play along with it. But it's not true, even when we wish it was.

DON'T GRIEVE FOR ME, MY ART REMAINS

I've done a couple of collaborations with Scarface, and they're always pretty intense. The first one was on the *Dynasty* album, a song with me and Beanie Sigel called "This Can't Be Life." The track we were rapping over was an early Kanye production, driven by a sample from "Miss You," by Harold Melvin and the Bluenotes, with big strings. Strings always pull me into a pretty deep place, in terms of the feelings and ideas they bring up. On my verse I went into some dark personal storytelling about a time in my life when I felt truly confused and lost, between worlds, the voice in my head screaming at me to leave the street shit alone, while outside I watched Big and Nas blowing up. On top of that, I've got heartbreaking personal issues dogging me.

It was a verse about fear of failure, which is something that everyone goes through, but no one, particularly where I'm from, wants to really talk about. But it's a song that a lot of people connect to: The thought that "this can't be life" is one that all of us have felt at some point or another, when bad decisions and bad luck and bad situations feel like too much to bear, those times when we think that this, *this,* can't be my story. But facing up to that kind of feeling can be a powerful motivation to change. It was for me.

On the day we were supposed to be recording Scarface's verse, we were all just sort of sprawled out, bullshitting in the front room at Bassline Studios, which was the home studio for Roc-A-Fella Records. We had a pool table and some couches and we were just shooting, joking around with my engineer, Guru, and getting ready to go into the booth. Then Scarface's phone rang, and as soon as he picked it up, the look on his face changed. He kept saying the same thing over and over again, "Nahh . . . nahhh, man . . ." Then he was quiet for a while. When he hung up, he told us what happened. His homeboy had called to tell him that a friend of theirs had just lost one of his kids in a fire. We're all just sitting there like, *Fuck.* Then Scarface was back on the phone to his own wife to tell her the news and to check on how his own kids were doing.

When he got off the phone I told him, "Yo, we'll get the verse another time." He shook his head. "Nah, Jig, nah, I'll do it now." He went off on his own for a while to compose his verse. When he came into the booth to record, he laid down the verse that's on the album in one take. His first lines were, *Now as I walk into the studio to do this with Jig, I got a phone call from one of my nigs.*

Scarface turned that moment of pain instantly into a great piece of writing, which he followed with a powerful vocal performance. It was incredible to watch. But really, what he did was to just compress the normal act of hip-hop songwriting into a matter of minutes. The raw material of life got mixed into that song, for real—in this case, the sudden sadness of life. But the great hip-hop writers don't really discriminate. They take whatever's at hand and churn it into their work. Whatever feeling demands a release at a given moment finds its way out in the songs. The music is as deep and varied as life.

REGRETS[1]

I sold it all from crack to opium,[2] **in third person**[3] / I don't wanna see 'em, so I'm rehearsin / **with my peoples how to g 'em**[4], from a remote location / **in the BM, scopin the whole situation**[5] like, "Dayamm!" / **Metamorphic, as the dope turns to cream**[6] / **but one of these buyers got eyes like a Korean**[7] / It's difficult to read 'em, the windows to his soul / are half closed, I put the key in / Pulled off slow, hopin my people fleein[8] / **Chink tried to knock the only link that tied me in**[9] / Coppers was watchin us through nighttime binoculars / This time they got us on tape, exchangin dope for dollars / Make me wanna holler back at the crib in the sauna / Prayin my people bailed out like Time Warner / **Awaitin call, from his kin not the coroner**[10] / Phone in my hand, nervous confined to a corner / Beads of sweat second thoughts on my mind / **How can I ease the stress and learn to live with these regrets**[11] / This time . . . stress . . . givin this shit up . . . fuck / This is the number one rule for your set / In

1. This is the last song on my first album, *Reasonable Doubt*. The album as a whole was like a conversation I was having with the listener about real feelings and emotions. The album went from the highs of the hustler's life in songs like "Feelin It" to the paranoid depths of "D'Evils." I wanted to end it with regret, that last feeling you have before you go to sleep, or feel when you wake up and look at yourself in the bathroom mirror.

2. This is something I do in a lot of my songs—I introduce the narrator with a declaration that lets you know who he is: In this case, he's obviously a boss, someone who "sold it all" and is speaking from that experience.

3. "In third person" means that I'm at least one person away from the actual transaction, which is, again, the way a boss would handle his business.

4. I'm teaching my people how to "g 'em," which was slang back in the day for game. All this means is that I've trained my people how to handle the negotiation.

5. This shows how thorough a boss the narrator is, and how thorough his worker is: I gave him the play before it happened, and now I'm watching the play from a BMW parked some distance away.

6. The metamorphosis happens when you exchange one product for another, the drugs for the money.

7. The narrator sees the buyer's eyes and they're like a Korean's—which is some ignorant shit, I'll admit—but the point is that to him they're hard to read, which makes him anxious, because something about the buyer is shut off. The eyes are the window to the soul, and his windows are closed.

8. Now I know something's up, and I'm hoping my people figured it out, too.

9. "Chink" refers back to the hard-to-read buyer (I told you it was ignorant) and now it's clear that the plan was to bag my worker, the link that connects me to the transaction.

10. I bailed out, like Time Warner bailed out of hip-hop when it sold Interscope under pressure. I'm hoping to get a call from his family to tell me he's okay, not that he died in a shootout with cops.

11. The emotion here is guilt, regret. I put him in the situation, I told him what to do. I showed him how to do it, and I watched it go down. And there was nothing I could do about it. Run down there and try to grab him? Then we're all locked up. So I had to leave. The guilt of leaving, the guilt of putting him in that situation and then not knowing what happened—it was just driving me crazy. I've seen situations like that in real life, and while I can paint a picture of it, the feeling itself is impossible to describe.

order to survive, gotta learn to live with regrets / On the rise to the top, many drop, don't forget / In order to survive, gotta learn to live with regrets / This is the number one rule for your set / In order to survive, gotta learn to live with regrets / And through our travels we get separated, never forget / In order to survive, gotta learn to live with regrets / As sure as this Earth is turning souls burning / **in search of higher learning turning in every direction seeking direction**[12] / My moms cryin cause her insides are dyin / her son tryin her patience, keep her heart racin / **A million beats a minute, I know I push you to your limit**[13] / but it's this game love, I'm caught up all in it / They make it so you can't prevent it, never give it / you gotta take it, can't fake it I keep it authentic / **My hand got this pistol shakin, cause I sense danger**[14] / like Camp Crystal Lake and / don't wanna shoot him, but I got him trapped / **within this infrared dot, bout to hot him and hit rock bottom**[15] / No answers to these trick questions, no time shit stressin / My life found I gotta live for the right now / Time waits for no man, can't turn back the

12. We're on to a second narrative. Once again I try to quickly define the character in the first line: He's a young hustler trying to figure out life.

13. When I started hustling, my mother knew I'd moved out, of course, and when I did come home it would be for a weekend at most, and I'd show up wearing a gold cable that weighed thirty-six ounces and real diamond studs in my ear, gold-plated fronts in my mouth. She never talked to me about it; she believed in letting her children make their own mistakes, plus what could she say?

14. The song shifts from a general description of his life to a specific situation of danger and decision.

15. I know once I shoot him, that's it for me. Not only will I be a drug dealer, but also a murderer. It's rock bottom. I'm in a situation where I'm literally shaking with fear and my gun is aimed right at his forehead.

hands / **once it's too late,**[16] gotta learn to live with re-grets / You used to hold me, told me that I was the best / Anything in this world I want I could possess / **All that made me want is all that I could get**[17] / In order to survive, gotta learn to live with regrets . . . (when I was young) / I found myself reminiscin, remember this one / **when he was here he was crazy nice with his son**[18] / I miss him, long as I'm livin he's livin through memories / He's there to kill all my suicidal tenden-cies / **In heaven lookin over me, or in hell, keepin it cozy / I'm comin**[19] life on these streets ain't what it's supposed to be / Remember Newton, mutual friend well me and him feudin / **On your life I tried to talk to him**[20] / But you know niggaz, think they guns can stop four niggaz / **Frontin like they're Big Willie but really owe niggaz / Hoe niggaz,**[21] this year I'm sho' niggaz think I'm slippin / **I'm 'bout to send you a roommate, no bullshittin / for my hustle's goin too well to hit him**[22] / You was right niggaz want you to be miserable wit em / Anyway, I ain't tryin to hear it, I think I'm touched / **this whole verse I been talkin to your spirit a little too much**[23]

16. These are the moments that move fastest but linger longest. This is a kid who starts the verse seeking—but not finding—guidance in every direction and ends it having to make a life-or-death decision while his body is flooded with adrenaline and his mind clouded with fear and time is ticking off, ruthlessly demanding an answer.

17. This is another example of how something seemingly innocent can take a turn. My mother's love and belief in me made me think that I could have anything I wanted in this world, but without direction that ambition led me into situations I wasn't ready for and decisions that I'd have to live with for the rest of my life. Here I tried to capture in a few words that turn from an innocent kid absorbing his mother's love to a young man old before his time burdened with unspeakable regrets.

18. This narrator is someone who's obviously thinking about a lost friend.

19. These lines capture the doomed feeling of the narrator. Not only is he suicidal from the stress of the life, but he's not even sure he'll find an escape in death, because he's going to go to hell for all the shit he's done.

20. Now the song moves to a one-sided conversation between the narrator and his dead friend.

21. The conversation is heating up, the narrator has left the reminiscing, and he begins to enter a rage about a current situation with Newton, another old friend turned enemy.

22. Killing Newton would fuck up his money, so he's got to resign himself to dealing with him in some other way. But it's going to be hard, because Newton is a problem.

23. By the end, he realizes that he's having a crazy conversation with someone who's not even there. He's so destabilized by stress and regret that he's become "touched," crazy enough to strategize with his dead homie about killing someone.

THIS CAN'T BE LIFE / FEATURING BEANIE SIGEL AND SCARFACE

[*Jay-Z*] / Geah . . . whassup? / Where's all my street niggaz, project niggaz / Real niggas, worldwide / Let's reflect . . . e'rybody got a story / We all ghetto B—here's mine / Geah / See I was—**born in sewage, born to make bomb music**[1] **Flow tight like I was born Jewish**[2] / Used the streets as a conduit—**I kept arms** / **38 longs**[3] inside my mom's Buick / At any given moment Shawn could lose it, be on the news / **Iron cuffs—arms through it;**[4] or stuffed with embalmin fluid / Shit, I'm goin through it—mom dukes too / Tears streamin down her pretty face, she got her palms to it / My life is gettin too wild / I need to bring some sorta calm to it / **'Bout to lose it; voices screamin "Don't do it!"**[5] / It's like '93, '94, 'bout the year / **that Big and Mac dropped;**[6] and *Illmatic* rocked / outta every rag drop, and the West had it locked / Everybody doin 'em, I'm still scratchin on the block / **like "Damn; I'ma be a failure"**[7] / Surrounded by thugs, drugs, and drug paraphernalia / Cops courts and their thoughts is to derail us / **Three-time felons in shorts**[8] with jealous thoughts / Tryin figure where your mail is, guesstimate the weight you sellin / So they can send shots straight to your melon; wait! / It gets worse, baby momma water burst / **Baby came out stillborn, still I gotta move on**[9] / Though my heart still torn, life gone from her womb / Don't worry, if it was meant to be, it'll be—soon / [*Chorus*] This can't be life, this can't be love / This can't be right, there's gotta be more, this can't be us / This can't be life, this can't be love / This can't be right, there's gotta be more, this can't be us / [*Scarface*] / Yeah . . . uhh . . . / Now as I walk into the studio, to do this with Jig' / I got a phone call from one of my nigs / Said my homeboy Reek, he just lost one of his kids / And when I heard that I just broke into tears / And see in the second hand; you don't really know how this is / But when it hits that close to home you feel the pain at the crib / So I called mine, and saddened my wife with the bad news / Now we both depressed, countin our blessings cause Brad's two / Prayin for young souls to laugh at life through the stars / Lovin your kids just like you was ours / And I'm hurtin for you dog; but ain't nobody pain is like yours / I just know that heaven'll open these doors / And ain't no bright side to losin life; but you can view it like this / God's got open hands homey, he in the midst of good company / Who loves all and hates not one / And one day you gon' be wit your son / I could've rapped about my hard times on this song / But heaven knows I woulda been wrong / I wouldn'ta been right, it wouldn'ta been love / It wouldn'ta been life, it wouldn'ta been us / This can't be life / [*Chorus*] / [*Jay-Z*] / This can't be life.

1. "Bomb" is a slang term for something that's not just good, but powerful. Something that cuts through normal life explodes like a bomb. When you come from the lowest rung of a society—from "sewage"—sometimes the only way to make noise is with an explosion.

2. When I use lines like this, I count on people knowing who I am and my intentions, knowing that I'm not anti-Semitic or racist, even when I use stereotypes in my rhymes, like here, where I'm playing off the stereotype that Jewish people are "tight," that is, frugal, as a way of talking about the tightness of my flows. Lyor Cohen and I joke about race and Jews and blacks every time we see each other. It's obviously something that's in all of our minds in one way or another, and it's better to get it out, make fun of it, instead of being silent about it and let it start to influence you.

3. "38 long" could be a sleeve length for arms, or it could be—and is, in this case—a type of arm, as in weapon, a .38 long handgun.

4. Another double entendre relating to a shirt—the cuffs that my arms go through here aren't cotton, though, they're iron. There's no deep hidden meaning to shirts in this song, but extending the metaphor helps to hold the thought together and make it more vivid.

5. The voice screaming in this case is the voice in my head. Normally you think about the voice in your head as whispering to you or, at worse, having a heated conversation, but you know shit is really out of control when your conscience needs to scream to get your attention, like, "Don't make me come out there!"

6. Big's *Ready to Die* dropped in 1994; his Bad Boy labelmate Craig Mack's *Project: Funk Da World* also dropped that year. *Illmatic* also dropped that year from Nas. The significance of those three records is that they launched the resurgence of East Coast hip-hop after the West Coast had dominated the game for years.

7. This was a sentiment that I didn't fully allow myself back in 1994. I was rhyming, but mostly hustling. It took me a while to come to grips with the fact that I really wanted to devote myself to music. Biggie and Nas were an inspiration—but the flip side is that no one was giving me a deal. There were times when I slowed down enough to tap into that true feeling, the feeling that maybe I was going to miss out on this thing I really wanted, deep down. That despite whatever success I had on the streets, I would be a failure because I never fully chased my dream.

8. "In shorts" shows you that these three-time felons were still just kids.

9. This refers to something that happened to me around that time, 1994, when my girl of five years got pregnant and lost the baby in a miscarriage. Now, obviously, miscarriages happen everywhere, to anyone, but the point is that on top of the especially acute paranoia and disappointment and exhaustion I'm feeling from the street life, friends getting shot, your family being broke, I have to deal with the everyday tragedies that stalk everyone. And when that hits you, sometimes it becomes clear that you have to get out, that this really can't be life, it has to be more.

SOON YOU'LL UNDERSTAND[1]

You're my best friend's sister, grown woman and all / **But you see how I am around girls; I ruin 'em all**[2] / Plus your mom call me son, around you since I was small / **Shit I watched you mature—nah, this ain't right**[3] / But still when your boyfriend ditched you, life's a bitch you cried / Over my right shoulder I told you to wipe your eyes / Take your time when you likin a guy / **Cause if he sense that your feelings too intense, it's pimp or die**[4] / I bought you earrings on your birthday / **Drove you to college your first day**[5] / It must be sad, though it hurts to say / We could never be a item, don't even like him / **You deserve better—this is ugly; Gina, please don't love me**[6] / There's better guys out there other than me / (You need a lawyer or a doctor or somebody like that you know) / Like a lawyer or a doctor with a Ph.D. / Think of how upset your mother and brother would be / **if they found that you was huggin me**[7] / My conscience is fuckin with me / Let him hold you, let him touch you / Soon you'll un-der-stand / Man, I look in the eyes of a . . . / this . . . a kid that stole life we made to-gether . . . / We're tryin, really tryin to make it work / I'm young, and I ain't ready, and I told you / Let him hold you, let him touch you / Soon you'll un-der-stand / It ain't like, I ain't tell you from day one, I ain't shit / When it comes to relationships, I don't have the patience / Now it's too late, we got a little life together / and in my mind I really want you to be my wife forever / **But in the physical it's like I'ma be trife forever**[8] / A different girl every night forever; told you to leave / but you're stubborn and you love him and, / no matter what despite all the fuckin and the cheatin, / you still won't leave him, now you're grievin / And I feel bad, believe me / **But I'm young and I ain't ready, and this ain't easy**[9] / Wasn't fair to tell you to wait, so I told you to skate / You chose not to, now look at the shit we gotta go through / **Don't want to fight, don't want to fuss, you the mother of my baby**[10] / I don't want you to hate me, this is about us / **Rather me; I ain't ready to be what you want me to be / Because I love you, I want you to leave, please**[11] / Let him hold you, let him touch you / Soon you'll un-der-stand / Mm . . . listen ma / I mean, I seen you workin two or three jobs / Daddy left . . . I thought I was makin things better / I made it worse / Let him hold you, let him touch you / Soon you'll un-der-stand / **Dear ma, I'm in the cell, lonely as hell**[12] / Writin this scribe, thinkin bout how you must feel inside / **You tried to teach me better, but I refused to grow**[13] / Goddamn I ain't the young man that you used to know / You said the street claims lives, but I wanted things like / bling bling ice I was wrong in hindsight / Shit we grew apart, try to blame it on your new spouse / I know it hurt like hell the day you kicked me out / But your house is your house, I ain't respect the rules / I brought crack past your door, beefed with rival crews / And who wants to be the mother of a son who sold drugs / Co-workers saw me on the corner slingin Larry Love / Meanwhile, you workin hard like, two or three jobs / Tryin to feed me and my siblings, makin an honest livin / Who am I kiddin I call myself easin the load / I made the load heavy, I need money for commissary / Try to under-stand, please / Let him hold you, let him touch you / Soon you'll un-der-stand

1. There's a lot of talk about misogyny in rap, and some of it is justified, but some of it misses the point. The world hip-hop describes is full of extremes and exaggerations, sometimes to make a dramatic point, sometimes to tell a more vivid story, sometimes for comic effect. It's the nature of storytelling, especially if it's done in verse, to use more dramatic language and bigger gestures than real life, and to focus on moments of extremity. But those extremes and exaggerations look ridiculous unless there's a core of truth. Songs like "Can I Get A . . ." where the chorus has me chanting *can I get a fuck you, from all of my niggas who don't love hoes / they get no dough,* is partially a comic exaggeration and partially reflective of reality. This is a slice of the world of male-female relationships: Niggas who want to fuck without paying, bitches who want to get paid and then fuck (maybe). This isn't the one and only way relationships work, but in the world I was in, I saw it. A lot. But in other songs, ranging from "Song Cry" to "Ain't No Nigga," I try paint other pictures, to show the complexities and nuances of relationships.

2. This is a conversation between a man and woman, obviously, but more specifically, it's a player trying to talk a friend out of turning their friendship romantic. The tricky thing is that if you take a female friend and add a sexual relationship, you have to be ready to ruin the friendship.

3. The girl is like a sister to him so the relationship is almost incestuous. When he says *this ain't right,* it's the rational, ethical part of him arguing with the part that just wants to hit it.

4. I gave her advice like a big brother who knows how careful you have to be around certain types of guys, which I know about because I'm one of them.

5. These details let you know that this is a "good" girl, someone who has potential outside of the Life.

6. I used the name Gina because of Gina Montana, a character in the movie *Scarface.* Gina was a good girl who was ruined by her closeness to the criminal underworld. Specifically, her big mistake was getting involved with Manny, the best friend of her brother, which mirrors the situation I'm describing.

7. In *Scarface,* Tony eventually kills Manny when he discovers he's involved with his sister, so there's another pragmatic reason for avoiding this kind of complicated relationship. Still, it's hard to be careful when it comes to your heart and it hurts to know that you're not good enough or ready enough to do something you want to do.

8. This is the song's second scenario. Trife meaning trifling, of course, and it comes through in all his justifications: I told you I wasn't ready, I don't have the patience, I want to do right.

9. "About 20 percent of men and 15 percent of women under 35 say they have ever been unfaithful." —*The New York Times,* October 27, 2008.

10. This is the big complication in so many relationships between young people. Cheating and broken hearts are just part of life when you're young, but when there's another life involved, the stakes are higher and things become so much more complicated and painful.

11. Now here's another nuance. There's two ways of looking at this line: One is to say that the speaker in this verse has real clarity about his own shortcomings and enough integrity that he's willing to give up the woman he loves in order to protect her. It's a situation that he could easily take advantage of—and lots of cats do—to have a wife at home who loves him and raises his child, while also having a "different girl every night." Or you can see this as a cop-out, a man who doesn't bother controlling his own lusts and then pulls a "it's not you, it's me" line to get out of a solemn commitment, a commitment that now includes a child. Maybe both are true.

12. The last verse is a letter from a prison cell from a kid to his moms.

13. This is the kind of insight people normally don't get until they've fucked up for good. It's so important that kids can at least get out of adolescence without ruining their lives, because it's not till you get older that you start to see the wisdom in what your mother tried to teach you. Before that, you ignore it until you do fuck up and the truth of it all comes crashing in, too late. Youth is wasted on the young, I guess.

INSTANT KARMA

BEACH CHAIR
Featuring Chris Martin
(Kingdom Come, 2006)

LUCIFER
(The Black Album, 2003)

My grandfather was a pastor—an Elder, they called them—in the Church of God in Christ, a Pentecostal denomination. He had the same name as my father, Adnis Reeves, so they called my father AJ, for Adnis Junior. My grandmother Ruby was a deaconess in the same church. My father came from a strict, religious household, but sanctified churches are rooted in African traditions, so music, especially drumming—even if it's only drumming by clapping your hands together—played a big part of the service. Worship is never a quiet thing in the Church of God in Christ congregation, people passing out, speaking in tongues, or tarrying for hours until they become possessed with the Holy Ghost and the church mothers, dressed in nurse's uniforms, come and revive them.

My father's parents were strict. Secular music like the Motown sound was forbidden in AJ's house, but he snuck and listened anyway. The whole family had to be in church all the time, like four, five days a week. His three sisters couldn't wear makeup or pants, and his two brothers spent most of the week in church, too.

Church wasn't a major part of my life growing up, as it had been for my father—soul in our house usually referred to the music. But when you grow up in a place like Bed-Stuy, church is everywhere. So is mosque. So are a thousand other ways of believing. Street corners were where all these different beliefs met—Pentecostals arguing scripture with Jehovah's Witnesses, clean-cut brothers in bow ties and dark suits brushing past cats wearing fezzes and long beards, someone with a bullhorn or a mic and an amplifier booming out a sermon. We were all just living life, trying to get through, survive, thrive, whatever, but in the back of our minds, there was always a larger plan that we tried to make sense of. I was always fascinated by religion and curious about people's different ideas. And like everyone, I've always wanted answers to the basic questions. Still, by the time I reached my teens, the only time I'd be anywhere near a church was when someone I knew died, and even then I wouldn't necessarily go in. But I wasn't looking for church, anyway; I was looking for an explanation.

YOU AIN'T GOTTA GO TO CHURCH TO GET TO KNOW YO GOD

I think for some people life is always like those street corners in Brooklyn, with everyone arguing for the superiority of their own beliefs. I believe that religion is the thing that separates and controls people. I don't believe in the fire-and-brimstone shit, the idea that God will punish people for eternity in a burning hell. I believe in one God. That's the thing that makes the most sense to me. There's wisdom in all kinds of religious traditions—I'll take from Christianity, Islam, Judaism, Buddhism, whatever. The parts that make the most sense feel like they're coming from the same voice, the same God. Most of all, I don't think what I believe should matter to anyone else; I'm not trying to stop anyone from believing whatever they want. I believe in God, and that's really enough for me.

I don't spend a lot of time on records talking about spiritual ideas in an explicit way, although I think a lot of my music sneaks in those big questions—of good and evil, fate and destiny, suffering and inequality. I think about life mostly in pragmatic terms: I think about behavior and intention in the here and now. But I also think about Karma. It's a complicated idea that I've tried to make sense of. At the heart of a lot of these competing ideas of the afterlife and heaven and hell and thug angels and all that is the idea that if the universe is just, things have to even out eventually, somehow. And sometimes that's a scary thought.

I've done things I know are wrong. There are times when I feel like I've suffered for those things, that I've paid back for my mistakes in spades. But then there are times when I look around me, at the life I have today, and think I'm getting away with murder. It's something a lot of us who come from hard places go through, and maybe we feel a certain amount of survivor's guilt for it. I never imagined I'd be where I am today. There's a line in *Fade to Black,* the concert film we did for *The Black Album,* where I say, "I sometimes step back and see myself from the outside and say, who is that guy?" Over time I've worked to get more clarity about my past and present and to unify my outside shell and soul, but it's ongoing. Inside, there's still part of me that expects to wake up tomorrow in my bedroom in apartment 5C in Marcy, slide on my gear, run down the pissy stairway, and hit the block, one eye over my shoulder.

SENSITIVE THUGS, YOU'LL ALL NEED HUGS

Sometimes this uneasiness comes out in my songwriting. I was on vacation when I started writing "Beach Chair." This was after my semiretirement with *The Black Album* and I was really trying to sit back for the first time in my life and get off the grind for a minute. My vacation of choice—even back before I got into music—has always involved water and warmth. I wanted to write a song that matched my mood, a song about the good life. But almost immediately, the song went left. It begins with the line *"Life is but a dream to me"* but turns into a meditation on ambition and the laws of the universe, on questions I can still only ask but not fully answer.

It's a song that I think of as one of the hidden jewels in my catalog. Some people absolutely love the song, but other people find it confusing and out of character. But just as I tried to do something a little different on my first album—get deep inside the conflicted mind of the hustler—I'm still trying to push hip-hop into new places. In the song "Regrets," off my first album, there's a line addressed to my mother—*you used to hold me, tell me that I was the best*—that can almost be taken as soft. But what, niggas are supposed to be so hard that their mothers never held them? It's kind of ridiculous. In "Streets Is Talking," off of the Dynasty album, in the middle of a pretty hardcore song I threw out a line about my father leaving me—*I ain't mad at you dad, holla at your lad*—which might seem odd, because shouldn't I just be saying, Fuck you, dad, I hope you die, instead of opening myself up to be played by the man who abandoned me? But that feeling was real; I couldn't deny it. Honest introspection has always been one of the tools I use in my rhymes. Songs like "Beach Chair" are just an evolution of that same technique applied to broader questions, the kind of questions that even the grimiest street cat wakes up wondering about at three in the morning.

I think for hip-hop to grow to its potential and stay relevant for another generation we have to keep pushing deeper and deeper into the biggest subjects and doing it with real honesty. The truth is always relevant.

BEACH CHAIR / FEATURING CHRIS MARTIN

Life is but a dream to me[1] / I don't wanna wake up / Thirty odd years without having my cake up / So I'm about my paper / **24-7, 365, 366 in a leap year**[2] / **I don't know why we here**[3] / Since we gotta be here / Life is but a beach chair / Went from having shabby clothes / **Crossing over Abbey Road**[4] / Hear my angels singing to me / **Are you happy HOV?**[5] / **I just hope I'm hearing right**[6] / Karma's got me fearing life / **Colleek are you praying for me**[7] / See I got demons in my past / So I got daughters on the way / If the prophecy's correct / **Then the child should have to pay**[8] / For the sins of a father / So I barter my tomorrows / Against my yesterdays / **In hopes that she'll be OK**[9] / And when I'm no longer here / To shade her face from the glare / **I'll give her my share of Carol's Daughter**[10] / and a new beach chair / Life is but a dream to me / Gun shots sing to these / Other guys but lullabies / **Don't mean a thing to me**[11] / I'm not afraid of dying / I'm afraid of not trying / Everyday hit every wave / Like I'm Hawaiian / I don't surf the net / No I never been on MySpace / Too busy letting my voice vibrate / **Carving out my space**[12] / In this world of fly girls / Cutthroats & diamond cut ropes I twirls / Benzes round corners / Where the sun don't shine /

1. This song is written like a will to an unborn child in anticipation of the day when I wake up from the dream of life.

2. What's clear here is that being "about my paper" is not me being all about money, but being all about the drive for success, 24-7, every day of the year. That drive is what got me where I am and in some ways is who I am. So already I'm sort of contradicting—or at least complicating—the idea that "life is but a beach chair."

3. On my first single, "In My Lifetime," the hook was *What's the meaning of life?* In the video I make a toast that gives some idea of what I was thinking back then: "May your glasses stay full of champagne, your pockets full of money; this world is full of shit."

4. I had recently been in London, where Abbey Road, famous from the Beatles album of the same name, is. But the real point here is the movement from the projects to walking the most famous streets in the world.

5. When you get the things you think you've always wanted, it doesn't stop the voice in your head's interrogation. If anything, it gets more insistent.

6. This is probably something everyone feels at some point. If the things that we feel are true—about the way the universe and God work—then we're good. But what if I'm going about it totally wrong? What if there's some price to pay that I haven't calculated?

7. Colleek is my nephew, who died in a car crash when he was eighteen—the car he was driving was a graduation gift I'd bought for him. It was one of the most devastating events in my life—my nephews are like sons to me—and in some ways I blamed myself. (I described that situation in the song "Lost One" on this same album.)

8. This is a familiar saying and something that's worked its way into a lot of religious traditions: the idea that our children pay for our sins. It's a frightening idea—we make most of our mistakes when we're still nearly children ourselves, before we've even fully figured out right and wrong, much less considered the effect of our behavior on lives that haven't even been born yet. I don't believe it's true. It's enough that we pay for our own mistakes. But who really knows?

9. This is me trying to make a deal with the universe: I'm hoping that if I live right through all my tomorrows it will pay for the fucked-up shit I did yesterday, so that she—the daughter I'm imagining—won't have to live in the shadow of my sins.

10. Carol's Daughter is a company that makes skin-care products ("to shade her face") but is also a company I invested in, which is a way of saying that I'll leave her whatever she needs, materially or spiritually, to protect her from the harshness of life.

11. In the projects, especially back in the eighties, things were so violent that you literally went to sleep to the sound of gunshots some nights. You grow up fast like that. The second meaning here is that Karma catches up to other guys—in the form of gunshots putting them to sleep—but not me, at least not so far. And I'm not going to let fear of death slow me down.

12. It's always been most important for me to figure out "my space" rather than trying to check out what everyone else is up to, minute by minute. Technology is making it easier to connect to other people, but maybe harder to keep connected to yourself—and that's essential for any artist, I think.

I let the wheels give a glimpse / **Of hope of one's grind**[13] / Some said HOV, how you get so fly / **I said from not being afraid to fall out the sky**[14] / My physical's a shell / So when I say farewell / My soul will find an even / Higher plane to dwell / So fly you shall / **So have no fear,**[15] just know that / Life is but a beach chair / Life is but a dream / Can't mimic my life / I'm the thinnest cut slice / Intercut, the winner's cup / With winters rough enough / **To interrupt life**[16] / That's why I'm both / The saint and the sinner / Nice / **This is Jay everyday**[17] / No compromise / No compass comes with this life / Just eyes / So to map it out / You must look inside / Sure books can guide you / **But your heart defines you**[18] / Chica / You corason is what brought us home / In great shape like Heidi Klum / Maricon, I am on / Permanent Vaca / Life is but a beach chair / This song is like a Hallmark card / Until you reach here / So till she's here / And she declared / The heir / I will prepare / A blueprint for you to print / A map for you to get back / A guide for your eyes / And so you won't lose scent / I'll make a stink for you to think / I ink these verses full of prose / **So you won't get conned out of two cent**[19] / My last will and testament I leave my heir / My share of Roc-A-Fella Records and a shiny new beach chair

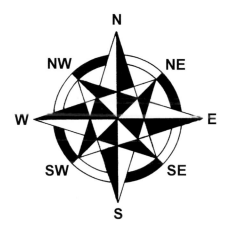

13. This is how it feels when you're in the hood hanging out and then a Benz rounds the corner. You see the dude in the Benz and you feel a surge of something, maybe hope. The guy who hops out of the Benz is familiar—a normal guy, like you, in some ways—but he got out of that tight situation you're still in. Where I'm from, that guy in the shining Benz was almost always a hustler, not a doctor or a lawyer or an engineer. Seeing that level of success is powerful. The image tells a dramatic story and drew a lot of us into lives of crime. But the good thing about it is it also gave us all a kind of hunger for success that motivated us to do *something* more than just hold down the project benches.

14. There's a double entendre here, but there's more, too: In Greek mythology, a character named Icarus and his father, Daedalus, tried to escape from their imprisonment. Daedalus built two pairs of wax wings for himself and his son so they could fly to freedom. Before they took off, he warned his son not to fly too close to the sun. But once Icarus got in the air, he forgot all about that and kept soaring higher and higher. He got too close to the sun, and his wax wings melted. He kept flapping his arms, but without wings he crashed into the sea, where he drowned. It's a great story, but sometimes we have to ignore the lesson of it, especially those of us who come from backgrounds where there's always someone telling you to quit or to keep a low profile. We can't be afraid to fly—or to be fly—which means soaring not just past our fear of failure but also past our fear of success.

15. This is why we shouldn't be afraid. There are two possibilities: One is that there's more to life than the physical life, that our souls "will find an even higher place to dwell" when this life is over. If that's true, there's no reason to fear failure or death. The other possibility is that this life is all there is. And if that's true, then we have to really live it—we have to take it for everything it has and "die enormous" instead of "living dormant," as I said way back on "Can I Live." Either way, fear is a waste of time.

16. In a way this captures the theme of my entire catalog—moments of triumph and success, the "winner's cup," intercut with dark, cold days, "winters" so severe they threatened my life.

17. This was also the chorus and last line of "Never Change" from *The Blueprint* album, whose opening lines capture the same sentiment—*Hov summer or winter, Hov dead or alive.*

18. This takes us back to one of the recurring questions I've been trying to figure out in my songs: How can we know what's right, what's wrong? You're born into this world in a random way. There are no guides. So much depends on where you're born and who your influences are. It's like in the song "Regrets" where the young kid is *in search of higher learning turning in every direction seeking direction* but doesn't find any. People give you books—the Bible, the Qu'ran—but they don't define you. All of the directional language in this verse: *compass, map, look, guide,* in the end point the listener inside, toward their own hearts.

19. A series of wordplays—*pro's* and *prose*; *cents* and *scents*—bring the song to its finish. Even though I've just said that it's your heart that defines you, I'm still trying to give this unborn child something more than that: a blueprint for life. A map, a guide, a scent to follow.

LUCIFER

Lucifer, son of the morning! / **I'm gonna chase you out of Earth** / **Lucifer, Lucifer, son of the morn-ing . . .**[1] / (I'm from the murder capital, where we murder for capital) / Lucifer, Lucifer, son of the morning! / I'm gonna chase you out of Earth / (Kanyeeze you did it again, you're a genius nigga!) / Lucifer, Lucifer, son of the morning . . . / So you niggas change your attitude / 'Fore they asking what happened to you / **Lord forgive him** / **He got them dark forces in him** / **But he also got a righteous cause for sinning**[2] / **Them a murder me so I gotta murder them first**[3] / Emergency doctors performing procedures / Jesus / I ain't trying to be facetious / **But "Vengeance is mine" said the Lord /** **You said it better than all**[4] / Leave niggas on death's door / Breathing off respirators / **for killing my best boy,**[5] haters / On permanent hiatus as I skate / In the Maybach Benz / **Flyer than Sanaa Lathan** / **Pumping "Brown Sugar" by D'Angelo**[6]**/ in Los Angeles.**[7] Like an **evangelist**[8] / I can introduce you to your maker / **Bring you closer to nature** / **Ashes after they cremate you**[9] bastards / Hope you been reading your psalms and chapters / **Paying your tithes being good Catholics**[10] / **I'm coming**[11] / Yes / This is holy war / **I wet you all with the holy water** / **spray from the Heckler Koch auto-** / **matic all the static shall cease to exist** / **Like a sabbatical I throw a couple at you** / **Take six** / **Spread love**[12] to all of my dead thugs / I'll pour out a little Louis 'til I head above / Yes Sir /

1. Kanye brought me this amazing track. The hook— *I'm gonna chase you out of earth / Lucifer, Lucifer, son of the morning*— comes from a classic roots-reggae joint from Max Romeo called "I Chase the Devil." Lucifer is a figure in the Old Testament book of Isaiah: "How art thou fallen, O Lucifer, son of the morning!" Interestingly, he's never directly identified as the devil in the Bible, just a fallen angel. I don't believe in the devil myself, or at least not in the guy with horns and a pitchfork. But I do believe we all have the potential for evil inside of us, which is very real.

2. This is another conversation with God, which is, as always, also a conversation with myself, trying to make some kind of ethical sense of my own choices.

3. If there is a justification for murder, it's that your own life is threatened. It seems obvious, but it raises questions: When can you be sure that the only way out is preemptive murder? Is violence the only way to prevent violence? Is murder ever a good answer? Even if you save your life, what about your soul?

4. I'm repeating the Lord's own words to him because he "said it better than all": If he can allow himself to take vengeance, then why can't I?

5. The "best boy" I'm referring to here is Biggie. This is actually a song about his death and the way it destroyed my sense of a just universe. Here's the thing about Big: when you got past all the grotesqueries in his lyrics, all the Richard Pryor comic exaggera- tions, he was one of the most decent, peaceful guys I knew. One night back in '96, maybe, we were hanging out together at Daddy's House, the studio that Bad Boy Records owned, and I played him "Streets Is Watching," a song I'd just finished for my second album. He played it twenty times in a row and gave me a sideways look: "Is the whole album going to sound like this?" He loved me, but at the end of the day, we're all MCs, all competing. He was mad that the song was so good, but happy for me at the same time. He had already started work on his own second album—he played "Hypnotize," "Downfall," and a few other songs for me that night. I was mad but happy, too. Anyway, we left the studio and had dinner with a couple of friends—Ty-Ty and D-Rock—and then we headed out to a club, maybe Mirage or Exit or Carbon, one of the hot clubs at the time in Manhattan. We pulled up to the club and saw some niggas out front who we knew had some problems with Big, crazy guys, the kind who would be happy to shoot up the club just to settle some tired beef or just for the fuck of it or to improve their reputation. Big looked at me and told me straight up: "I'm not going in there." I was young and dumb, and my ego wouldn't let me drive away. I thought Big was scared. I told Ty-Ty, *Fuck it, we're going in.* And we did. But Big wasn't playing. He pulled right away from that club and went the fuck home. He wasn't scared; he just didn't want to waste his time with that kind of bullshit. He had bigger goals and wasn't going to get derailed on some silly shit. He had started on the streets but developed greater insight and clarity about the futility and wastefulness of that kind of petty violence. For someone like that to get shot and killed the way he did tore me up. The whole Tupac beef was so pointless. Big just tried to avoid the whole thing. He never did anything wrong in that situation. His death was so senseless, so wrong, that it drove me crazy with rage and sadness.

6. *Brown Sugar* was a movie starring the fly Sanaa Lathan (and based in part on the life of my collaborator dream hampton, coincidentally).

7. I'm in Los Angeles because that's where Big was murdered.

8. Although *evangelist* shares a bar with and picks up the rhyme from *Los Angeles,* it's actually the beginning of the sentence that continues in the next bar, or after the line break when you read it in print. The sentence is: *Like an evangelist I can introduce you to your maker.* But when you hear it it sounds like *In Los Angeles, like an evangelist.* But what could that possibly mean? It plants something strange in the middle of the song and adds weight to those words *Los Angeles* and *evangelist,* even if they're out of context. I like playing with the line breaks like that to create strange lyrical effects.

9. Being reduced to ashes brings you "closer to nature" by returning you to the dust, which is also another indirect biblical echo.

10. They need to hope their debts are paid up and they're all square with whatever god they worship, because it's over. I've played a lot with the language of the threat in my songs— I even have a whole song called "Threats"—but in this song, there's something more sinister about the threat, something more serious, which is partially conveyed by the use of biblical and religious imagery.

11. The "I'm coming" is another near-religious phrase. It implies that I'm not just plotting and planning to get you and you can maybe plot and plan to escape. This is serious. You killed my nigga. I'm coming like a force of nature, or even something supernatural, something you can't oppose or prevent, because my cause is righteous and my intent is pure. All you can do is make sure your casket's picked out and you've gotten right with God because death is inevitable. It's a dark sentiment, but that's how revenge can feel, like it's so right and just can't be stopped. It's the perfect feeling for this song.

12. The lines here are staggered and the references come in a fusillade. The bullets in the Koch automatic spray, and the holy water you get wet with is your own blood. A sabbatical is one way to refer to taking a break, so is "taking six"—but the break I'm talking about is permanent: you'll "cease to exist." Take Six is also the name of an a cappella gospel group—another religious reference—whose big hit was "Spread Love." I used to freestyle over that song when I toured with Big Daddy Kane as a teenager, the a cappella rhythms they created with their voices were like a harmonic human beat box.

And when I perish / The meek shall inherit the earth / Until that time it's on a poppin, **Church!** / **Like Don Bishop**[13] / the fifth upon cock either / Lift up your soul or give you the holy ghost please / **I leave ya in somebody's Cathedral**[14] / For stunting like Evel Knievel / I'll let you see where that bright light lead you / The more you talk the more you irking us / The more you gonna need memorial services / *The Black Album*'s **second verse is like devil's pie please save some dessert for us**[15] / Man I gotta get my soul right / I gotta get these devils out my life / These cowards gonna make a nigga ride / They won't be happy 'til somebody dies / Man I gotta get my soul right / 'Fore I'm locked up for my whole life / Every time it seems it's all right / Somebody want they soul to rise / (I'll chase you off of this Earth) / I got dreams of holding a nine milla / **To Bob's killer**[16] / Asking him "Why?" as my eyes fill up / **These days I can't wake up with a dry pillow**[17] / Gone but not forgotten homes I still feel ya / So . . . curse the day that birthed the bastard / Who caused your Church mass / **Reverse the crash**[18] / **Reverse the blast** / **And reverse the car** / **Reverse the day, and there you are**[19] / Bobalob / **Lord forgive him we all have sinned**[20] / But Bob's a good dude please let him in / And if you feel in my heart that **I long for revenge**[21] / **Please blame it on the son of the morning**[22] / **Thanks again**[23]

13. Another staggered line. The previous line's emphatic *church* ties to this line's reference to Don Bishop, the pimp/pastor whose catchphrase is *chuuuurch!*

14. At your funeral, of course.

15. This connects back to the first line in the verse where I mention "Brown Sugar" by D'Angelo; "Devil's Pie" was another song by D'Angelo from his *Voodoo* album. That song starts off *fuck the slice want the pie / why ask why till we fry*. This verse is like a Devil's Pie, a complete indulgence in evil thoughts.

16. I'm now talking about Biggs's brother, Bobalob. We called him that because of his ball skills. He could jump really high so they threw him an alley oop or lob passes a lot.

17. This last verse is more autobiographical. I'm no longer the killing machine of the first two verses, now I'm just someone suffering through the loss of a friend, dreaming of revenge but waking up with just sadness.

18. Bob was driving a car in the Bronx when he was shot—the car crashed after the bullets connected.

19. This series of reverses is a more honest account about how I'm thinking about the deaths of these two friends. Revenge as a fantasy feels glorious in a dark way, but doesn't solve the real problem, which is that they're gone. The only thing that would bring them back is this impossible prayer to reverse time.

20. Just as I started the song with a prayer—*Lord forgive him*—I'm ending it with one. The first prayer asks for forgiveness for an act of murder; the last asks God to forgive the victim of a murder and make a way for him through the proverbial pearly gates of the afterlife.

21. I believe that intentions are a form of reality. Even having that idea of murderous revenge in your heart is dangerous.

22. Why do people trip over into the dark side, into murder and vengeance? It's not the "Devil." It could stem from all kinds of things: abandonment, deprivation, the loss of a loved one. All those things can make you question your faith in the universe or in the idea of a just God. But that evil inside is something we all have to find a way to deal with, or it'll take us over.

23. Some people have used this song as evidence that I worship the devil, which is another chapter for the big book of stupid. It's really just laughable. But the sad part is that it's not even remotely a song about devil worship! It's a song about the intersection of some basic human emotions, the place where sadness meets rage, where our need to mourn meets our lust for justice, where our faith meets our inclination to take matters into our own hands, like karmic vigilantes. People who hear the word *Lucifer* and start making accusations are just robbing themselves of an opportunity to get in touch with something deeper than that, something inside their own souls.

DECEMBER 4TH
(The Black Album, 2003)

HISTORY
Featuring Cee-Lo
(Unreleased)

When I made my first album, it was my intention to make it my last. I threw everything I had into *Reasonable Doubt,* but then the plan was to move in to the corner office and run our label. I didn't do that. So instead of being a definitive statement that would end with the sound of me dropping the mic forever, it was just the beginning of something. That something was the creation of the character Jay-Z.

Rappers refer to themselves a lot. What the rapper is doing is creating a character that, if you're lucky, you find out about more and more from song to song. The rapper's character is essentially a conceit, a first-person literary creation. The core of that character has to match the core of the rapper himself. But then that core gets amplified by the rapper's creativity and imagination. You can be anybody in the booth. It's like wearing a mask. It's an amazing freedom but also a temptation. The temptation is to go too far, to pretend the mask is real and try to convince people that you're something that you're not. The best rappers use their imaginations to take their own core stories and emotions and feed them to characters who can be even more dramatic or epic or provocative. And whether it's in a movie or a television show or whatever, the best characters get inside of us. We care about them. We love them or hate them. And we start to see ourselves in them—in a crazy way, become them.

SCARFACE THE MOVIE DID MORE THAN SCARFACE THE RAPPER TO ME

In hip-hop, there's practically a cult built up around the 1983 remake of *Scarface,* the one starring Al Pacino. Lines from that movie are scattered all over hip-hop, including my own songs:

All I got is my balls and my word.
The world is yours.
I always tell the truth, even when I lie.
Don't get high on your own supply.
You fuck with me, you're fuckin with the best!
Say goodnight to the bad guy.
Okay! I'm reloaded!
You gotta get the money first. When you get the money, you get the power.
When you get the power, you get the women.
Who do I trust? Me, that's who!
and of course
Say hello to my little friend!

So many people saw their story in that movie. No one literally looked in the mirror and saw Tony Montana staring back at them. I hope. But there are people who feel Tony's emotions as if they were their own, feel the words he speaks like they're coming out of their own mouths.

I've always found this a little strange because—I hope I'm not giving anything away here—at the end of the movie, Tony gets shot. He's wasted. His life is in ruins. His family is destroyed. It's funny that so many people use the phrase "the world is yours" as a statement of triumph, when in the movie the last time the words occur, they're underneath Tony's bloody body in a fountain. But that's not what people identify with. It seems like the movie ends in some people's memory about two-thirds of the way through, before it all goes to shit for Tony. And for those two-thirds of the movie, they are Tony. And after the movie, Tony is still alive in them as an inspiration—and maybe a cautionary tale, too, like, Yeah, I'll be like Tony but not make the same mistakes. The viewer inhabits the character while the movie runs, but when it's over, the character lives on in the viewer. So instead of passing judgment on Tony, you make a complete empathetic connection to the good and bad in him; you feel a sense of ownership over his character and behavior. That's how it works with great characters.

HOW YOU RATE MUSIC THAT THUGS WITH NOTHIN RELATE TO IT?

People connect the same way to the character Jay-Z. Like I said, rappers refer to themselves a lot in their music, but it's not strictly because rappers are immodest. Part of it is about boasting—that's a big part of what rap is traditionally about. But a lot of the self-reference has nothing to do with bragging or boasting. Rappers are just crafting a character that the listener can relate to. Not every rapper bothers with creating a big first-person character. Chuck D, a great MC, never really makes himself into a larger-than-life character because his focus is on analyzing the larger world from an almost objective, argumentative point of view, even when he's speaking in a first-person voice. You rarely *become* Chuck D when you're listening to Public Enemy; it's more like watching a really, really lively speech. On the other hand, you have MCs like DMX for whom everything comes from a subjective, personal place. When he growls out a line like *on parole with warrants that'll send me back the raw way* the person rapping along to it in their car is completely living the lyrics, like it's happening to them. They relate.

When Lauryn Hill came out with *The Miseducation of Lauryn Hill,* for a while it was the only thing I listened to. Lauryn is a very different person

from me, of course, but I felt her lyrics like they were mine. She was also one of the few contemporary female MCs I could even rap along to in my car. I love Lil' Kim, but I'd be a little nervous pulling up to a light and having someone see me rapping along to "Queen Bitch." Lauryn's lyrics transcended the specifics of gender and personal biography, which is why she connected to so many people with that album. All kinds of people could find themselves in those songs and in the character she created.

MY CORPORATE THUGS BE LIKE, YEAH JIGGA TALK THAT SHIT

There's a funny Dave Chappelle bit, one of his "When Keeping It Real Goes Wrong" sketches. Chappelle plays a young black guy named Vernon who works as a vice president at a major corporation. At the end of a meeting, a bald white colleague tells him, "Vernon, you da man," and the Chappelle character snaps. He stands up and gets in the dude's face. *"Allow me to reintroduce myself. My name is Hov!"* He ends up working at a gas station. It's funny, but the truth is I do hear about guys in corporate offices who psych themselves up listening to my music, which sounds odd at first, but makes sense. My friend Steve Stoute, who spends a lot of time in the corporate world, tells me about young execs he knows who say they discovered their own philosophies of business and life in my lyrics. It's crazy. But when people hear me telling my stories, or boasting in my songs, or whatever, they don't hear some rapper telling them how much better than them he is. They hear it as their own voice. It taps in to the part of them that needs every now and then to say, Fuck it, allow me to reintroduce myself, nigga. And when I'm really talking shit, like in this piece from the song "Threats" off *The Black Album*—

Put that knife in ya, take a little bit of life from ya
Am I frightenin ya? Shall I continue?
I put the gun to ya, I let it sing you a song
I let it hum to ya, the other one sing along
Now it's a duet, and you wet, when you check out
the technique from the 2 tecs and I don't need two lips
To blow this like a trumpet you dumb shit

I don't think any listeners think I'm threatening them. I think they're singing along with me, threatening someone else. They're thinking, *Yeah, I'm coming for you.* And they might apply it to anything, to taking their next math test or straightening out that chick talking outta pocket in the next cubicle. When it seems like I'm bragging or threatening or whatever, what I'm actually trying to do is to embody a certain spirit, give voice to a certain emotion. I'm giving the listener a way to articulate that emotion in their own lives, however it applies. Even when I do a song that feels like a complete autobiography, like "December 4th," I'm still trying to speak to something that everyone can find in themselves.

I'LL TELL YOU HALF THE STORY, THE REST YOU FILL IT IN

Of course, *Reasonable Doubt* wasn't my only album. But as I was moving into my early thirties, I wanted to challenge myself in new ways. I was looking forward to building a label from the ground up, starting from scratch. Roc-A-Fella's deal with Def Jam was set to expire and I saw it as the perfect time to move on. When I announced plans to begin recording *The Black Album,* I said it would be my last for at least two years, and that story grew into rumors about retirement. I considered an all-out retirement out loud to the media, and that was a mistake even though I definitely gave the idea a lot of space in my head.

When I first started planning *The Black Album,* it was a concept album. I wanted to do what Prince had done, release an album of my most personal autobiographical tracks with absolutely no promotion. No cover art, no magazine ads, no commercials, nothing; one day the album would just appear on the shelves and the buzz would build organically.

Like my dream of *Reasonable Doubt* being my only album, that idea quickly evaporated. But I stuck to the idea of making the album more explicitly autobiographical than anything I'd done before. "December 4th," the song that opens the album, is itself a capsule autobiography. I took my mother out for her birthday and on the way to the restaurant I made her take a detour to Bassline and tell some stories about my life. These were stories that were already legend in my family; I'd heard them all a million times: My painless ten-pound birth. How I learned to ride a bike at a young age. The time she bought me a boom box because I loved rapping so much. The thing I love about these stories is that they're unique to me, of course, but they're also the sort of minor mythologies that every family has, the kind of stories that everyone hears from their parents and aunts and uncles, if they're lucky enough to have parents around. In the song I played that near-universal mother-love against the content of the verses, which was the story about how I went from a kid whose world was torn apart by his father's leaving to a young hustler in the streets who excelled but was scarred by the Life and eventually decided to *try this rap shit for a living.* The parts where my mother's voice comes in to the song are surrounded by swirling orchestral fanfare that make the little stories feel epic. And that's how it feels for everyone, I think, to hear our mothers proudly tell those little stories about what made us special over and over again.

My final show for *The Black Album* tour was at the Garden. Playing Madison Square Garden by myself had been a fantasy of mine since I was a kid watching Knicks games with my father in Marcy. I arrived and the sight of my name in lights on the marquee got me in the right frame of mind. I began to visualize the whole show from beginning to end; in my mind it was flawless. Security at the Garden was nuts; my own bodyguard couldn't even get in. Backstage I watched my peers come in one by one. Puff was there in a chinchilla. Foxy showed up wearing leather shorts. Slick Rick was there wearing his truck jewelry. Ghostface had on his bathrobe. I had asked Ahmir and the Roots band to join me for the few shows I did before the Garden so we could get the show in pocket, and that night he was extra nervous, but I told him to act like it's any other show. We both knew that was a lie. Michael Buffer, who announces all the boxing matches in the Garden, announced me, and I did my signature ad-libs. The crowd went bananas.

I started my set off with "What More Can I Say" and I ended the night with "December 4th," the song I named for my birthday. I ended the concert by "retiring" myself, sending a giant jersey with my name on it up to the rafters. As it was making its way to top of the Garden, I looked into the crowd and saw a girl in the audience crying, real tears streaming down her face. It was all I could do to stop looking at her and focus on the person next to her. My songs are my stories, but they take on their own life in the minds of people listening. The connection that creates is sometimes overwhelming.

[Jay-Z's mom] / *Shawn Carter was born December 4th* / *Weighing in at 10 pounds 8 ounces* / *He was the last of my four children* / *The only one who didn't give me any pain when I gave birth to him* / *And that's how I knew that he was a special child*[1] / [*Jay-Z*] / They say "they never really miss you till you **dead or you gone"**[2] / So on that note I'm leaving after the song / So you ain't gotta feel no way about Jay so long / At least let me tell you why I'm this way, Hold on / I was conceived by Gloria Carter and Adnis Reeves / Who made love under the sycamore tree / Which makes me / **A more sicker MC,**[3] my momma would claim / At 10 pounds when I was born I didn't give her no pain / Although through the years I gave her her fair share / I gave her her first real scare / **I made up for birth when I got here**[4] / **She knows my purpose wasn't purpose**[5] / I ain't perfect I care / But I feel worthless cause my shirts wasn't matchin my gear / Now I'm just scratchin the surface cause what's buried under there / **Was a kid torn apart once his pop disappeared**[6] / I went to school got good grades could behave when I wanted / But I had demons deep inside that would raise

1. My mother actually narrated these stories on the record. She's got a beautiful voice, like Maya Angelou or something.

2. It's like the line from the Joni Mitchell song "Big Yellow Taxi" (which Janet Jackson and Q-Tip sampled), *you don't know what you got till it's gone.*

3. A reference to Biggie's line in "You're Nobody (Til Somebody Kills You)": *My sycamore style, more sicker than yours.*

4. I didn't give her pain in childbirth, but I made up for it later. My mother didn't talk about it a lot, but she was scared for me when I really hit the streets. At the same time, she knew I had to figure some things out for myself.

5. My behavior was purposeful, but it was never my purpose to cause her pain.

6. I'm making the point here that poverty, as bad as it is, was one reason why I ended up hustling, but there were deeper reasons, demons that I had stemming from abandonment.

when confronted / Hold on / [*Jay-Z's mom*] *Shawn was a very shy child growing up / He was into sports / And a funny story is / At four he taught himself how to ride a bike / A two-wheeler at that / Isn't that special? / But I noticed a change in him when me and my husband broke up* / [*Jay-Z*] Now all the teachers couldn't reach me / And my momma couldn't beat me / **Hard enough to match the pain of my pop not seeing me,**[7] SO / **With that disdain in my membrane**[8] / Got on my pimp game / Fuck the world my defense came / Then DeHaven introduced me to the game / Spanish José introduced me to cane / I'm a hustler now / **My gear is in**[9] and I'm in the in crowd / And all the wavy light-skinned girls is lovin me now / **My self-esteem went through the roof man I got my swag**[10] / Got a Volvo from this girl when her man got bagged / Plus I hit my momma with cash from a show that I had / **Supposedly knowin nobody paid Jaz wack ass**[11] / I'm getting ahead of myself, by the way, I could rap / That came second to me moving this crack / Gimme a second I swear / **I will say about my rap career** / **Till '96**[12] came niggas I'm here / Goodbye / [*Jay-Z's mom*] *Shawn used to be in the kitchen / Beating on the table and rapping / And um, until the wee hours of the morning / And then I bought him a*

7. The sample that Just Blaze used for this track is a song from the Chi-Lites, a seventies soul group in my parents' collection. The sample includes an ad lib from that song: *What's wrong, you look like you lost your best friend, is it something that I've done again?*

8. This is a reference to "Insane in the Brain," by Cypress Hill.

9. Now the shit matches my shirt.

10. The money isn't just about money. It's about finding a sense of worth in the world—after you've been told you're worthless. Status—and self-esteem—are really what the money buys you.

11. I would hit my mother with cash and tell her I picked it up from shows I was doing—a transparent lie since Jaz and I weren't exactly raking in big money for performing back then.

12. Of course, '96 was the year *Reasonable Doubt* came out, and more importantly for this song, it was the year that my rapping stopped coming "second to me moving this crack."

boom box / And his sisters and brothers said that he would drive them nuts / But that was my way to keep him close to me and out of trouble / [*Jay-Z*] Goodbye to the game all the spoils, the adrenaline rush / **Your blood boils you in a spot knowing cops could rush**[13] / **And you in a drop you're so easy to touch**[14] / No two days are alike / **Except the first and fifteenth pretty much**[15] / And "trust" is a word you seldom hear from us / **Hustlers we don't sleep we rest one eye up**[16] / And a drought can define a man, when the well dries up / **You learn the worth of water without work you thirst till you die**[17] / YUP / And niggas get tied up for product / **And little brothers ring fingers get cut up**[18] / To show mothers they really got em / And this was the stress I live with till I decided / To try this rap shit for a livin / I pray I'm forgiven / For every bad decision I made / **Every sister I played**[19] / Cause I'm still paranoid to this day / And it's nobody fault I made the decisions I made / **This is the life I chose or rather the life that chose me**[20] / If you can't respect that your whole perspective is wack / Maybe you'll love me when I fade to black / If you can't respect that your whole perspective is wack / Maybe you'll love me when I fade to black

13. This is a song that strips all the glamour out of the drug game. The best thing I say about it is that it was a source of adrenaline and "spoils," which is a word with two opposite meanings, of course: Spoils can be a reward, but the word itself implies that the reward is tainted, spoiled, by what you have to do to get it.

14. A "drop" is a convertible, which makes you easy to touch.

15. The first and the fifteenth are the days when government checks went out, and the fiends would rush drug dealers to get fixed, blow their whole check on a weekend of smoke.

16. *I keep one eye open like C-B-S*—this is a line from "Can I Live?"

17. A drought is when your drug supply runs low. That's when you really find out who you are in the streets, because you have to figure out some way to survive it. It's also when things can get especially hectic and violent—in "Public Service Announcement," on the same album, I make the point: *I get my / by any means on / whenever there's a drought / get your umbrellas out / because that's when I brain storm.*

18. This is the sort of dramatic touch that you might see in a movie and think it's over the top, but this kind of thing really did happen, literally in the case of a famous gangster named Rich Porter. There was a high level of threat in the drug game, a high degree of ruthlessness and brutality, and, at its worst, it could reach this level, where your moms is getting your body parts in the mail.

19. I'm not talking strictly romantically here—I'm talking about all the women who were in the game with me, who transported drugs and money, opened towns, and made connects.

20. This line resolves one of the central contradictions in my thinking about my life. I always felt like I kept my eyes a little bit more wide open than other people around me did—not that I was smarter, but that I saw some things very clearly. I wasn't blind to the damage that I was causing myself and other people when I was in the game. I wasn't deluded about the fact that my motivations went beyond satisfying my basic material needs—that I also loved the excitement and the status of that life. I'll never say that, in the end, I got into the game because I wanted it; it was the *life I chose*. On the other hand, I chose it in part because I didn't have a lot of other choices. I was born into a community that this country was trying to make disappear; was born at a time when drugs and guns were everywhere and jobs and education were much harder to find. In that sense, it was a life that chose me, a life I never would've pursued if I'd been born in different circumstances. But ultimately, the point of this song is that I don't blame anyone, I'm just trying to explain myself, tell you why I'm this way. It's my story, and I'm willing to own it.

HISTORY[1] / FEATURING CEE-LO

Now that all the smoke is gone / (Lighter) / And the battle's finally won / (Gimme a lighter) / Victory (Lighters up) is finally ours / (Lighters up) / History so long so long / So long so long / **In search of Victory[2] she keeps eluding me[3]** / If only we could be together momentarily / **We can make love and make History[4]** / Why won't you visit me? until she visit me / I'll be stuck with her sister her name is Defeat / She gives me agony so much agony / She brings me so much pain so much misery / Like missing your last shot and falling to your knees / **As the crowd screams for the other team[5]** / I practice so hard for this moment Victory don't leave / I know what this means I'm stuck in this routine / **Whole new different day same old thing[6]** / All I got is dreams nobody else can see / **Nobody else believes nobody else but me[7]** / Where are you Victory? I need you desperately / Not just for the moment to make History / Now that all the smoke is gone / (Lighters) / And the battle's finally won / (Lighters) / Victory is finally ours / (Yeah) / History (yeah) so long so long / So long so long / So now I'm flirting with Death **hustling like a G[8]** / While Victory wasn't watching took chances repeatedly / As a teenage boy before acne before **I got proactive[9]** I couldn't face she / I just threw on my hoodie and headed to the street / That's where I met Success we'd live together shortly / **Now Success is like lust she's good to the touch[10]** / She's good for the moment but she's never enough / **Everybody's had her she's nothing like V[11]** / But Success is all I got unfortunately / But I'm burning down the block hoppin' in and out of V / But something tells me that there's much more to see / **Before I get killed because I can't get robbed[12]** / **So before me Success and Death ménage[13]** / I gotta get lost I gotta find V / We gotta be together to make History / Now that all the smoke is gone / (Lighters. Up.) / And the battle's finally won / (Lighters. Up.) / Victory is finally ours / (Lighters. Up.) / History so long so long / So long so long / Now Victory is mine it tastes so sweet / She's my trophy wife **you're coming with me[14]** / We'll have a baby who **stutters repeatedly[15]** / We'll name him History he'll repeat after me / He's my legacy son of my hard work / **Future of my past he'll explain who I be[16]** / Rank me amongst the greats either one two or three / If I ain't number one then I failed you Victory / Ain't in it for the fame that dies within weeks / Ain't in it for the money can't take it when you leave / I wanna be remembered long after you grieve / Long after I'm gone long after I breathe / **I leave all I am in the hands of History[17]** / **That's my last will and testimony[18]** / This is much more than a song it's a baby shower / **I've been waiting for this hour History[19]** you ours / Now that all the smoke is gone / And the battle's finally won / Victory is finally ours / History so long so long / So long so long

1. I wrote this song after President Obama won the 2008 presidential election and performed it at one of the inaugural balls. It's a song like "I Know" and some other songs I've done, in that it's a sustained metaphor that I never break. It's a song that talks about victory and success and history in the largest, communal sense, but it does it, like most of my songs, through metaphors and deeply personal storytelling. It's a song that came out of the same ambition I had when I started: to use the specific stories of my life and the world I grew up in to tell the broadest story possible about what it means to be alive.

2. This is a song that metaphorically turns the concepts of Victory, Defeat, Death, Success, and History into personalities—the first four are women, the last an unborn child.

3. The song is autobiographical: Victory for me was being an artist, making my living as a rapper. But it was elusive: for years I couldn't get a record deal.

4. In the metaphor, if I made love with Victory, the woman, we'd make History, the child; in real life, if I could become an artist, I'd have a chance to leave behind a legacy.

5. Here, Defeat, my mistress, is the most painful kind of failure, the near miss. That's why Defeat is Victory's sister, they're close to each other, but also entirely different. That's how it felt to me—I felt so close to my dream, but fell just short.

6. I was already in the routine: I was working hard for Victory and when I failed, I had to find the strength to start the pursuit again.

7. At the end of the first verse, I'm living with Defeat, which meant I was still hustling in the streets. I didn't talk to other people about my dreams, I kept them to myself. But that didn't make me any less desperate for them to come true.

8. I've taken another step away, beyond Defeat, Victory's sister. Now I'm just like *fuck it,* living like a G, flirting with my new girl, Death.

9. A double-entendre: I was proactive, "headed to the street,"; but like a kid with acne who needs Proactiv, the skin medication, I couldn't face my old girl, Victory. So the line combines the boldness of a kid taking his fate into his hands, with the sense of shame that same kid has—"I couldn't face she"—for turning his back on his true dream.

10. Another new relationship enters: Success. This is what happens after the kid starts hustling. He finds "success," money, girls, a reputation, a nice car. But it's a cheap relationship and he knows it.

11. The two references to "V" point to the two competing ideas of happiness: one is about Victory, a prize that no one else has touched; the other is about having enough money to get a V, a car that I could afford from "burning down the block."

12. Way back when I recorded "Streets Is Watching" I first made the point that if you let yourself get robbed, you're as good as dead—when people see you're soft, they're coming in for the kill anyway.

13. Success—meaning winning on the block as a hustler—and Death and me are like three lovers.

14. Once I achieved the life of an artist, I never let it go.

15. The "stutter" is the baby, History, repeating itself. Victory is not just a matter of coming out with one hit, it's about trying to build a true legacy.

16. The body of work you create is like the future of your past—it's the thing that tells people who you were, even after you're gone.

17. This is something we all think about sometimes. How will we be remembered? In this song, I'm talking about creating a legacy that will speak for me after I'm gone, that will tell my story after I'm dead.

18. My last will and testimony is the work I've done. It's imperfect, but there's no truer statement of who I am. The reason this book is ultimately about my lyrics, instead of being a typical autobiography, is that my creative work is my truest legacy, for better or worse.

19. This song, at its most basic, is about a hustler becoming a rapper. But I performed it at President Obama's inauguration, and it worked there, too. Beyond the specifics of my story, it's about a desire to get past defeat, to even get past the kind of success that leaves you feeling empty. It's about not compromising your ultimate ambition, no matter how distant the dream might seem. Electing a black man named Barack Obama president in the same country that elected George W. Bush—twice!—is as far-fetched as a hustler from Marcy performing at that president's inauguration. But it happened.

EPILOGUE

I was over at L.A. Reid's house in New York for a dinner party a couple of years ago when I first met Oprah Winfrey. I've met a lot of powerful people, but Oprah, as everyone knows, is in her own stratosphere. She's also some-one who's been vocally skeptical about hip-hop for a long time because of the violence and rawness of a lot of the imagery and language, particularly the use of what she'd call the "n-word." It's ironic that she's also been a champion of other kinds of writing—from poets like Maya Angelou to novelists like Toni Morrison—that also use violent and raw images and language (includ-ing the dreaded n-word!) to get at true emotions and experiences. But for her, rap was different, and dangerous, in a way that other forms of art weren't.

Oprah and I ended up talking for a while at that dinner. Somehow, it came up that I'd read *The Seat of the Soul*, a book that really affected the way I think about life—the book is about Karma and what it means to do the right thing and the power of intention. It turns out that the author, Gary Zukav, had been a guest on Oprah's show on multiple occasions, and Oprah expressed surprise that I was also a fan of his work. She didn't expect that of a rapper. I could tell that the way she saw me shifted in that moment; I wasn't exactly who she thought I was.

Oprah and I have since gone on to become friendly acquaintances, after having only observed each other warily from a distance. But it was a fasci-nating moment to me. Rap, as I said at the beginning of the book, is at heart an art form that gave voice to a specific experience, but, like every art, is ultimately about the most common human experiences: joy, pain, fear, desire, uncertainty, hope, anger, love—love of crew, love of family, even romantic love (put on "The Miseducation of Lauryn Hill" some time and tell me rap can't be romantic—or if you want to keep it street, put on Mary J. Blige and Method Man's "I'll Be There for You/You're All I Need to Get By"). Of course, in the end, it may not be the art form for you. Oprah, for instance, still can't get past the n-word issue (or the *nigga* issue, with all apologies to Ms. Winfrey). I can respect her position. To her, it's a matter of acknowledging the deep and painful history of the word. To me, it's just a word, a word whose power is owned by the user and his or her intention. People give words power, so banning a word is futile, really. "Nigga" becomes "porch monkey" becomes "coon" and so on if that's what's in a person's heart. The key is to change the person. And we change people through conversation, not through censorship.

That's why I want people to understand what the words we use—and the stories we tell—are really about.

    And that's why I wrote this book. I love writing rhymes. There's probably nothing that gives me as much pleasure. There have been times in my life when I've tried to put it to the side—when I was a kid, so I could focus on hustling in the streets, and when I was an adult, so I could focus on hustling in the boardroom—but the words kept coming. They're still coming and will probably never stop. That's my story. But the story of the larger culture is a story of a million MCs all over the world who are looking out their windows or standing on street corners or riding in their cars through their cities or suburbs or small towns and inside of them the words are coming, too, the words they need to make sense of the world they see around them. The words are witty and blunt, abstract and linear, sober and fucked up. And when we decode that torrent of words—by which I mean really *listen* to them with our minds and hearts open—we can understand their world better. And ours, too. It's the same world.

AFTERWORD TO
THE EXPANDED EDITION

THIS IS YOUR SONG, NOT MINE

I KNOW
AMERICAN GANGSTER, 2007

YOUNG G'S
Puff Daddy, the Notorious B.I.G., and Jay-Z
NO WAY OUT, 1997

LOST ONE
KINGDOM COME, 2006

A month before the hardcover edition of *Decoded* hit the shelves, a poet named Kathleen Norris saw unbound pages of the book—production proofs—lying on the desk of my publisher. She picked them up out of curiosity and started reading. Norris isn't exactly part of the hip-hop generation: She's an award-winning poet who has spent much of her adult life in South Dakota, and her most famous books are meditations on the spiritual life, based on her experiences in a monastery in North Dakota. I'm not sure she knew who I was at all when she started reading those pages. When she ultimately sent my publishers an email in response to the book, I think she may have spelled my name Jay-Zee. But her response was humbling and gratifying—the first suggestion that maybe the book would achieve what we'd set out to accomplish. Here's what she wrote, in part:

> I'll always be fairly hopeless when it comes to hip-hop. . . . You
> know me, if I'm given a choice between going clubbing to hear

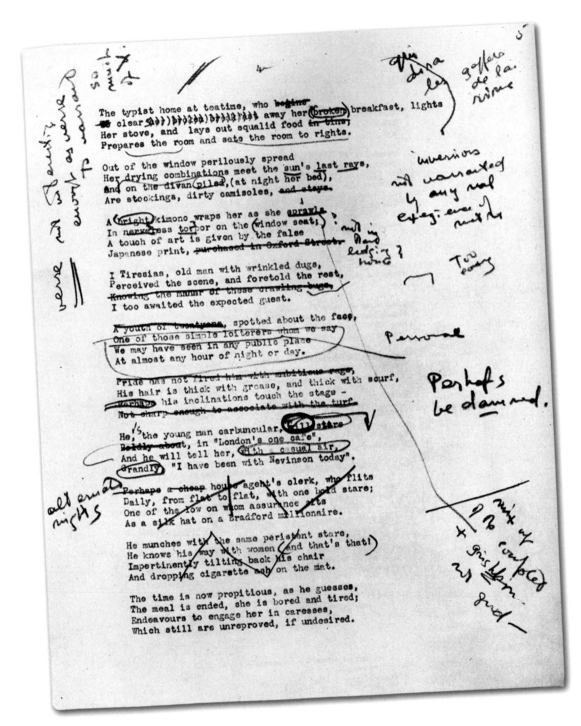

hip-hop and going to a monastery to chant the Psalms with Benedictine monks, the monks will win out every time. But as a poet, I am just so pleased to be given a better sense of the workings of this vital art form. Just from the few hip-hop/rap lyrics I'd heard, I knew there was something important going on—street news, social history, life stories of people who are so often invisible. But I had no idea how rich they were. I find myself making connections of my own—Jay-Z's comments about both poets and hustlers "bending" language, for instance, and I'm recalling Emily Dickinson's "tell the truth, but tell it slant." The notes to the lyrics had me riffing on T. S. Eliot's notes to *The Waste Land.* Most of all, this book has reconnected me with *The Autobiography of Malcolm X.* A teenage hustler in jail, realizing that his vocabulary is limited to street slang, sets out to learn English by reading the dictionary! It's really the story of a life saved, and a book written so that other kids that our society considers "throwaways" might find a way out, another way to live. Well, Malcolm's book did that for many young people, and I hope that this book will as well.

I would never compare this book to *The Autobiography of Malcolm X*—and I've never read T. S. Eliot's notes to *The Waste Land,* but I'll just go ahead and say that I wouldn't compare myself to T. S. Eliot or Emily Dickinson, either. But the gratifying part of Norris's response was that for her the book opened up the conversation about the art of rap and gave some insight into the lives of the people "society considers 'throwaways,'" as Norris puts it. In other words, for her, the book wasn't a passive, one-way experience. She closed it hungry to make *more* connections. This was all I'd hoped for when I first decided to write a book. When my publisher sent me Norris's email, I emailed them back: Take the books off the shelves, I'm good.

Of course, I didn't mean that literally.

The book did actually hit the shelves a few weeks later and there were more responses—many more, including many very positive responses. But I was probably most moved by the tweets I read from kids who wrote things like, *This is the first book I've ever read all the way through.* For all the other accolades the book received, the thing that makes me happiest is knowing that it's working as a gateway drug for kids to get into reading and into thinking about new ways to use their own voices and experiences.

The first thing I had to do when writing *Decoded* was to figure out which songs to include, which wasn't easy. I went through all the songs released on my albums, all the guest verses, and all the mixtapes, and came up with the selection you've just finished reading. But for reasons of time and space, we left some good ones out. To mark the release of this new edition, I'm adding three additional songs, for different reasons.

The first song I'm adding is "I Know," from my *American Gangster* album. There are many songs in this book that tell stories and explore ideas, but there's another kind of song that's underrepresented: conceptual songs, for lack of a better term. For example, "History" is what I'd call a conceptual song. In that song I personified words like "history," "victory," and "defeat," turning the concepts into characters. It wasn't just a gimmick; playing with the words like that made them into even more powerful tools for storytelling. Rappers often emply this kind of technique for a few bars, but to extend it for the length of a song—as on "History" and "I Know"—is an exciting challenge as a writer.

With "I Know," the concept is to tell the story of drug abuse as a love story—to mix the metaphors of addiction and romance. Specifically, the song extends the metaphor of heroin addiction to describe a toxic love affair. To add another twist, I also play on the relationship between music and drugs, between craving music and fiending for dope. It's not that far-fetched: Music, sex, and drugs all release the same chemical, dopamine, in your brain, and create a similar feeling of ecstasy and, on the downside, dependence. One of the interesting things about this song is how often people hear it as a straight love song, a rap song you can slip into your Quiet Storm mix on date night. If that's your thing, cool; just don't listen too closely, it might fuck up your groove.

"Young G's" is another new decoding here. This is a song I recorded with Biggie and Puff for Puff's 1997 *No Way Out* album. *No Way Out* was one of the most successful rap albums of the era—or any era—and transformed Puff from a rap impresario into a global star; the irony, of course, is that the album is suffused with mourning and a sense of loss. It came out in the aftermath of the deaths of Biggie and Tupac, and its biggest hit, "I'll Be Missing You," was a eulogy. It was a tough moment for me, too. Big was a genius poet and storyteller and an explosively charismatic character. And we were friends. But even more than that, for Brooklyn MCs like me, Biggie represented the dream fulfilled. We were peers, but he was the one blazing the trail from the streets to a place where he could support himself and his family through his art—and then beyond that to building new businesses, bringing his crew along, and conquering a world he'd only just started to discover. And then he was gone.

"Young G's," which features a devastating verse from Biggie, was obviously the last song I'd ever make with him. My verses on it capture a lot of the feeling that was running through me at that time. I'd released my own first album, *Reasonable Doubt,* already and was working on my second, which would feature a lot of production from Puffy's team. I was still transitioning to my new life, still trying to figure out how to balance all of the elements of my past and present. *I been rich, I been poor, I saved and blown bread.*

My first collaboration with Big, "Brooklyn's Finest," was a strangely joyful song, given all the violent, confrontational language. But beneath all that what you hear is two competitive MCs pushing each other verse by verse to come up with more creative metaphors, sicker punch lines, and more outrageous images (all over Clark Kent's great production, which is what drew Biggie to the song in the first place). That song was the foundation of the friendship we'd develop. "Young G's" is the bookend to "Brooklyn's Finest": It's darker and moodier, but once again Biggie pushed me to go harder. *Solemnly we mourn, all the rappers that's gone.*

The final new decoding is the reader's choice: "Lost One." This is a song a lot of listeners have wanted to know more about for a long time, specifically, the real-life identity of all the people in the song. Which brings me to one of the dilemmas of writing a book that "decodes" lyrics.

Let me go back to the beginning: I sat in my studio one night at the start of the process of writing this book, trying to decide which songs to include. Throughout the night, different people came through the studio, including some of the people I've worked with closest throughout my career—my engineer, Young Guru; Memphis Bleek; Pharrell; Steve Stoute; dream hampton; and others. I was taking a break from finishing up the *Blueprint 3* album, and hung out there for hours while people came and went, playing songs and telling stories, some of which made it into this book. Memphis Bleek told his side of the story of how we worked together on "Coming of Age," Young Guru remembered that moving moment when Scarface rewrote his verses for "This Can't Be Life," Steve told us about how young corporate guys he knew were psyching themselves up for business meetings by listening to "Public Service Announcement" (and dream remembered the Dave Chappelle "When 'Keeping It Real' Goes Wrong" bit where a character did the same thing and got fired).

I loved talking about the stories behind the songs, but as we were listening to the songs that night I found myself drawn over and over again to the words—the metaphors and rhythms and structural choices, not the gossip behind the songs. It was the little things that got me nodding my head, lost in the songs like I was hearing them for the first time. For instance, at one point Guru cued up "What We Do," a song by Freeway with me and Beanie Sigel on it, and set it rumbling through the studio. In an instant, I was lost in Freeway's remarkable flow. Do yourself a favor and listen to the first verse of that song, where Free ends every bar with some variation of the word "up" or "down." It's a simple thing, but the flow it creates is mesmerizing. I was still in the studio, but I was gone. That, I thought, is what an MC in the zone can do—turn language as simple as "up" and "down" into a magic spell.

Much later in the process of creating this book, I reviewed the final pages of the book with my editor in my office for the last time. It was right before I left for Detroit for the first of the huge "Home and Home" stadium shows I did with Eminem. As we were going through the pages, we eventually got to "Young Gifted and Black," and I started reading through the lyrics: *Y'all was in the pub having a light beer / I was in the club having a fight there / Y'all can go home / Husband and wife there / My momma at work trying to buy me the right gear.* Before I knew it, I was standing up, walking around my office, half speaking, half rapping out the rest of the lyrics: *China White right there / Right in front of my sight like here, yeah / There's your ticket out of the ghetto / Take flight right here / Sell me, you go bye-bye here, yeah / Damn there's a different set of rules we abide by here / You need a gun niggas might drive by here / You're having fun racing all your hot rods there / Downloading all our music on your iPods there / I'm Chuck D standing in the crosshairs here.* I meant every repetition of "here" and "there" to be another brick in the wall that separated the two lives in the song, till the wall was high and real. Again, it was a simple device: "here" and "there" repeated over and over, with some double entendres slipped in to pack in more meaning, but the rhythm it created was like an incantation—I wasn't in my office anymore, I was somewhere else, lost in the words and images and rhythm. That's hip-hop. That's poetry. That's magic.

I don't want to be the guy in the mask who gives away all the magician's tricks. I also don't want to reduce the songs to the gossip behind them (however interesting that gossip might be). "Lost One" is a very personal song, but the thing I love about it is the way it takes three episodes from my life—intimate and, in many ways, painful incidents—and turns them into poetic fables about loss that I hope anyone can relate to. I don't want people to listen to "Lost One" after reading the decoding and say, *Oh, that verse is about so-and-so;* what I really want is for them to listen to the song and say, *Oh, that verse is about me.*

It comes back to the reason I wanted to write a book in the first place, and to the idea Kathleen Norris picked up on in her email: It's about *connections*. What still excites me about rap is that it's an open thread, a cipher that listeners find their own meanings in. The point of this book is not to settle arguments or transform rap songs into neat stories with a beginning, middle, and end. Rather, I'm trying to point readers to some ideas and information, get them to see deeper into the music than they saw before and learn more about worlds different from their own (or find new ways of looking at the worlds they already know)—to find their own meanings and connect them back to their own lives. I want readers to see the craft and learn the context—and I want them to still be able to feel the magic, and enjoy the show.

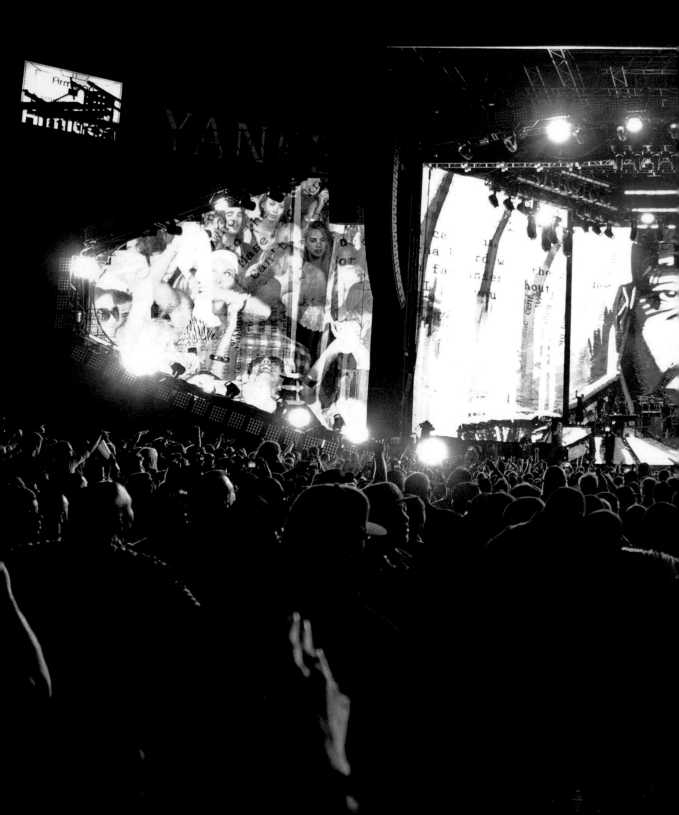

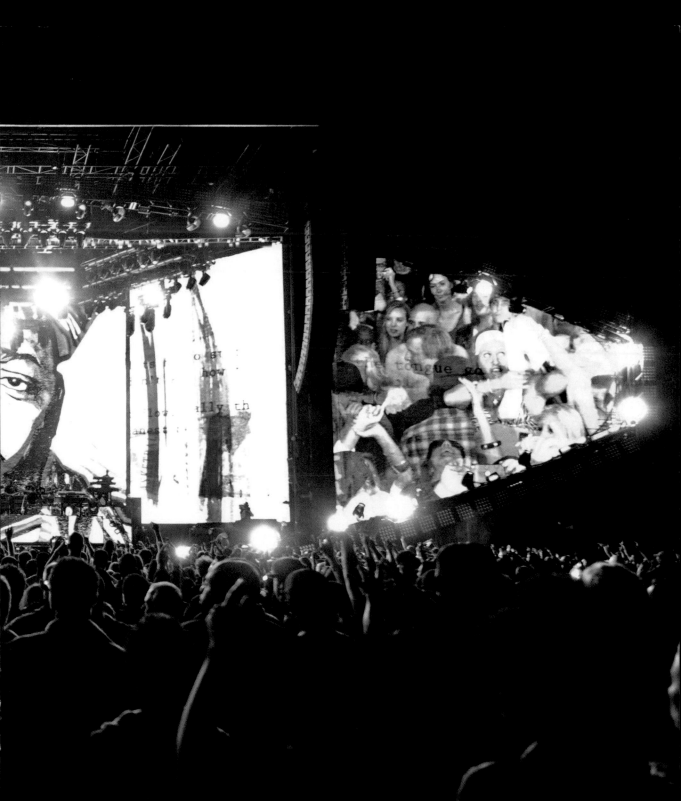

I KNOW

[*Chorus*] / And I know and I know / I know what you like / Everything you love / [*repeat*] / Baby you love . . . HOV / Uh- / She wants that old thing back / Uh-uh-uh- / She want those **heroin tracks**[1] / She likes **me**[2] / She fiends for me nightly / She **leans**[3] for me / Morning she rush for my touch / This is about **lust**[4] / **Cold sweats**[5] occur when I'm not with her / My presence is a must-must-must / **Bonita Applebum, I gotta put you on**[6] / If I didn't when **we cutting the feeling would be too strong**[7] / In any form, I'm giving you **sweet dreams** / That **Sugar Hill,**[8] she call me her sweet thing / That **Black Rain** that take away your pain / Just for one night, baby, **take me in vein**[9] / Now that feeling got you tripping / You no wanna feel no differently / Said lust has got you itching / **Nose wide open and it's dripping**[10] eh-eh-eh-eh / I know what you like, I am your prescription / I'm your physician, **I'm your addiction**[11] // [chorus] // I am so **dope**[12] / Like **Louboutins with the red bottoms**[13] / You gotta have 'em, you glad you got 'em / Like every color **Giuseppes,**[14] your guilty pleasure is me / It's so much fun, you **shun therapy**[15] / Although it never be, the feeling is fleeting / Shopping's like copping, you constantly need it / I'm never around, you constantly seek it / You'll never be down, **I know where your peak is**[16] / **Nine and a half weeks is better than twelve steps**[17] / I keep trying to remind you to keep telling yourself / **Now your conscience is interfering,**[18] like "Better yourself!" / Like you better get help / But when that medicine's felt? / **We're back together**[19] / Don't ever leave me / Don't ever let 'em tell you that you'll never need me / My **China White,**[20] till we **D.O.A.**[21] / It's **Montega**[22] forever, baby, let's get away . . . // [chorus] // **How could you leave me?**[23] / I thought that you needed me! / When the world got too much and you pleaded with me— / Who helped you immediately? / How speedy of me! / How could you deny me so vehemently? / Now your body is **shaking trying to free it of me**[24] / And your soul is in control, trying to lead it from me / And your heart no longer pledge allegiance to me / Damn, I'm missing the days when **you needed the D**[25] / [chorus]

This is the first drug/music/love double entendre. "Heroin tracks" are the scars left behind by dirty needles; they're also a way to describe addictive music. Rappers use the drug/music metaphor all the time—Kanye has a song called "Crack Music," for instance—but I wanted to push the metaphor as far as I could here. I chose heroin because it's the most addictive of all commonly sold street drugs. Also, this was on my *American Gangster* album, inspired by the movie about the life of heroin drug lord Frank Lucas.

The "me" here defines the narrator as the love interest or as the drug personified.

The dope-fiend lean was famous on the streets in the 1970s and early '80s when heroin was at its peak. People high on dope would always be nodding right on the edge of consciousness, their bodies still aware enough to keep them from falling over, but they'd lean at crazy angles. It looked comical and pathetic from the outside, but who knows what the leaner was experiencing inside, exquisitely balanced at the peak of their high.

There's a quick night/morning play here to create a parallel between the nightly lean and the morning rush. But whether it's drugs or toxic love or music, the impulse is greedy and out of control—a rush of lust.

This is another love/drug parallel: in the rush of new or crazy love, the absence of your lover can feel like withdrawal.

This is the chorus to A Tribe Called Quest's classic song "Bonita Applebum." I played with the last "must" from the previous line to make it sound like "Miss," as in Miss Bonita Applebum.

Cutting drugs stops the feeling from being "too strong" because it dilutes them. "When we cutting" can also refer to having sex, which keeps the drug/love metaphor going. Even diluted, though—"in any form" in the next line—I'm still giving you "sweet dreams."

Sweet Dreams, Sugar Hill, and Black Rain are all street names for heroin.

This could be a reference to the vein you take the drug in or to the phrase "take me in vain," that is, take me for granted.

Again, comparing the physical effects of addiction to love. "Nose wide open" is old black slang for someone in love—but her nose is open and dripping, a sign of coke addiction.

Here the drug/lover sounds like a pimp. There's something sick in this love affair, where one lover cultivates the other's sick dependence and exploits her weakness. It describes the place where seduction and control meet.

The mother of all drug double entendres.

Louboutin shoes are known for their signature red soles.

"Giuseppes" are Giuseppe Zanottis—another shoe reference. Shoes are often thought of as a woman's addiction (*shopping's like copping*), and they add material consumption to the collection of addictions the song mixes.

Another connection between a sick relationship and drug use: In either case, the addiction has you convinced that you don't need rehab or therapy.

More taunting, controlling language—the drug knows better than you how to make you happy and so does the lover. And, by the way, so does HOV; the other undercurrent in the song is that music is a drug.

Nine and a Half Weeks is another heroin brand name. It's also a reference to the Mickey Rourke and Kim Basinger movie *9½ Weeks*, about a sick, manipulative sexual relationship. Both the drug and the sick relationship are better than "twelve steps," which refer to recovery and escape.

The drug/lover tries to control the user by reminding her to tell herself that she doesn't need help—but it's now in conflict with her conscience, which is sending out alarms.

When she's on the verge of escape, the narrator hits her with that medicine—love, drug, music—and we're back together. Dopamine is a helluva drug.

Another brand name for heroin.

D.O.A. is another heroin brand name. This line adds a morbid twist to the romantic oath "till death do us part."

A seventh heroin brand name worked into the lyrics.

In the final verse, she tries to break away, and the manipulation goes into overdrive as the drug/lover fights for its survival.

The symptoms of withdrawal are kicking in, but she holds firm through it, and resists the final attempts to control her.

The "D" stands for drugs. Or sex. Either way, the need is gone. The song completes the the the arc of addiction and recovery from the perspective of the drug, the rejected lover.

YOUNG G'S

[Second verse] These here's the **dog years**[1] 'cept mother-fuckers don't shed / I try to bring you life but mother-fuckers want dead / So I travel with the **barrel, with the chrome, with the lead**[2] / 'Cause when it's on, then it's on, till shots flown through your head / I been rich I been poor I saved and blown bread / Some say I been here before because of the way I zone / Some said, Jigga zone is like the falling of Rome / Reoccuring, that he thinks like that cause he's observant / Won't be known until I'm gone and **niggas study my bones**[3] / Mentally been many places, but I'm Brooklyn's own / In the physical, unseen, like a lost body / In fact my thoughts don't differ much from that of **God body**[4] / But it's **the R shottie,**[5] that got cats likening me / To the mob **John Gotti,**[6] rap dudes biting me 'cause / I got it locked like the late Bob Marley / Pardon me y'all, the great Bob Marley / Solemnly we mourn, all the rappers that's gone / Niggas that got killed in the field and all the babies born / Know they ain't fully pre-pared for this **New World Order**[7] / So I keep it ghetto like **sunflower seeds and quarter waters**[8] / You walk 'em through it, you know, talk 'em through it / Know these beats is more than music whenever I talk to it / Destined for great-ness and y'all knew this, when I doubled the pie / Had a shorty and a girdle coming out of **BWI**[9] (in school) / I hated algebra but I loved to multiply / And I told my nigga Big I'd be **multi before I die**[10] / It's gonna happen whether rapping or clapping have it your way / 'Cause if that's my dough you're trappin, I'm clappin your way

1. These are dog years—hard times.

2. This might seem redundant—each of these, the barrel, the chrome, and the lead, is talking about the same thing—but breaking them down into their components allows the image to build in the listener's mind, like the *aw shit* scene in every action movie where the hero assembles his gun, locks, and loads.

3. This "zone" I'm describing is the way people are unnerved by someone who moves in silence and with calculation. There's an intimidating air of mystery around the type of person who seems more

interested in watching closely and tapping into secret knowledge about the cycles of human behavior and history than in just reacting immediately to everything that comes. That's the kind of person whose true motives and thinking you can't discover till you study their bones, which refers to reading about them in books or hearing their legends passed down in the streets.

4. Here I'm comparing my own knowledge and style to a "God body," a Five Percenter.

5. Refers to a .30-06 shotgun, known as a thirty-aught. We pronounced "aught" like it was "r." We didn't even know the proper names of the guns we carried; like with most things, we were improvising our way through, doing the best we could with the information we had.

6. I may be like a "God body" in some respects, but the "shottie"—a blast from a shotgun—makes me closer to John Gotti, a gangster.

7. "New World Order" was a phrase used by George H. W. Bush to describe the postcommunist world, but many of us understood it as a code phrase for the secret societies that controlled governments and economies. The suspicious deaths of our great heroes—from Bob Marley to the "rappers that's gone," all "killed in the field" of battle, the battle between good and evil, to put it simply—was part of that New World Order's agenda. This kind of conspiracy theory was commonplace where I'm from; it may have been borne of paranoia, but, as they say, just because you're paranoid doesn't mean someone's not out to get you. Biggie and Pac could testify to that.

8. The ghetto breakfast of champions, fresh from the dusty bottom shelf of the bodega: sunflower seeds in a plastic pack and quarter waters, sugar and colored water sold in tiny bottles for twenty-five cents.

9. BWI is the Baltimore/Washington Airport, where the song's narrator had a girl ("shortie") coming in with drugs strapped to a girdle under her clothes, a common method of moving drugs.

10. I came back to this promise to Big—that I'd be multiplatinum before I died—in "Renegade," with the lines "B.I.G. I did it / multi before I die."

LOST ONE

It's not a diss song, it's just a real song / Feel me? // I heard motherfuckers saying they made Hov / Made Hov say, **"Okay so, make another Hov"**[1] / Niggaz wasn't playing they day role / So we parted ways like Ben and J-Lo / I shoulda been did it but I been in a daze though / I put **friends over business**[2] end of the day though / But when friends, business interests is they glow / Ain't nothing left to say though / I guess we forgot what we came for / Shoulda stayed in food and beverage / Too much flossing / Too much **Sam Rothstein**[3] / I ain't a bitch but I gotta divorce them / Hov have to get the shallow shit up off him / And I ain't even want to be famous / Niggaz is brainless to unnecessarily go through these changes / And I ain't even know how it came to this / Except that fame is / The worst drug known to man / It's stronger than, heroin / When you could look in the mirror like, "There I am" / And still not see, **what you've become**[4] / I know I'm guilty of it too but, not like them / You lost one // Lose one, let go to get one / Left one, lose some to win some [You lost one] / Sorry I'm a champion, sorry I'm a champion / You lost one // I don't think it's meant to be, be / But she loves her work more than she does me / And honestly, at twenty-three / I would probably love my work more than I did she / So we, ain't we / It's me, and her / 'Cause what she prefers over me, is work / And that's, where we, differ / So I have to give her / Free, time, **even if it hurts**[5] / So breathe, mami, it's deserved / You've been put on this earth to **be** / **All you can be,**[6] like the **reserves** / And me? My timing in **this army**, it's served / So I have to allow she, her, **time to serve** / The time's now for her / In time she'll mature / And maybe we, can be, we, again like we were / Finally, my time's too short to share / And to ask her now, it ain't fair / So yeah, she lost one // Lose one, let go to get one / Left one, lose some to win some [Oh yeah, she lost one] / Sorry I'm a champion, sorry I'm a champion / You lost one // **My nephew died in the car I bought**[7] / So I'm under the belief it's partly my fault / Close my eyes and squeeze, try to block that thought / Place **any burden on me,**[8] but please, not that lord / **Time don't go back, it go forward**[9] / **Can't run from the pain, go towards it**[10] / Some things can't be explained, what caused it? / Such a beautiful soul, so pure, shit / Gonna see you again, I'm sure of it / Until that time, little man I'm nauseous / Your girlfriend's pregnant, the lord's gift / **Almost lost my faith, that restored it**[11] / It's like having your life restarted / Can't wait for your child's life, to be a part of it / So now I'm childlike, waiting for a gift / To return, when I lost you, I lost it // Lose one, let go to get one / Left one, lose some to win some [Colleek, I lost one] / Sorry I'm a champion, Colleek, you're a champion / I lost one /

1. I recorded this song after a professional breakup, when a lot of things were being said about who was responsible for my success and how things would go in the future now that our initial team had broken up. I owe a lot of my success to a lot of people, but ultimately, no one made me. This is the kind of lie that people get told all the time, sometimes in romantic relationships, sometimes in their professional lives: that somehow who they are is a result of other people's investment in them. It's vital to resist that or you risk losing yourself; as I say in another song, *Remind yourself / nobody built like you / you design yourself.*

2. It's tricky to be in business with your friends; it can test the strength of your friendship and your business acumen. I still do business with my friends, but over time I've developed a clearer sense of the difference between business "friendships" and true friendships. Loyalty is what sets them apart.

3. Sam Rothstein is a character in the movie *Casino*. In the film he pretended to be the "food and beverage" manager of a casino, while running the operation for the mob behind the scenes. The movie turns when Rothstein makes an appearance on television and starts drawing publicity for himself, a shift into the limelight that destroys everything he'd worked for.

4. Watching people evolve as they become richer and more famous is fascinating; as I said earlier in the book, extreme situations don't change us, they reveal us. But the worst is when we can't even see what we've allowed ourselves to become—or rather, we can't see what parts of ourselves we've allowed to grow out of control. It can happen to anyone. It happens to me, as I point out in the next line. But you have to find ways to check yourself.

5. These lines are about trying to have a real, serious relationship with another ambitious professional. In a lot of ways, this is the flip side of the songs in my catalog like "Big Pimpin'," where women exist almost completely as predators or objects. This is about how difficult it is to respect a lover as an autonomous human being, with separate needs and goals and timelines than yours. It's one of the hardest things about a real relationship of equals. But it's worth it.

6. Starting with this—"Be All You Can Be" was a longtime Army slogan—I play off military images, like the "reserves," "army," "time to serve," to describe two people at different stages in their lives.

7. My nephew Colleek died in a car accident while driving the car I bought him for his high school graduation.

8. My feeling of responsibility for his death, no matter how irrational, was for a while inescapable. Even when we know in our minds that we're not responsible for a thing, the guilt of it can be overwhelming.

9. This echoes the sentiment in another song mourning a loved one lost in a car crash. In "Lucifer" my fantasy is to *reverse the crash / reverse the blast / reverse the day / and there you are.* Here I force myself to avoid that fantasy and come to grips with the truth, that time only moves forward, no matter how painful it is.

10. The only way through such searing pain is to "go towards it," to allow ourselves to feel it, to reckon with it, and, eventually, to let it go.

11. Just when you're on the verge of giving up hope and losing faith, the universe reveals unexpected consolations. My nephew's girlfriend was just a couple months pregnant when he died, which none of us knew, maybe not even him. But the son she gave birth to looked just like his father, like Colleek reborn. The last verse is the most powerful example of the paradox of the song's chorus, that even the greatest loss holds the possibility of redemption.

ACKNOWLEDGMENTS

First and foremost I'd like to acknowledge dream hampton. How can I thank you enough? You've lived my words and life for so long that you might need therapy to get back to yours (sorry, Nina). Dream, thanks again for suffering for my art (I mean, you were in Martha's Vineyard but still, ha). You are a GODSEND.

Chris Jackson for your dedication, appreciation of detail, and your tireless work—even following me around Coachella (and missing your flight home).

I'd also like to thank all of the people at Spiegel & Grau, Random House, and Rodrigo Corral Design who worked themselves ragged to produce this beautiful book, including Julie Grau, Mya Spalter, Greg Mollica, Evan Camfield, Richard Elman, Penelope Haynes, Rodrigo Corral, Rachel Bergman, Steve Attardo, Laurie Carkeet, Deb Wood, Dean Nicastro, and Sally Berman.

PERMISSIONS ACKNOWLEDGMENTS

Ignorant Shit

Words and music by Shawn Carter, Ernest Isley, Marvin Isley, O'Kelly Isley, Ronald Isley, Rudolph Isley, Christopher Jasper, and Dwight Grant

Copyright © 2007 EMI April Music, Inc., Carter Boys Music, Bovina Music, Inc., Bug Music-Music of Windswept, Hitco South, and Shakur Al Din Music

All rights for Carter Boys Music and Bovina Music, Inc., controlled and administered by EMI April Music, Inc.

All rights for Hitco South and Shakur Al Din Music controlled and administered by Bug Music-Music of Windswept

All rights reserved. International copyright secured. Used by permission.

Contains elements of "Between the Sheets"

I Know

Words and music by Shawn Carter and Pharrell Williams

Copyright © 2007 EMI April Music Inc., Carter Boys Music, EMI Blackwood Music Inc., Waters of Nazareth, and Songs for Beans

All rights for Carter Boys Music controlled and administered by EMI April Music Inc.

All rights for Waters of Nazareth and Songs for Beans controlled and administered by EMI Blackwood Music Inc.

All rights reserved. International copyright secured. Used by permission.

Lost One

Words and music by Shawn Carter, Chrisette Michele Payne, Mark Batson, Andre Young, and Dawaun Parker

Copyright © 2006 EMI April Music Inc., Carter Boys Music, EMI Foray Music, Four Kings Productions, Inc., Chrisette Michele Music, Bat Future Music, WB Music Corp., Ain't Nothing But Funkin' Music, Warner-Tamerlane Publishing Corp., Alien Status Music, and Psalm 144 Verse 1 Music

All rights for Carter Boys Music controlled and administered by EMI April Music Inc.

All rights for Four Kings Productions, Inc., and Chrisette Michele Music controlled and administered by EMI Foray Music

All rights for Bat Future Music controlled and administered by Songs of Universal, Inc.

All rights reserved. International copyright secured. Used by permission

Meet the Parents

Words and music by Shawn Carter and Justin Smith

Copyright © 2002 EMI April Music, Inc., Carter Boys Music, and F.O.B. Music Publishing

All rights for Carter Boys Music controlled and administered by EMI April Music, Inc.

All rights reserved. International copyright secured. Used by permission.

Minority Report

Words and music by Shawn Carter, Shaffer Smith, Mark Batson, Andre Young, and Dawaun Parker

Copyright © 2006 EMI April Music, Inc., Carter Boys Music, Universal Music-Z Songs, Super Sayin Publishing, Songs of Universal, Inc., Bat Future Music, WB Music Corp., Ain't Nothing But Funkin' Music, Warner-Tamerlane Publishing Corp., Psalm 144 Verse 1 Music, and Alien Status Music

All rights for Carter Boys Music controlled and administered by EMI April Music, Inc.

All rights for Super Sayin Publishing controlled and administered by Universal Music-Z Songs

All rights for Bat Future Music controlled and administered by Songs of Universal, Inc.

All rights for Ain't Nothing But Funkin' Music controlled and administered by WB Music Corp.

All rights for Psalm 144 Verse 1 Music and Alien Status Music controlled and administered by Warner-Tamerlane Publishing Corp.

Used by permission from Alfred Music Publishing Co., Inc., and Hal Leonard Corporation

All rights reserved. International copyright secured. Used by permission.

Contains elements of "Non Ti Scordar Di Me" (DeCurtis/Furno)

Moment of Clarity

Words and music by Shawn Carter and Marshall Mathers

Copyright © 2003 Carter Boys Music and Eight Mile Style

All rights for Carter Boys Music controlled and administered by EMI April Music, Inc.

All rights reserved. International copyright secured. Used by permission.

Most Kings

Words by Shawn Carter

Copyright © EMI April Music, Inc., Carter Boys Music

All rights for Carter Boys Music controlled and administered by EMI April Music, Inc.

My 1st Song

Words and music by Shawn Carter and Germain de la Fuente

Copyright © 2003 EMI April Music, Inc., Carter Boys Music, and EMI Music Publishing Chile

All rights for Carter Boys Music controlled and administered by EMI April Music, Inc.

All rights for EMI Music Publishing Chile in the United States and Canada controlled and administered by Beechwood Music Corp.

All rights reserved. International copyright secured. Used by permission.

Contains elements of "Tú y Tu Mirar . . . Yo y Mi Canción"

My President Is Black

Words and music by Justin Henderson, Christopher Whitacre, Jay Jenkins, and Nasir Jones

Copyright © 2008 Songs of Universal, Inc., Nappypub Music, Henderworks Publishing Co., Universal Music Corp., Nappy Boy Publishing, West Coast Livin' Publishing, Universal Music-Z Tunes, Universal Music-Z Songs, EMI Blackwood Music, Inc., and Young Jeezy Music, Inc.

All rights for Nappypub Music and Henderworks Publishing Co. controlled and administered by Songs of Universal, Inc.

All rights for Nappy Boy Publishing and West Coast Livin' Publishing controlled and administered by Universal Music Corp.

All rights for Young Jeezy Music, Inc., controlled and administered by EMI Blackwood Music, Inc.

All rights reserved. Used by permission.

ILLUSTRATION CREDITS